Hiking Trails of the Santa Monica Mountains

by
Milt McAuley

Illustrated by

JANET WILSON SOLUM

Canyon Publishing Co.

TABLE OF CONTENTS

Where the Mountains meet the Sea

ACKNOWLEDGMENTS

Many people contributed to the writing of this book; so many that I cannot hope to acknowledge each one. However, I do want to name those who have contributed to this edition of the book, either with updated information or support.

• Maxine who endured the disruption of our home during the preparation of this guide, typed the original manuscript and did the final typesetting. Authors have a disturbing habit when writing. We believe the world should stand still while we write. Without giving up her independence, Macky supported this project from beginning to end. And I learned to tread lightly at times.

• Ron Webster has been a driving force behind our trail building efforts to improve recreational use of the Santa Monica Mountains. In my estimation he has no peer when it comes to designing a trail, enlisting volunteer workers, and guiding the construction to com-, pletion. With strong support from Mary Ann, Ron's team has a 25-year record of devotion to our mountains.

• Dave Brown is a commanding force as an activist in the environmental protection of the Santa Monica Mountains. A goal is to preserve the land for the future. Dave is steadfast in obtaining this goal. He is a Bulldog.

• Anthony Beilenson, after many honorable years of public service has withdrawn from the political arena, so I can speak up without influence. California Senator, Anthony Beilenson, in February 1971, introduced legislation in Sacramento that made a change in California's State Park system. One major change emphasized the "preservation of unique environmental features." After this precedent-setting decision, Richard Danielson offered 5800 acres of land adjacent to Point Mugu State Park at 50% its appraised value. The preservation of the Santa Monica Mountains was underway. We all know that Tony Beilenson as a United States Congressman later guided legislation that formed the Santa Monica Mountains National Recreation Area. One person can make a difference and I consider that day in 1971 as a turning point in history for the future of our recreation area.

- Jim Kenney shares his knowledge of plants with all of us in slide shows and lectures as well as taking groups out on "Wildflower Walks." Jim has organized and prepared the list of plants of the Santa Monica Mountains found in the back of this book.

- Pat Romolo, our daughter, for her dedicated interest and time involved working with us on this book.

- Bill Harris has hiked these trails for many years and has shared his knowledge with me. Just because I write books doesn't mean that some trails aren't still hidden. Also, one should not hike alone and Bill, with his optimism and ready wit is a dependable hiking companion.

- Doug Kirk has done a lot of work to bring a new recreational activity to the Santa Monicas — Kayaking. The time and effort put into coordinating areas of beaches for landings, approved camping areas, and a miscellaneous array of information is helpful.

- Patti Keenan wrote hike #89 (see page 326). We had talked on the phone a few days earlier and I asked a lot of questions about the condition of the trail. Patti and two of her friends answered all my questions by . . . . .well, you read about the trail on page 326.

- Linda Palmer lives in the heart of the mountains and for many years has worked as a volunteer for any cause that promotes recreational use of the Santa Monicas. As a long time President of the Santa Monica Mountains Trails Council she promoted trail building as a condition of major development. She established a trail maintenance program and is active. When we walk the Secret Trail, Stunt High Trail, and Stoke's Ridge — Linda was an activist in the building of each trail.

- Everyone with whom I have hiked these mountains, all of the good friends that have given me information in casual conversation.

I thank you all.

Milt McAuley

INTRODUCTION

Welcome to this mountain range — bound on the north by valleys, on the south and west by the Pacific Ocean, and on the east and southeast by the Los Angeles Basin. A rugged bastion holding out against the population expansion, the Santa Monica Mountains offer lofty crags, cascading waterfalls, rugged boulder-filled canyons, beaches, and more.

Ancient home of Indians, landing site of Juan Rodriguez Cabrillo, site of surrender ending California's part in the U.S.-Mexican War, location of Mexican land grants, destination of early settlers, and now the Santa Monica Mountains National Recreation Area, here are the Santa Monica Mountains. (Cabrillo landed on the coast, 10 October 1542. After a brief, friendly meeting with Chumash Indians, he sailed on. Several months later Cabrillo died as a result of an accident on San Miguel Island. He is buried there.)

Conceived as ocean deposits and born of compressive land forces, the Santa Monicas have grown through volcanic action, fire, flood and earthquake. For centuries, Chumash, Fernandiño, and Gabrieleno families hunted and gathered seeds in the mountains, fished along the ocean shore, and built their villages near the major watercourses.

Wild animals still haunt the rugged back country. Deer can be expected any time at any place; a coyote yip just after sundown will trigger a response from a dozen more; bobcats usually keep to themselves, but will occasionally surprise us by nonchalantly walking across a trail or across a road. Red-tailed hawks soar overhead; mountain lions exist but are seldom seen; at night owls hoot, crickets chirp and frogs croak. This is a rugged pristine panorama of mountain, animal, and plant life into which humankind has been invited.

The Santa Monica Mountains offer a unique opportunity for recreation, exercise, and the pure enjoyment of the out of doors. It is my desire that this guide book will open up new vistas, that you might savor and enjoy this unique range of mountains. So come on an adventure, walk the trails, absorb the history, and experience the beauty and friendship that is waiting for you.

THE SANTA MONICA MOUNTAINS

TOPOGRAPHY

The Santa Monica Mountains are an east-west trending range located in Los Angeles and Ventura Counties of Southern California. Including Griffith Park on the east and Point Mugu State Park on the west, the range is 46 miles in length. Bounded on the north by the San Fernando Valley, the Conejo Valley and the Oxnard Plain, and on the south by the Pacific Ocean, the range averages nearly 10 miles in width. There are 36 miles of Pacific Ocean shoreline, 29 intermittent streams entering the ocean, and a lesser number to the north. Sandstone Peak at 3111' is the highest point in the mountain range, Malibu Creek has its origin in the Simi Hills north of the central part of the Santa Monica Mountains, and is the only stream that cuts through the range. All other streams drain the same side of the mountains on which they originate.

Access to the trailheads in the mountain range is provided by a series of roads that parallel and traverse the mountains. Fireroads, firebreaks, and trails, provide further access to the hiker or equestrian.

PLANT LIFE

Vegetation is a vital natural resource to the area. It stabilizes the soil from erosion by providing a screen from rain. Root systems hold the soil in place, aiding in the prevention of slides, and by retaining much of the water from storms, reduces the chance of floods. Vegetation also forms the basis for the food chain for the animal community. And of course, I can't resist pointing out the beauty of Ferns, Oaks and Sycamores along the streams, the riot of flowers found in the secluded glens as well as open fields. Nothing compares with the chaparral in spring when thousands of acres of California Lilac overpower us with their beauty of sight and scent.

The plant references in this guide will usually be in a common name. These names are listed alphabetically in the appendix and are further classified as to genus and species. For more information either the botanical name or common name may then be referenced to *"Wildflowers of the Santa Monica Mountains"* by Milt McAuley, where each plant that grows locally is described, and most are pictured. *"Flora of the Santa Monica Mountains, California"* by Raven, Thompson, & Prigge is a technically oriented and authoritative work of the area.

PLANT COMMUNITIES

The plant life of the Santa Monica Mountains can be placed into a number of different Plant Communities, each having characteristics setting them apart from one another. All naturalists do not agree on the nomenclature and specific communities so I will try to describe plant life from the eyes of a hiker, as I see it. To read of other points of view, see any of the wildflower books dealing with California or the Santa Monica Mountains. At the outset I will omit plants growing in the ocean (Kelp, Surfweed, etc) and in quiet salt water (Eelgrass). I will list eleven communities: (1) Coastal Strand (Littoral zone), (2) Coastal Salt Marsh (and Brackish Marsh), (3) Freshwater Marsh, (4) Coastal Sage Scrub, (5) Southern Oak Woodland, (6) Chaparral, (7) Riparian Woodland, (8) Valley Grassland, (9) Vernal Moist Habitat (includes ponds that dry up in summer and intermittent streams), (10) Cactus Scrub, (11) Cliffside.

COASTAL STRAND

Coastal strand includes a narrow interrupted sand dune and green belt along the ocean from Santa Monica to Point Mugu. Much of this area has been altered or removed from the environment by construction. Pacific Coast Highway travels through the area. Some characteristic plants are: Sand Verbena, Silver Beachweed, Yerba Mansa, Sea Rocket, Beach Primrose, Beach Morning Glory, Dudleya and Ice Plant.

COASTAL SALT MARSH

A saltwater marsh is in the tidewater zone of the ocean. We have two of them — Mugu Lagoon and Malibu Lagoon. All plants of this habitat have adapted to survival in saltwater, at least part of the time. Hollow spaces in stems and leaves let air go to the roots.

Salt concentration in roots reverses osmotic flow so that moisture is absorbed by the plant. Glands on the leaves and stems excrete salt. Some characteristic plants are: Salt Bush, Saltwort, Pickleweed, Jaumea, and Dodder.

Fresh water flowing into saltwater marshes places an extra demand on plants in that they must adapt to both salt and fresh water. Some characteristic plants are: Brass Buttons, Juncus, and Ditch Grass.

FRESHWATER MARSH

A freshwater marsh contains either standing or slowly moving water. Plants adapt to water living by having air tubes from leaves to roots, air pockets for bouyancy, and a concentration of photosynthesizing bodies in the upper leaves of floating plants. The edges of ponds, pools of slow-moving streams, and seepages are examples. Some characteristic plants are: Pond Lily, Cat-tail, Rush, Swamp Knotweed, Water-cress, and Common Knotweed.

COASTAL SAGE SCRUB

Coastal Sage Scrub is found on lower elevations in the mountains, both coastal and inland. It occupies drier locations than does Chaparral. Coastal Sage Scrub plants have shallow root systems, are spaced rather far apart and are much smaller plants than Chaparral. Some characteristic plants are: California Sagebrush, Bush Sunflower, California Buckwheat, Sawtooth Goldenbush, White, Purple, and Black Sage, and Laurel Sumac.

SOUTHERN OAK WOODLAND

Southern Oak Woodland is dominated by trees usually on north-facing slopes in heavy soil. Broad valleys having more than average ground moisture will often be covered with Southern Oak Woodlands. Some characteristic plants are: Coast Live Oak, Bay, Walnut, Poison Oak, and Woodfern.

CHAPARRAL

Chaparral is composed mainly of evergreen shrubs that are adapted to fire and summer drought. The name comes from "chaparro" which describes oak thickets of Spain. The growing environment is characterized by poor, rocky soil, hot dry summers, and limited rainfall (12-14 inches) all falling in the winter. Only five places in the world meet this criteria: (1) coastal southern California and Baja, (2) the Mediterranean, (3) central Chile, (4) south Africa, and southwest Australia. Most growth occurs during winter.

Chaparral is typically found on the higher ridges and slopes, sometimes in almost pure stands of Chamise or Ceanothus but usually as a mixture of shrubs and understory. Nearly all Chaparral plants have the ability to crown-sprout after a fire or physical removal. Some plants protect their immediate environment from competitive germination by putting chemical toxins in the soil as an inhibitor. Characteristic plants are: Chamise, Ceanothus (6 species), Manzanita, Red Shanks, Mountain Mahogany, Scrub Oak, Laurel Sumac, and Sugarbush.

RIPARIAN WOODLAND

Riparian Woodland occurs in canyons and streambeds. Shores of man-made lakes (Century Lake in Malibu Creek State Park) support Riparian Woodlands. A perennial source of water or subterranean moisture is required. Characteristic plants are: White Alder, Sycamore, Cottonwood, Willow, Bay, Blackberry, Poison Oak, Horsetail, and Stream Orchid.

VALLEY GRASSLAND

Valley Grassland is located throughout in well-drained areas at all elevations. Most communities are small but a 600 acre grassland is found in upper La Jolla Valley. Introduced species of grasses and herbs have permanently altered the composition of the original grasslands and overgrazing has also had an effect. A lessened frequency of fires probably has changed the composition to some extent; cultivation most certainly has. Characteristic plants are Needlegrass, Wild Oat, Foxtail Brome-grass, Rye-grass, Mariposa Lily, Tarweed, Blue-eyed Grass, Black Mustard, and Filaree.

VERNAL MOIST HABITAT

Vernal Moist Habitats are sinks or annual ponds that fill with water during winter then dry up in summer. Areas along intermittent streams can often fall into this habitat.

Some plants tolerate fluctuations of water level, in fact, may require it. Under these conditions plants that need submersion for germination and a lowering of the water level to flower and set seed have a competitive advantage over others. Trees, shrubs, and stem succulants do not prosper in this habitat. Some characteristic plants are: Long-leaved Ammania, Waterwort, Lowland Cudweed, Loosestrife, Woolly Heads, Alkali Mallow, Bull Clover, and White-tipped Clover.

CACTUS SCRUB

Cactus Scrub is a small community of one species of cactus (*Opuntia littoralis* or *Opuntia oricola*) of up to 200 feet in diameter. Normally on a south or west facing slope in an otherwise Coastal Sage Scrub community, Cactus Scrub is readily identified as a distinct habitat. Usually inhabited by ground squirrels and rabbits and possibly snakes, the community is structured so that coyotes and similar predators cannot enter. The rabbits and squirrels forage on grasses and herbs in the community and around the perimeter, probably aiding the expansion of the cactus patch by reducing other plant competition.

Individual plants are also found scattered in some Coastal Sage Scrub communities and on cliffsides.

CLIFFSIDES

Cliffs and the rock debris at their base provide a harsh environment for most plants, but some plants seem to thrive on rocks. Rock outcroppings are found throughout the mountains and "Rupicolous plants" (by definition, "live or grow on rocks") are usually found in the habitat. These same plants are also found in other areas. Some characteristic plants are: Dudleya, Golden Yarrow, Shrubby Bedstraw, Tejon Milk-aster, Spike Moss, Santa Susana Tarweed, Brickellbush, and Fuchsia.

ANIMAL LIFE

The wildlife of the Santa Monica Mountains makes every effort to remain hidden — and with just cause. People, dogs, and cats have encroached upon the terrain of the native animals and caused severe losses. It has been more than forty-five years since a giant California condor soared overhead or made a dive down into a canyon; bears no longer range their 100 square mile territory (thank goodness); and even the California mule deer is hard to find in some areas. The urban dream continues to take its toll; but if you walk into the mountains often enough, you are bound to find wildlife.

California quail are found in the fringe area between chaparral and riparian woodland as well as in coastal sage. Sometimes they are found near homes, especially when water is available. Deer are full of surprises. I've seen them crossing Mulholland Drive during mid-day, as a silhouette at night on a ridge, and as a flash up from a stream that I was walking along. Seldom seen, but often heard, is the kr-r-r-eck-ck of the Pacific tree frog. Most intermittent streams and even small temporary ponds are places to look and listen.

The coast horned lizard is often seen in the fringe area of the chaparral. This 3 to 4 inch long, flat, wide lizard is active during the daytime and will be seen in rocky, sandy, or gravelly places. It can change color from a dark to a light phase in only a few minutes and often closely matches the color of the background. This refugee from prehistoric times looks ferocious, but is really tame. This lizard feeds on insects, including bees. Beekeepers who place hives near the chaparral have reported that occasionally a horned lizard will take up a station near a hive entrance and grab a bee now and then.

Four kinds of salamanders live in the Santa Monicas: the arboreal salamander, the California slender salamander, Eschscholtz's salamander, and the California newt.

The California newt lives on land most of its life but returns to water to breed. The migration to water usually occurs in winter and spring during or after a rain. The eggs are attached to rocks, sticks, or other objects in the water, and hatch 5-10 weeks later. The California newt spends its larval state in the water, usually a coastal stream. Transformation takes place late in the summer and the young newt leaves the water and hides in damp areas nearby.

The other three salamanders are terrestrial through all phases of life. During the dry part of the year they stay under rocks, in burrows in the ground, or other subterranean retreats that afford some protection from becoming dry. When the ground becomes wet from the winter and spring rains these salamanders emerge and may be found under leaf litter and other surface material. Courtship and breeding may occur anytime that they are out on the surface. The California slender salamander lays eggs in late fall and winter, with hatching in the spring. The eggs are deposited under rocks and other underground places. The arboreal salamander deposits eggs in rotten logs or hollows in trees in late spring or early summer. Hatching takes place in fall and early winter. The eggs of the Eschscholtz's salamander are usually deposited underground. The young of all three terrestrial salamanders hatch as miniature adults, the transformation from larvae having taken place in the egg.

You will seldom see, but often note, the presence of coyotes in the mountains. If you are high on a ridge at evening you may hear the staccato yipping and then howling down in a valley; if you are in the valley they will likely be on the ridge. Also watch underfoot. Coyote "scat," characteristically containing the big Islay seeds will often be deposited right on the trail. There is no modesty about coyotes; they find an open spot away from trees and bushes, usually in the middle of the trail, and make their deposit. Unknowingly, this insures the optimum condition for the Islay seed to sprout, processed whole through the intestinal tract, placed in an open, sunny spot and provided with its own fertilizer! October ends the Holly-leaf Cherry season and the Toyon season begins for the coyote. Walnuts, Acorns, and Laurel seeds are not on the coyote diet.

The Southern Pacific rattlesnake is an important resident of the Santa Monicas. They are seen often enough that it is prudent to be aware of their characteristics. Because they are unable to control body temperature as mammals do, they seek an area in their temperature range between 64° and 89° F., with a preference for the mid 80's. This means that during the heat of the day in summer the rattlesnake will find shade and wait for late afternoon or evening to move around. They hibernate in the winter, coming out in early spring, and are then likely to be seen during the day.

Most snakes stay in an area for their lifetime rather than traveling great distances. Over a period of months it is not likely that a snake will travel more than 100 feet or so from home, with some exceptions.

Breeding usually takes place during March or April with the young being born alive 6 months later. A brood of 11 is average. The recognition of a sexually receptive female by an active male appears to be by sight and smell. Some snakes have a 2-year reproductive cycle, the ripe female copulating in the fall and ovulating the following spring.

The mating act as witnessed by me on one occasion, involved an entwining in slow but constant twisting and swaying motion. The heads and about 1/3 of the bodies were off the ground. A hiking group out on Sullivan Ridge came upon two mating rattlers about 9:30 p.m. on 16 August. Both snakes were rattling rather gently and did not appear to change their activity, nor seem to be threatened by the presence of a group of people shining flashlights.

Rattlesnakes sense the presence of warm animals by heat sensi-tive pits that are located below and forward of each eye. Good depth perception in locating prey is important because most foraging is done when visibility is poor at dusk or after dark.

Rattlesnakes do not hear in the normal sense. They probably detect ground-borne vibrations through their body or head if in contact with the ground, but do not hear air-borne vibrations. Rather unique, but they don't "hear" their own rattle.

Smelling is done in a pair of spherical chambers in the roof of the mouth. The forked tongue flicks out, picks up odorous particles from the air and transfers these samples to the chambers where sensory cells transmit the information to the brain.

To conclude this segment on the rattlesnake, it can be noted that the pupil of the eye is vertically elliptical and that the pupil of all other Santa Monica Mountain snakes is round. If you are close enough to note this difference, you are TOO CLOSE.

GEOLOGY

The Pacific Plate — the part of the earth's crust under the Pacific Ocean and as far inland as the San Andreas Fault — has been slowly moving against the North American Plate. This action is a major cause of mountain building in California. The land was forced up to become the Santa Monica Mountains less than 10 million years ago. Most of the geologic history prior to then happened as sedimentary deposits on the ocean floor. Land rose above the ocean on several previous occasions and later subsided. Volcanic activity resulted in massive igneous intrusions about 16-12 million years ago (mya), but for the most part the land was at the bottom of the ocean.

Although nowhere exposed, the 200 million year old ocean floor — the crustal section of the Pacific Plate — is the oldest formation in the Santa Monica Mountains. Santa Monica Slate, the first sedimentary deposit, was laid down in a shallow sea during the Jurassic Period, 190-135 mya. Santa Monica Slate is found in roadcuts in Sepulveda Pass and as far west as Sullivan and Rustic Canyons where outstanding examples may be seen. During late Jurassic and early Cretaceous Periods (about 135 mya) granite intruded into the slate.

The Tuna Canyon Formation, an Upper Cretaceous, 135-70 mya, marine sediment of sandstone, siltstone, and conglomerate, overlies the Santa Monica Slate. The land rose above the ocean during several significant periods of time, only to subside again. One such time occurred in the Early Paleocene Epoch, 70 mya, when the Simi Formation nonmarine conglomerate was deposited. This layer, characterized by rounded cobbles and boulders of quartzite, granitic, rhyolitic and gneissic rocks, is limited in its occurrence — the best known exposure is in Upper Solstice Canyon on private property.

Later, during Lower Paleocene and Eocene times, 60-50 mya, a fossil bearing marine sequence of pebbly conglomerate, sandstone, and siltstone was deposited on the Tuna Canyon Formation. Examples of this Coal Canyon Formation are found in Carbon (formerly Coal) Canyon.

The Llajas Formation is a marine sequence of sandstone, siltstone, and pebbly conglomerate that overlies the Coal Canyon Formation in a few places in the Santa Monica Mountains. A well exposed 1300' thick section of this Eocene, 50-40 mya, formation is seen in upper Solstice Canyon along part of the trail that goes west from the parking lot at the end of Corral Canyon Road.

During the late Eocene, Oligocene, and early Miocene times, 40-25 mya, the land again rose above the ocean and the nonmarine Sespe Formation of pebbly sandstone, mudstone, and coarse grained sandstone was laid down in flood plains. Examples may be found on Corral Ridge and Upper Solstice Canyon above the Llajas Formation. A prominent ridge is seen along East Topanga Fireroad.

The marine Vaqueros Formation containing shellfish fossils, characteristically TURRITELLA INEZANA, overlays the Sespe. This fine-grained sandy siltstone, mudstone, medium-to coarse-grained well-sorted formation was deposited during the Lower Miocene Epoch, 25-20 mya. Upper Trancas Canyon is one of many places to find this rock.

The Topanga Group is a Middle Miocene, 20-12 mya, sequence of sedimentary and volcanic rocks totalling about 18,000 feet in thickness. It is divided into three formations: a lower formation of sedimentary rock (Topanga Canyon Formation), a middle formation of volcanic rock (Conejo Volcanics) and an upper formation of sedimentary rook (Calabasas Formation) that intertongues with and overlies the volcanic. Examples of Topanga Group formations are widespread and common. A well-known collecting area for a variety of molluscan fauna is from the Topanga Canyon Formation along Old Topanga Canyon Road. The Conejo Volcanics are widespread in the central and western part of the mountains. Good examples are Goat Buttes in Malibu Creek State Park, but many other volcanic rocks are found throughout. The Calabasas Formation is a thick wide-spread sequence of sandstone, siltstone, and breccia. It receives its name from an exposure in Stokes Canyon about 2 miles west of Calabasas Peak. (The rock on Calabasas Peak is the Topanga Canyon Formation.)

The Modelo Formation was laid down during the late Miocene and early Pliocene Epochs, 12-8 mya, when the land was under a deep sea. Diatomaceous shale, siltstone, shale, and sandstone overlies the Topanga Group. The north slope of the central part of the mountains is made up of Modelo shale. Good examples can be seen in the roadcuts along Topanga Canyon Blvd. south of Mulholland Drive to the summit and 1/3 mile beyond.

The Malibu Coast Fault runs east-west from the mouth of Carbon Canyon to Leo Carrillo Beach. South of the fault the sequence of rock differs from that found in the rest of the Santa Monica Mountains. A 4000' exploratory well drilled near Point Dume determined the sequence, starting with the oldest rock: Catalina Schist, Trancas Formation, Zuma Volcanics, and Monterey Shale.

Catalina Schist of late Mesozoic Era is the underlying formation, and is not found anywhere on the surface.

The Trancas Formation is sandstone, mudstone, shale, claystone, and breccia of the early and middle Miocene epoch, 25-15 mya. Zuma Volcanic is of about the same age and interbedded with the sedimentary Trancas Formation. Neither formation is exposed at their base, and most of the information regarding thickness comes from core samples from oil well drilling.

Monterey Shale is of middle and late Miocene ages, 18-11 mya, of marine clay shale that is variably diatomaceous, bituminous, siliceous, and sandy. Dolomite and chert are common. The formation is about 3000 feet thick at Point Dume. Much of the area is overlain by marine terrace deposits of upper Pleistocene age, 3 mya and less.

GEOLOGIC COLUMN - SANTA MONICA MOUNTAINS

Eras	Periods / Epochs	Time in million years	Event or formation	Where to find examples
	Quarternary		Continued mountain building	
	Holocene	0.01		
	Pleistocene		Faulting Erosion	Everywhere
		3		
Tertiary			Mountain Building	
	Pliocene			
		11	Modelo	North slope of Mts
	Miocene		Topanga SS	Calabasas Pk
			Conejo Volc.	Mulholland HWY NW of Calab. Pk
			Vaqueros	Upper Trancas Cyn East Topanga F.R.
	Oligocene	25	Sespe	Upper Solstice Cyn
		40	Llajas	Upper Solstice Cyn
	Eocene		Carbon Cyn	
		60	Coal Cyn	Los Flores Cyn
	Paleocene		Simi Congl.	Upper Solstice Cyn
		70	Garapito Cyn	
Cretaceous			Tuna Cyn	Pena/Tuna Cyn
		135	Granite	Griffith Park
Jurassic			Santa Monica	Rustic Cyn Sullivan Cyn
		180	Slate	Sepulveda Cyn
Triassic		200	Floor of the ocean	

UPWARD FOLD OF STRATIFIED ROCK
caused during uplift of Santa Monica Mountains
(located in roadcut on south side of Mulholland
Highway near Malibu Creek State Park)

THE PEOPLE THAT CAME TO THE SANTA MONICA MOUNTAINS

THE INDIANS

Southern California experienced a decisive climatic change at the end of the Pleistocene Age about 11,500 years ago. The period of lessening moisture caused competition for water and plant food sources among the large land mammals that man used as a source of food. Over a period of several thousand years many of the large mammals became extinct causing man to experiment with new food sources and population movement. The selective processes resulted in man being forced to move out of a less productive desert environment into a new area.

The archaeological evidence shows that the Santa Monica Mountains were not extensively used prior to 7500 years ago. The earliest inhabitants were probably hunters that followed game through the valleys. This period coincides with the shortage of water that was evident in the desert region and coastal rivers of Southern California. The Santa Monica Mountain coastal area provided a highly productive environment for plant food as well as fish, and made for an attractive settlement area.

Most of the village sites of this time period are found on the coast rather than inland, usually located at low elevation near the mouth of a major stream in grassland and sagebrush plant communities. Four main areas along the coast show permanent occupation beginning about 7000 years ago: Malibu Canyon, Point Dume, Little Sycamore Canyon, and La Jolla Valley. The plant food sources were mainly the hard seed variety (grass and sage) which were available through much of the year. Walnut, Toyon, and Holly-leaf Cherry were available during fall and winter. It was later that acorns, with the need for processing, became a major part of the diet.

The year-round subsistence system of living in a permanent site and foraging for plant foods continued without any major change of strategy until about 3500 years ago. During this period of time many minor changes occurred. About 5000 years ago the processing of acorns for food became known and with this plentiful food source, there was an increase in population. Village sites expanded in size and number with some developing inland. This period of permanent settlement and vegetal subsistence system was given the name Millingstone Horizon, and is quite descriptive of the processing of the basic food which consisted of hard seeds.

The gradual transition from dependence on seed gathering from a permanent site to a subsistence system that included divergence in settlement pattern may have taken 1000 years. An increase in hunting, particularly resources from the ocean, and a decrease in the proportion of seed use, is characteristic. Fish became an important source of food. During this period, some significant improvements in fishing technique were made. A circular shell fishhook was developed. This allowed fishing from shore by hook and line. New coastal villages evolved and around 2300 years ago, the pattern of village distribution was established that remained constant until the time of the Spanish invasion. Many inland sites were also settled.

This middle period of history lasted until about 1500 years ago and is called the Intermediate Horizon. This 2000 year period of cultural evolution is characterized by a shift from almost total dependency on vegetal foods to one that included hunting, the increase in the use of seafood in the diet, the development of large spear points, (the bow and arrow came late in the period) and shell ornaments.

At this time (Late Horizon) the Chumash culture emerged. The heritage of the people did not change but a definite change occurred in the social structure. Nucleated villages developed, each supporting several smaller living sites away from the main village. These smaller sub-villages in turn temporarily allocated foraging areas to sub-groups. This concept intensified the exploitation of the natural food that was available, and was not abandoned until after the Spanish invasion. Land ownership became recognized, first as village-owned and in some cases family-owned.

Task specialization developed actively and the Chumash traded goods with their neighbors; technological changes occurred in such basic improvements as the evolution of pestle shape from heavy and short, to slender with increased efficiency; fused shale was discovered in Grimes Canyon and elsewhere, resulting in its use in projectile point making.

The Chumash had a well established political organization that stood the test of centuries. The technical accomplishments of the Chumash were noted by the Spanish and the records show that they were amazed at the finely made tools and equipment. They had a serviceable economic system.

A discussion of the Chumash society would not be complete without noting that their advancement in the fields of astronomy and cosmology can be considered highly developed.

The Chumash language is related to other languages of central and northern California yet is uniquely distinctive, showing a separation from other languages for thousands of years. Although not known, it is likely that the people that occupied the area 7000 years ago and more are the ancestors of the Chumash people.

There is some evidence to show that about 3000 years ago Shoshonean speaking people moved into the Los Angeles basin area, displacing the people there.

At the time of the Spanish invasion, the Santa Monica Mountains and adjacent area were home for two different Indian language groups, the Chumash speaking people in the west, and the Shoshonean speaking people in the east. The division line was between the Malibu Creek watershed and the Topanga Creek watershed. The Chumash were represented by the Ventureños whose territory included the west end of the Santa Monicas and basically Ventura County. The Shoshonean family in the mountains was represented by the Fernandeños east of the Ventureño territory except for the Griffith Park area occupied by the Gabrielinos.

THE SPANISH

Upon the overthrow of the Aztec empire by a Spanish force under Hernando Cortez between 1519 and 1521, there was a rapid expansion of the exploration and occupation of Mexico. Immediately a succession of explorers fanned out from Mexico City, one of whom was Juan Rodriguez Cabrillo who arrived off the coast of the Santa Monica Mountains in 1542.

This expedition marks the first known view of the Santa Monica Mountains by Westerners.

On the return trip from sailing north along the California Coast, Cabrillo anchored at San Miguel Island and spent the winter. In 1543 Cabrillo died as a result of an injury sustained when on the island before. It is supposed that he lies somewhere under the drifting sand of San Miguel.

Periodically, ships on the trade route from the Philippines to Mexico sailed past the Santa Monica Mountains. Sebastion Vizcaino sailed the coast in 1602, then for 167 years the Spanish ignored the area. Then Gaspar de Portolá made his first historic trip north.

Upon reaching the Santa Monica Mountains, scouts were sent out to find a way around or thru the mountains. A high, steep cliff down to the ocean prevented passage along shore. On Saturday, 5 August 1769, the party went over the mountains thru a rough and difficult canyon. The route was over Sepulveda Pass. The mountains were named after Saint Monica.

After reaching the north side of the mountains they crossed the San Fernando Valley and went on to Castaic, then followed the Santa Clara River to the coast.

On the return trip from searching for Monterey Bay, Portolá came inland from the Oxnard Plain staying close to the north edge of the Santa Monicas, crossing the mountains thru Cahuenga Pass along the route of an Indian trail — now the Hollywood Freeway.

This expedition introduced the missionization of the coast of southern California. No missions were built in the Santa Monica Mountains but all of the Indians were within mission influence.

The contact of Indian culture with Westerners can be conveniently divided into four chronological periods:

> Spanish Exploration (1542-1769)
> Mission (1769-1834)
> Rancho (1834-1848)
> American (1848-   )

During the exploration period the effect on the Indian culture was minimal.

The culture impact of the missions was significant. When the Spanish arrived in California they brought an inherent cultural concept very different from the Native Americans. The Spanish subjects belonged to an authoritarian state, had a history of religious intolerance and conformity, for centuries had been embroiled in almost constant war with other peoples, usually with conquest as a goal, and had a manic zeal to impose their culture

26

upon others. The Native Americans of southern California were almost the opposite in that they functioned in small political groups whose leaders did not have strong authority, were not warlike, tolerated other people's religious beliefs, and had no desire to exploit others.

Coupling these basic differences with the duplicity exercised by the Spanish speaking invaders, and the mass deaths because of introduced diseases, the Indians lost their land, their culture, and their lives.

THE MEXICANS

After Mexico declared independence from Spain in 1821, a shift in authority took place with the missions losing their vast land holdings and political domination. The Mexican colonization law of 1824 and the Reglamento of 1828 were passed and land grants were made. By 1834 the transition from religious to civil control was complete; mission lands had been sold and large ranchos established. Most of the Santa Monica Mountain area was claimed — current 7½ minute series topographic maps show boundaries and names of these Mexican land grants.

The Rancho period was of short duration because the Mexican-American War of 1846-1848 ended with California passing into the hands of the United States. The Ranchos remained but an era passed.

THE AMERICANS

The Mountain Men in search of beavers had entered Spanish territory as early as 1817, and then Mexican territory in the 1820's, affecting a degree of commercial annexation. Efforts were made to keep them out. Despite some jail sentences and forced ejections from the area, the intruders kept coming. Jedediah Smith arrived at the San Gabriel Mission in 1826; James Pattie made it to a mission in Baja in 1827; Ewing Young came to Los Angeles in 1832; Joseph Walker and many others explored the State: and in the early 1840's, immigrant parties were coming to California. Most of the settlers went to the San Joaquin and Sacramento Valleys.

John C. Fremont led an Army force into California in 1845 and was in position when the Mexican-American War began in 1846. Sporadic fighting for California lasted until 13 January 1847, when the peace treaty was signed at Campo de Cahuenga, at an adobe building at the foot of Cahuenga Pass in the Santa Monica Mountains. Another year was to pass before California became United States Territory, but a new page in history had been turned.

On 2 February 1848, the United States and Mexico entered into an agreement that officially ended the war, with negotiations being conducted at Guadalupe Hidalgo on the outskirts of Mexico City. A part of the treaty included the securing of California by the United States.

The "Gold Rush" of 1849 brought thousands of people to California and made a significant change in the way of life that had existed in the Rancho period. Flourishing towns developed overnight; local law became the rule; most of the population consisted of men without families, and the pastoral scene that characterized life was temporarily stayed. California was admitted as the 31st State in 1850.

The concept of land ownership made a dramatic shift. During the Indian occupation the land belonged to the people as a group, and usage was for all. There were some use agreements between families, but land titles as we know them today were not the rule. Under Spanish rule the land belonged to the King of Spain with the Church administering much of it. Usage permits were issued to ex-military men, but title to the land was not transferred. Under Mexican rule large land grants were made giving ownership of ranchos to relatively few individuals with the majority of the people living and working on someone else's land. The title to lands held under Mexican rule was honored by the United States upon obtaining California. Additionally, there was a strong demand for private ownership by the incoming settlers. Limited access to ownership of public property was available from the time that the United States acquired California, but the Homestead Act of 1862 made it possible for any adult citizen or applicant for citizenship who was the head of a family, to apply for 160 acres of unappropriated public land. This act, coupled with the growth of stage lines and established emigration routes, brought a lot of people to California.

The growth of population in the area surrounding the Santa Monica Mountains has had its effect on the mountains. The building of roads and the pressure to build more; the building of homes and the constant subdivision of new areas; the use of canyons as garbage dumps; the need to crisscross the mountains with power lines, telephone lines, water pipe lines, and gas lines; the demand for parks, equestrian trails, hiking trails, camping areas, picnic grounds and other recreation uses; and the desire to preserve the hundreds of archaeological sites that have survived thousands of years — all place a great demand on the mountains and those of us who use them.

HOW TO ENJOY THE HIKING EXPERIENCE

"Study nature, not books" is an old axiom that suggests that we emphasize the personal experience of observing nature rather than reading what others have written on the subject. The intent of this book is to help us to enjoy what the Santa Monica Mountains has to offer us as a participant. What I write here is done with the intent of our having a safe and interesting hiking experience. Others have known some of us to get carried away and describe nature as we would like it to be rather than as it is. My "thundering cascade" over a waterfall as witnessed during a heavy rain may seem extravagant to one who arrives late in summer and finds a mere trickle down the face of the rock. What I am trying to say is that to hike these trails is to enjoy nature at its fullest; read this book to get us out there!

SELECTING A TRIP

This book describes more than 75 hiking trips. Some are easy. Some are very challenging. We should choose a trip that we believe we can enjoy and is within our hiking ability. Unless the drive is especially appealing, we might want to select a trip near where we live. The heading of each trip includes information on the type of terrain, the distance, the elevation gain and the expected walking time. If hiking is a new experience for us, visit Topanga State Park and do the Eagle Spring Loop Hike. This is a safe hike in that we may turn back without doing the complete loop and still have an enjoyable experience. Any trip on a good trail with not more than 1000' elevation gain and in the five or 6-mile distance range would be suitable. As we gain experience, we can expand our horizons.

OBSERVE THE AREA

The beauty of the trip is not so much in the trail underfoot as it is in the landscape about us. The benefits of looking about and mentally noting the landmarks and features of the terrain are twofold at least. Not only will we see more of the physical sights that the mountains offer, but we will become familiarized with the area to the point that we will know the trails, points of interest, and can find our way.

DON'T GET LOST

Who can get lost? Anyone can, all ages, both sexes, people alone or in groups. Upon discovering that we might be lost, stop and sit and think. Then we mark our location, try to signal, relax.

Or to state it poetically: —

When lost or confused
and when in doubt
Don't run in circles
Just wave and shout.

FOOTGEAR

We can take many of these hikes wearing tennis shoes or jogging shoes; a friend of mine wears hush puppies. The evidence leads us to believe that the Indians were barefoot or at best had fiber sandals or leather moccasins. These facts aside, my recommendation for any but the short hikes on a good trail is to wear a sturdy hiking boot. Wear wool socks winter and summer. Have someone knowledgeable fit your boots. We should break them in on the shorter trips. It may sound as I am overdoing foot protection. Nevertheless, a blister, stone bruise, or twisted ankle sure takes much of the fun out of a good hike.

CLOTHING

Choices of clothing will depend on the season, weather and hiking terrain. My choices for warm weather open trail day hiking is shorts, T-shirt and a hat that keeps some sun off my face. Cooler weather requires more protection so wear long pants and a long sleeved shirt. A lightweight windbreaker will give added protection, and carry it in the pack. Bushwhacking through chaparral is another matter. Wear close-weave long pants and a long-sleeved shirt, gloves and goggles. Very few of the trips suggested in this book deliberately get off an established trail but once in awhile, like on the "Lemming Hike," we encounter chaparral; so if we plan to go through it, be prepared. We will encounter some rain in the winter. This should not be an absolute deterrent to hiking because hiking in the rain adds a new dimension to the experience. Various types of rain gear are available, probably none of which work perfectly. I expect to get wet and have muddy feet.

EQUIPMENT

The tendency is to carry more than one needs, but we could term some items essential. Needed is a day pack, water, a first aid kit, a map and a compass for some hikes. Cameras, binoculars, books on birds, plants, animals and geology and other items can add to the hiking experience. Take a little something to eat if we like. We might prefer to carry "The Ten Essentials" in a small bag and throw it in the day pack when needed. The ten essentials are:
For our protection, (1) Extra clothing, (2) Spare food and water, (3) Sunglasses.
To find our way, (4) Map, (5) Compass, (6) Flashlight (spare bulbs and batteries).
For emergencies, (7) First Aid Kit, Waterproof Matches, (9) Candle, (10) Knife, (11) Toilet paper.

FOOD

What can I say about food that we have not said often before? Anything goes — just since no one needs fire to heat the food. I've seen some very exotic meals out on the trail and some austere ones. For myself, I prefer to keep it simple and light. A large lunch discourages vigorous hiking. Sandwiches, carrot sticks and apple would do it. Or if we are not serious about hiking, some day take a loaf of sourdough French bread, a chunk of cheese and a bottle of Chablis.

WATER

Take some water. Generally avoid water from streams and ponds; we don't know for sure what is happening upstream. Water is necessary during exercise, so be on the comfortable side and bring a canteen.

ROCK CLIMBING

Most of the hiking we are likely to do will be on a fireroad or trail. Occasionally we will do some off trail travel to reach an area like middle Zuma Canyon. When we encounter this type of terrain on the described hikes, I will sometimes use a classification such as class 2 or class 3. The difficulty increases with the class:

CLASS 1 Walking upright usually on a trail but not necessarily so. We would not require special footgear.

CLASS 2: Use of hands is required for balance. We wear proper footgear.

CLASS 3: Climbing technique is required. Hands are also used for climbing. Rope belay should be available. Proper footgear is essential. I will state Class 3 in the heading of any hike that falls into this category.

None of the hikes described call for climbing techniques more difficult than class 3.

A word of explanation is in order. The classification is made under the assumption that the weather is good and that we follow the prescribed route. Rain or darkness can increase the difficulty so planning for a margin of safety is best.

DOGS, HORSES, BICYCLES, and PEOPLE

With some exceptions dogs are not allowed in any of the State Parks. Seeing Eye dogs are allowed. A few posted areas are open for dogs on a leash. None of the back country is available to dog use. The National Park Service allows dogs on leash where posted. For safety some trails are closed to horse use. In general, however, horses are allowed on most trails and roads.

Horses, bicycles, and people use trails differently and at widely divergent speeds. This mixed use presents problems to all users. A great deal of effort has focused on ways to make trail use safe and enjoyable for all. We have a long way to go, but if each of us does our best to be considerate of other trail users, we can continue to enjoy these mountains.

HIKING COMPANIONS

Last but not least is the people we hike with. We try to find a compatible group that hikes our speed and ability. Most people that hike are there because they want to be, and are easy to get along with. Occasionally circumstances provide difficult conditions that might test a group's compatibility, such as becoming lost in chaparral while it is raining. Being in the company of optimists is better than pessimists.

Some of us hike alone quite often. This reduces the safety factor some. Leaving word as to your proposed itinerary and time of return is sensible. (I usually carry a phone.)

ENVIRONMENTAL HAZARDS

Because these mountains are close to civilization, we might have tendencies to overlook the fact that it is wild country. A much different environment is out there — probably safer than downtown but still with some unique hazards of which to be aware.

FIRE

Much of the hiking in the Santa Monicas is in the chaparral area. Dry winds for an extended period with several months without any rain causes a potential fire hazard. Under these conditions a rampaging fire can sweep up a slope faster than we can climb out. They post fire closures during periods of extreme fire danger, both to reduce the possibility of starting a fire and to prevent danger to people in the area. Nearly all fires in the Santa Monica Mountains are man caused; of course, we of the hiking community should make sure that we do not contribute.

SUN

We have often heard that chaparral is "too high to see over, too thick to go through, and too low to give shade." The next time that the sun beats down on your unprotected head, give some thought to protection. Summer calls for a hat. Depending on the state of your tan, we should shade the rest of our body from the direct rays of the sun. I repeat, wear a hat.

Overheating causes both .heat exhaustion and heat stroke, Sunshine is not necessarily a cause, but can be. Differences exist between the two ailments. Heat Exhaustion occurs to someone that has perspired heavily during exertion or because it is very hot and the body loses both water and salts. The person feels tired, faint, has a headache, nausea, has moist skin, or may be pale. The body temperature is normal, fast and a feeble pulse, possibilities of cramps. The treatment is to find a cool place and lie down, loosen clothing, raise feet, drink fruit juices, or water with some electrolytes added. Drink 1/2 cup every 15 minutes.

Recovery is probable but get medical advice.

Heat Stroke can occur on a hot, humid, windless day that doesn't allow sweat evaporation to cool the body. Restlessness, confusion, and sometimes unconscousness, identify Heat Stroke.. The skin is hot and red, and becomes dry at the onset of trouble. Pulse is fast and strong, body temperature is high. Treat by getting the person to a cool place. Remove the clothing and sponge the body with water to bring the temperature down a few degrees. The condition is very serious — we should get medical help.

WATER

Flash floods such as occur in the desert are rare in the mountains. A heavy downpour will swell the streams and occasionally cause a mudslide, so we must use care. Travel along some streambeds becomes virtually impossible when the water is high and crossings become hazardous. Rocks rolling down into the canyons are definite hazards.

Automobile travel along the Pacific Coast Highway and on nearly all of the mountain roads is hazardous because of falling rocks during a storm.

PLANT LIFE

Immediately what comes to mind but Poison Oak? The juices from the leaves, stems or any part of the plant can cause a persistent rash. Washing with soap and cold water when possible after contact will prevent the rash. Also, a native plant, Mugwort, is a favorite "rub-on" antidote.

A similar plant called Squaw Bush, also belongs to the Sumac family, but is nonpoisonous. It resembles Poison Oak closely, and because it can grow in the same area, is frequently mistaken for Poison Oak. Other plants such as Phacelia and nettles cause a temporary skin irritation.

ANIMAL LIFE

Most people never see a rattlesnake. I have talked with people that have hiked the Santa Monicas frequently over a long period — 20 years or so — and some have never seen a rattler.

Nevertheless, as for myself, I have seen dozens of them. A reason for this apparent disparity exists.

Much of my hiking is late afternoon and night. During the hot summer, rattlesnakes keep in the shade during the day and begin to move around when the temperature drops. Having no temperature regulating device, as mammals do, they must seek a spot that keeps them in their preferred temperature range. Somewhere between 64° and 89° F. — with a real preference for the mid 80's.is normal. This means that from late spring until late fall they are often nocturnal. Occasionally I have seen a rattler lying in the hot noonday sun during the middle of summer, but not for long. When a rattlesnake absorbs heat, he'll become active and head for shade. So look for snakes in late afternoon or evening from late spring to late fall, and during the day at other times, except in the winter when they stay underground.

Also, it is very important to look where we step and avoid probing around in clumps of grass or around rocks unless we can see clearly. If we spot a snake, avoid him and nothing will happen. If we come close, the snake will move away or take a coiled defensive position, depending upon the threat. I have had only one snake move toward me, which was early April, and from a coiled rattling position.

One thing further — if I owned a dog I'd either leave him at home or keep very close track of him while hiking. A dog's curiosity can cause trouble very quickly — for the dog.

They recommend several methods for treating snakebite. The following method appeals to me: Lay the person down; wipe venom away from the puncture area; wash with soap and water; pat dry, do not rub; apply a clean dressing; give pain pills; carry the person to a hospital when possible, keeping the bitten area low. Do not apply a tourniquet; do not cut into the area; do not apply chemicals; do not suck the wound. Keep calm. Do not let the patient exercise.

Also, avoid the small animals: gophers, rabbits, mice, etc., alive or dead. Fleas that sometimes carry germs may be looking for a new host and though the chance is remote, nobody needs the bubonic plague. (The State Dept. of Public Health recognizes this as Sylvatic [wild rodent] plague since the term "bubonic" refers to only one of the three clinical forms.) Also, the pustules on a diseased animal are a source of infection. The larger animals:

deer, coyotes, bobcats, all will avoid people and are not a usual hazard.

Insects live in the Santa Monica Mountains and can be a factor in your enjoyment. The usual flies, mosquitoes, and other bothersome insects are evident, although not to the degree they would be in a damper environment. Trail descriptions will normally omit any discussion of insect life because the distribution of any species is random, and their presence doesn't appear to cause a problem. Well, those "bee trees" down in Santa Ynez and Rustic Canyons bear watching.

I have some general words of advice, however. Such as — don't become so engrossed in watching the behavior of a colony of Harvester ants that we allow one of these 1/4" long red ants to crawl up our leg and bite. It's quite interesting to watch one group of ants gather seeds from the Buckwheat plant and carry them down a hole in the ground while other ants from the colony bring up the chaff and deposit it. Though each ant seems to have an assigned work role, it appears anyone can bite.

Mites (chiggers, "red bugs") are not a serious problem in the dry areas and people only occasionally become a target. Ticks climb to the tips of blades of grass or brush and wave their eight legs when disturbed, thus attaching to an unsuspecting host. I use a recommended procedure for removing a tick that has become attached. Using a pair of tweezers or a piece of paper or leaf or just your finger and thumb to hold the tick as we exert a straight steady pull. The tick will release its hold. The time for this to occur varies; my experience has been that some ticks persevere longer than others, but eventually give. Then apply antiseptic. My Dad added a counterclockwise twist of one revolution while steadily pulling on the tick. It always worked. If all of the tick doesn't come out, then it will probably become infected and come out in a couple of days. Once a tick is firmly attached and beginning to swell up, a drop of alcohol every minute or so for 10 minutes will cause him/her to relax enough for easy removal. Another method is to cover the tick with oil — any kind — for half an hour, then gently remove the tick. We see a physician if we become ill after a bite. Ticks are carriers of Lyme disease (named from Old Lyme, Connecticut) which they have reported in California, mostly in northern, wetter counties. Case reports in Los Angeles County are infrequent. Dogs, deer, coyotes, horses and people seem main hosts for ticks. Some good news is that a UC/Berkeley insect biologist has reported ticks having a Western fence Lizard for a host can be disinfected of the Lyme disease bacteria. The bad news is that dogs are a carrier and without control could introduce Lyme disease to a clean area. A vaccine for dogs is available. Recently a vaccine for people has been developed. Reports are that it is effective to a degree but with decreasing effectiveness as a person reaches 60 years.

The cone-nosed bug can cause a serious allergic reaction in some people. Normally the cone-nose bug lives in a wood rat den so one can avoid the possible encounter by not poking around any large pile of sticks and twig.

HOW TO USE THE GUIDE

"Pick up the book, turn to a trip that appeals to you, and follow the instructions." At least that is my intention in the preparation of this guide. So — a trail that exists today may not necessarily be the same a few years from now.

In addition, trails that hikers have used for years may suddenly become unavailable for use because of land ownership transfer, or the owner may just get tired of picking up beer cans and decide to post a "no trespassing" sign. One property owner told me that in 5 years 3 fires have been started on his property by hikers. I have seen people light up a cigarette while sitting on dry grass and the wind is blowing. Admittedly, these instances are rare, but for someone who loses a house, once is more than enough. A lot of the Santa Monica Mountains is privately owned and the owner of property has the right to use of the property. None of the hikes I have described deliberately trespass; but times and conditions change, so be alert to posted notices and abide by them.

Temporary closures also exist on both public and private land. Point Mugu State Park, Malibu Creek State Park and Topanga State Park are frequently closed for fire hazard during warm or windy weather. Flood conditions will also close a park. A daily updated recorded status of the State Parks may be obtained by dialing the local State Park Office.

Most of the hikes are over land in the State Park system and are open to the public, sometimes for a fee. Rules and regulations are posted and available as handout information. Except in designated campgrounds, dogs and other pets are not allowed; smoking and other fires are not allowed in the back country; camping is permitted only in designated campgrounds; removal of flowers, rocks or other natural items is prohibited; littering or defacing the environment is not allowed; and all motorized vehicles are banned from the roads and trails.

Each trip writeup has information as to the maps used, the distance travelled, the elevation gain and loss, the terrain, and the walking time for an average person. I have included a brief explanation of getting to the trailhead — this can be further clarified in some cases by referring to the map and charts showing main driving roads and the charts showing distances. The trip writeup itself describes the general concept of the hike with specific attention to the detail of road forks, landmarks, and items of interest.

Other information is occasionally included in the trip writeup. Plant life, geologic information, historical, or archaeological facts may sometimes be a part of the hike and provide interesting background. My intent has been to place the emphasis on describing how to get into and out of the mountains.

The trips in this book are listed from west to east; that is, trip number one is in Point Mugu State Park at the western end of the Santa Monicas and the last trip is in Griffith Park at the eastern end. How to judge the time required to walk a given trail takes some experience. Some of us with a good steady pace on level ground slow down when going uphill. Some even slow down going downhill. Your own speed can be determined by timing yourself while walking a measured distance on level ground, then doing the walk with a hill added. If your level trail hiking speed is 3 mph and it takes an extra 30 minutes to gain 1000 feet, then the walking times listed in these trip writeups will match your speed close enough.

Another type of factor that enters in is the type of terrain. Boulder-hopping and bushwhacking throw this system out of balance. Some of us really slow down under these conditions. A good stand of chaparral will stop me completely.

One other factor is the size of the hiking group, If there are a dozen people on the hike, I automatically add 20 minutes to every hour estimated. If the hike walking time is listed at 3 hours, it will take a group of 12 about 4 hours. This takes into account waiting for people as they bunch up for bottlenecks such as crossing a stream or a log, or for someone who decides to stop and take off a sweater. All these things slow down the group.

The times shown on the individual hikes are the actual time that it took me to walk the trip, modified by time-outs I may have taken for picture-taking or investigating some local item of interest. Short rest stops are included in the hiking time. My hiking speed is just under 3 mph and I am slower going uphill. Since my hiking speed undoubtedly varies on different days, absolute accuracy is not possible.

MAPS

Don't get lost! This is not as impossible as you may think. The Santa Monica Mountain range is surrounded by civilization and there are some roads and also small communities, but the terrain in between is quite rugged. The possibility of losing your way is real, so a good map and the knowledge of how to use it will add to your enjoyment of hiking.

This guide book is written so that you may conveniently take a number of established trips, using the book as reference, but when the time comes that you want to explore on your own, you should carry a map.

Maps of this area are available from a number of sources. Many of the backpacking stores carry the topographic maps published by the U. S. Geological Survey. The 7.5 minute "topos" have a scale of I inch = 2000 feet, the contour interval of 25 feet makes it possible to estimate elevation gains and losses accurately. The maps do not have an explanation of the symbols used — a booklet describing topographic maps and symbols is available, free from the Geological Survey. In the event that local sources of maps cannot supply your needs, order directly from Distribution Section, Geological Survey, Federal Center, Denver, Colorado 80225.

Some of the State and National Parks give away maps of their own area, showing the trails and major points of interest.

Street maps of the local metropolitan area are helpful in locating the roadheads of the hikes described in this book. I have found the Street Atlas published by Thomas Bros. Maps to be convenient.

Tom Harrison's Trail Maps of the Santa Monica Mountains are used as a major source of information. Three maps: West, Central, and East sections apply to our mountains.

And of course this book is written so that by reading the trip descriptions and referring to the maps included, all will go well.

Road guides are also important in locating the trailhead. On occasion it will be helpful to understand some of the signs that are posted alongside highways. Following these signs can sometimes become a two person affair; one to pay attention to the driving, the other to read the map and the signs. You may have already developed superior route finding techniques but I shall list some traditional methods for those that have difficulty.

A logical and mathematically correct method is to note mileage at the passing of some checkpoint then project ahead to the mileage at the next checkpoint. As any of us who has used this method knows, it has limitations. Watching the odometer very closely can cause you to miss the scenery and even the landmarks. And for some unknown reason there is accuracy of 0.l mile. Also if somehow you lose track of either a checkpoint or mileage the system deteriorates quickly.

So instead of complete reliance on this mileage method I will attempt both on highway or trail, in auto or afoot, to augment mileage with prominent features that can be used to crosscheck position.

Many of the highways in California are lined by small metal markers, 8x24 inches, set on a three foot post. Usually white, often with reflectors mounted on the side facing traffic, but sometimes with lettering and numbers in black. This will identify the County, the highway number, and the distance in miles, from either the county line or the beginning of the highway or some other reference point. As an example: the accompanying figure reads 27 LA 7.01. This is interpreted as being being Hwy #27 (Topanga Cyn Blvd.) in Los Angeles County and 7.01 miles from some reference point — in this case 7.01 miles from the Pacific Coast Highway. Bridges and overpasses are marked the same, with the added benefit of naming the stream or roadway. Wherever it may be of help, I'll include this road marker information.

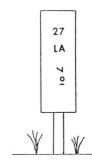

I am recommending Tom Harrison's maps and will list the appropriate one for each hike scheduled. These maps include symbols, parking areas, camp grounds, topographic information, roads, and trail information. A set of his maps should always be in our packet of 10 essentials.

TRAILS INDEX

HIKE 1

Route:	By kayak from the north side of Mugu Rock to Santa Monica Pier
Maps:	The one illustrated here
Distance:	36 miles

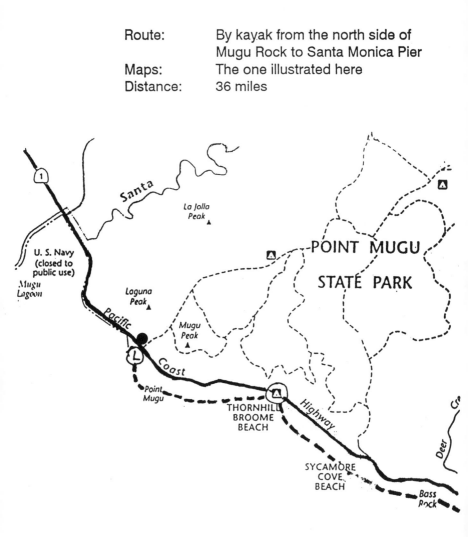

Can you believe this? Hike #1 in this hiking book is a kayak route on the ocean offshore of the Pacific Coast highway!

Tomol is the Chumash Indian name of their planked canoe. It is unique to southern California. When Cabrillo arrived off the coast of the Santa Monica Mountains in 1542 he was met by Chumash Indians in planked canoes. The Spanish gave glowing written reports of these seaworthy and maneuverable crafts. It seems fitting that an ocean route takes the name of Lower Tomol Trail.

Doug Kirk has paddled this section of the coast extensively. His enthusiasm for kayak travel and his willing approach to coordinate the opening of this trail has made it possible for kayaking along our coast.

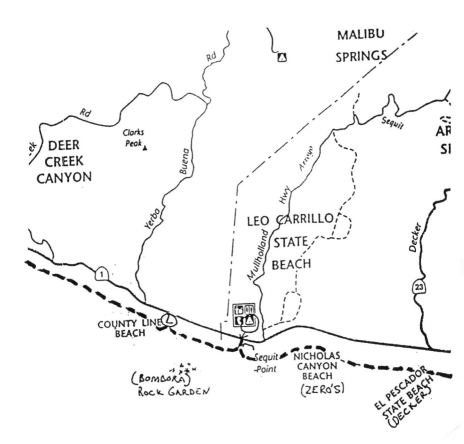

Doug is finalizing his book on the trail and is including considerable detail. Serious kayakers should use it as a reference. Doug Kirk introduces us to this trail in his own words:

"The Lower Tomol Trail is an ancient paddling trail which connects the inter tidal zone and kelp forests with the beautiful Santa Monica Mountains. Before the Pacific Coast Highway the Chumash had their Tomols and this trail. The lower portion of this trail has been officially reopened for the modern day paddler. Paddling this trail you will see these mountains from a wonderful new prospective. You will also get acquainted with very large marine mammals, sea birds, and spectacular sunsets.

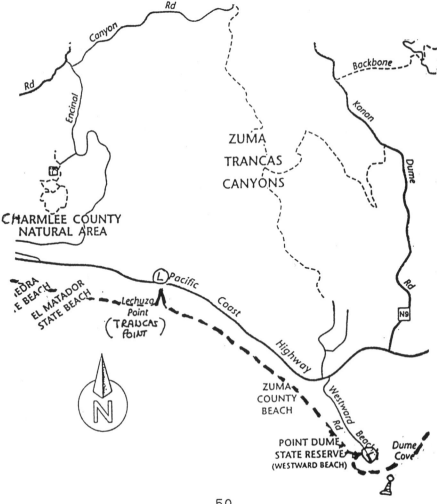

The coast in this area varies from gradual sandy beaches to the striking cliffs of the headlands textured with Giant Coreopsis. Trailheads are located at Mugu Beach (2.5 miles down the coast from Las Posas road in Mugu State Park) and at the Santa Monica Pier. Many approved landings and two overnight paddle camps have been provided by the many agencies protecting our beaches.

As with many trails this thirty-six mile trail can be done as a through trip or as many short day trips. Prevailing winds and mild currents are down the coast (west to east). The portion from Santa Monica to Trancas offers bus service for a shuttle. Sorry, paddlers only, no boats on the bus.

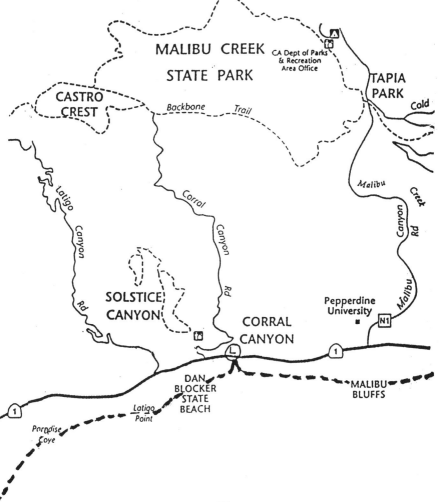

This is a beautiful part of our world and is well worth the effort. Have the appropriate skill level and safety equipment. The Tomol Trail can be calm and peaceful or dangerous and challenging. Conditions can change quickly so be alert and choose conditions that you can easily handle.

If you like big wild mammals, soaring birds, colorful fish and scenery in an almost pristine setting this is your trail. The Tomol Trail never is the same. It changes not only with the weather and the season but also the waves and tides."

The Lower Tomol Trail brings another perspective to the Santa Monica Mountains National Recreation Area. As with hiking and biking, this trail places an emphasis on the human-powered form of using the recreational resources of our park system. We will look at beaches from a new viewpoint. A kayak trip down the coast brings us closer to prehistoric and historic uses of the land. Let's challenge the sea and reap the rewards of our ancestral relation to the ocean.

The coast between Mugu Rock and Santa Monica pier runs west to east.

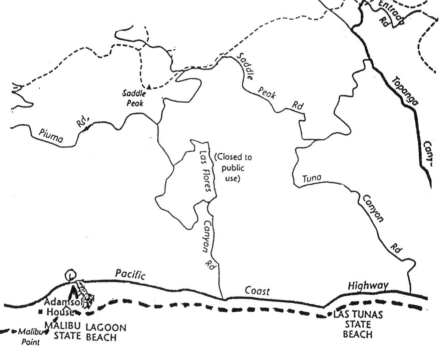

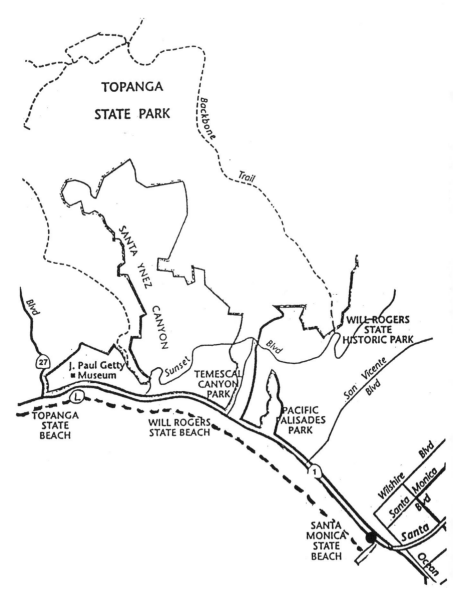

TOPANGA
STATE PARK

Backbone

Trail

SANTA YNEZ CANYON

Blvd

WILL ROGERS
STATE
HISTORIC PARK

27

J. Paul Getty
■ Museum

Sunset

Blvd

San Vicente Blvd

L

TEMESCAL
CANYON
PARK

TOPANGA
STATE
BEACH

WILL ROGERS
STATE BEACH

PACIFIC
PALISADES
PARK

1

Wilshire

Santa Monica Blvd

Santa

Ocean

SANTA
MONICA
STATE
BEACH

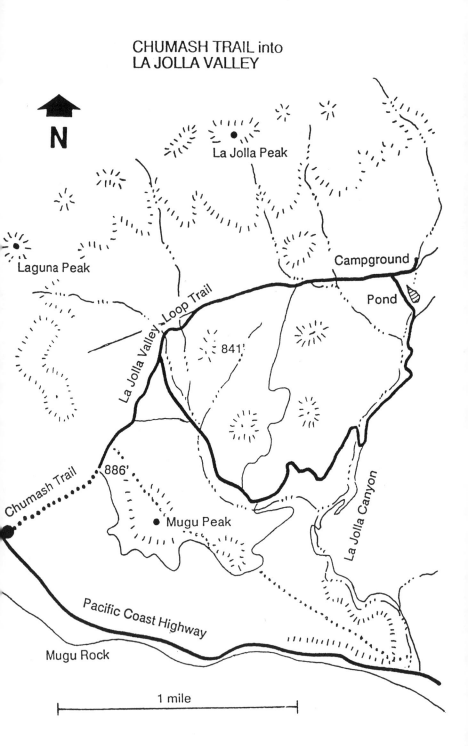

CHUMASH TRAIL into
LA JOLLA VALLEY

N

La Jolla Peak

Laguna Peak

Campground

La Jolla Valley Loop Trail

Pond

841'

Chumash Trail

886'

Mugu Peak

La Jolla Canyon

Pacific Coast Highway

Mugu Rock

1 mile

HIKE 2

LA JOLLA VALLEY LOOP
from the Pacific Coast Hwy
via The Chumash Trail

Maps:	Point Mugu, topo
	Point Mugu State Park
Distance:	6 miles roundtrip
Elevation:	1200' gain and loss
Terrain:	Trail; some steep,
	some easy
Time:	2¾ hours
Trailhead:	Pacific Coast Hwy

Indians lived in La Jolla Valley early in man's occupation in the Santa Monica Mountains. We don't know for sure but they probably settled in the mountains and along the coast seven thousand years ago. During the mission expansion period in the late 1770s and early 1800s many Native Americans moved to the missions. A trail into the valley comes up from the east end of Mugu Lagoon. This was one route used as a corridor between the people living in the valley and the coast. This trail could very well be the oldest trail in the world with continuous use for 7,000 years. We can envision daily trips from several inland villages to the seashore. Mussels and other seafood were available all along the coast. Because this trail may become a national treasure, we must care for it now. 'By care for" I suggest we do not try to improve upon the heritage we find here. For seventy centuries it has had no formal maintenance, and has survived in benign neglect. If a few of us walk the trail once a year we will not forget the way. We should not build a trail to modern standards, let's experience the path walked by countless Native Americans.

To reach the beginning of the trail, go 24 miles west of Malibu on the Pacific Coast Highway. Park two miles beyond the La Jolla Canyon Road in a large parking area on the right. The road marker nearby reads 8⁰⁷. The Trailhead is across the highway from a military small arms firing range.

We willl go straight up the hill to the east without any

switchbacks. This is characteristic of the Indian trails — steep and direct — no frills. In a little more than 1/2 mile just northwest of Mugu Peak, the trail crests at a saddle. The altitude is 886'. Broken seashells litter the route, giving mute evidence of its previous use.

Take time to look back at the sprawling Pacific Ocean. On occasion it will storm, but usually we will see gentle rolls of waves softly caressing the shore below. Off to the right and out at sea are the Channel Islands. Indian tradition says that when a certain type of cloud forms over Anacapa that rains will follow in a few days.

La Jolla Valley extends northeast of the crest of the trail. It is a surprisingly large area of grassland cut by the two main forks of La Jolla Creek. Trees line the streambeds and in a few places oakgroves offer shade for resting or lunch. Once Chumash villages and camps dotted the valley. Springs and permanent running water made this an attractive living area for the Indians the ranchers that followed.

Several trails in La Jolla Valley give us an opportunity to crisscross the valley and to see the canyon downstream. This hike will guide you on a loop trip around the upper part of the valley.

Continue on the trail as it heads northeast from the saddle. The gentle downhill grade takes us through a mountain rimmed savannah, rich in Indian history and valuable as a preserve for rare native grasses. Several trails come up the valley from the right and join ours. A trail that comes from the direction of Laguna Peak enters on the left. (Laguna Peak supports a radar facility in a fenced-in area and is "off limits.") About a mile after leaving the saddle, the trail goes through an area of head high mustard plants, crosses two tributaries of the west fork and turns east. As we continue east for another mile, several trails come up the valley from the south. These all come in from the main trail that starts at the Ray Miller Trailhead in La Jolla Canyon parking lot.

The La Jolla Valley Walk-in Camp is on the left. This camp is a primitive overnight camping spot with drinking water and restrooms. Campers may obtain permits for an overnight stay from a ranger at the Sycamore Cove administration building. Find the building on the ocean side of the highway at Sycamore Canyon.. The campground is in an oak grove with lots of shade and level grassy areas. It's a good place for a lunch stop.

Continue the loop of the valley by backtracking a short distance and branch off the trail to the south, along a pond. That black bird swimming among the tules is a coot. Just after passing the pond, the trail intersects the main La Jolla Canyon Trail as it gently follows downstream along the east bank. Turn right and walk this trail for about 3/4 mile until reaching another well marked and clearly visible trail on the right. (If we happen to miss it we will soon start dropping down into the splashing waters of La Jolla Canyon and arrive at the wrong roadhead.) Take this trail, initially heading northwest. .Cross the stream and follow the trail through a left turn as we begin a climb along the hillside. Upon reaching an overlook point we stop for a rest and look south to see the canyon trail below and the ocean beyond. About one-half mile west of the overlook we come to an oak grove on the left. A trail branches left giving us option #1 of taking it. We cross the stream and climb around the south and west shoulders of Mugu Peak then to the top of Chumash Trail. (We can take a side trip to Mugu Peak by using a narrow trail on the right). Or back at the grove we can take option #2 and continue ahead. We follow up-stream taking care to notice that the trail forks again. Take the left fork, and in about one mile we intersect the Indian trail on which a left turn takes us back to the trailhead.

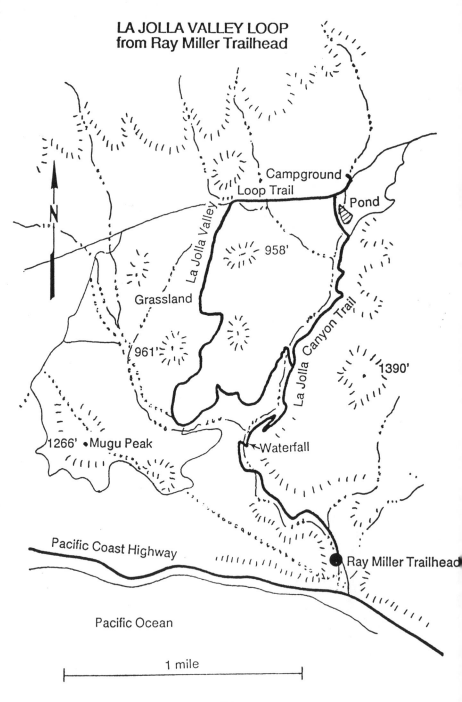

**LA JOLLA VALLEY LOOP
from Ray Miller Trailhead**

Campground
Loop Trail
Pond
La Jolla Valley
958'
Grassland
961'
La Jolla Canyon Trail
1390'
N
1266' •Mugu Peak
Waterfall
Pacific Coast Highway
Ray Miller Trailhead
Pacific Ocean
1 mile

HIKE 3

LA JOLLA VALLEY LOOP
from Ray Miller Trailhead

Maps:	SMMTS, Western Section
Distance:	6½ miles roundtrip
Elevation:	1000' gain and loss
Terrain:	Trail, some very steep, some level
Time:	3 hours
Trailhead:	Ray Miller Trailhead in La Jolla Canyon

Drive west on the Pacific Coast Highway, 22 miles from Malibu to the La Jolla Canyon parking lot. As we drive along, the lazy Pacific surf noses in on our left. Up ahead Mugu Peak is still shaking the morning mist from its crest. LaJolla Canyon is east of Mugu Peak.

Walk north from the parking lot at the Ray Miller Trailhead, going upstream on the La Jolla Canyon Trail. An old road, built in the '20s and used to haul rock for building the Pacific Coast Highway, goes about 3/4 mile into the canyon. We can see the quarry on the left as the trail starts up to the two waterfalls. Stop in the shade at the upper waterfall and notice the red roots of willow trees growing in the water. A rocky, steep, narrow segment of the trail lies ahead for a few hundred yards so we use an added amount of caution until the tread underfoot becomes wider. The waterfall is at an elevation of about 250', we level off after the two big switchbacks at an elevation of 500'. We will have gained one quarter of the entire hike's elevation in just a few minutes.

At this temporary high point look at the sandstone along the trail — look for a layer of fossil shells. Sedimentation embedded these shells in sand when the land was an ocean floor. Giant Coreopsis plants are in bloom during February through April. Come here then, if for no other reason. Continue along the trail for a few minutes and reach a side trail branching left. Maxine calls this a "Frying Pan Loop Trail." We have just done the handle and will spend the next hour and a half, doing the loop. Take the left trail and it immediately drops down to the stream in the shade of oaks before making a left turn to climb along the shoulder of the mountain. A viewing spot lets us look down on the trail we hiked earlier. We have an exceptional view of the ocean if it is a clear day. On the uphill side of the trail look for a Cholla cactus, a rarity in the Santa Monica Mountains.

Our trail heads west toward the approach to Mugu Peak, then turns north for an uphill climb to LaJolla Valley. Our first view of the upper valley is an astonishing sight. We see a Valley Grassland plant community that we include in the Inventory of California Natural Areas. It is one of the best existing relict stands of native California grassland, anywhere. Chumash Indians lived here for thousands of years, then it became part of a provisional Mexican land grant to Isabel Maria Yorba in 1836. Mexico awarded the grant of 30,594 acres, called Rancho Guadalasca, in 1846. In 1871 Isabel Yorba sold 22,000 acres of the Rancho to a land company that resold to William R. Broome in 1873. Under the Broome family, Rancho Guadalasca has functioned as a ranch into the present. Part of the ranch, including LaJolla Valley, sold to the State of California in 1966 for recreational use. In February 1971 the State Park and Recreation Commission, renamed the land Point Mugu State Park, and adopted a pristine use plan.

One of our favorite lunch spots is on a knoll east of the trail. We have a good view of the ocean and the vegetation recovery gives us a windbreak. Continue north on the trail and we are on the eastern edge of the grassland. Not all of the vegetation is

Millingstone and Muller

native, we will recognize introduced grasses mixed with the natives, and in springtime might even taste the waist-high Mustard flowers. For the first ten seconds or so mustard flowers have a slightly sweet taste. Then hot!

Our trail intersects a trail coming from a saddle on the western horizon north of Mugu Peak. Turn right and follow this trail until reaching a walk-in campground on the left. Restrooms, water, and shade under the oaks are available. If the sun was too hot to have lunch back along the trail, this is a good spot for eating.

To return we walk about 150 yards back on the trail we came on, then turn left onto a narrow trail and stay left until we pass by the pond, then angle right and meet the main trail down into La Jolla Canyon. A brisk 45-minute walk takes us back to our cars.

POND, La Jolla Valley

OVERLOOK TRAIL/RAY MILLER TRAIL
Loop, from Ray Miller Trailhead

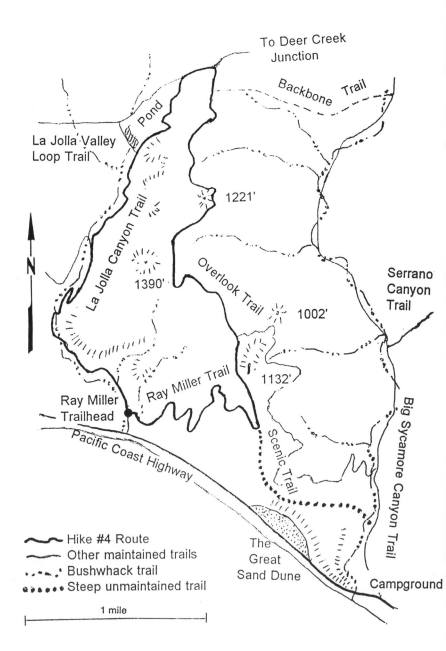

To Deer Creek Junction

Backbone Trail

Pond

La Jolla Valley Loop Trail

La Jolla Canyon Trail

1221'

1390'

Overlook Trail

Serrano Canyon Trail

1002'

Ray Miller Trail

1132'

Ray Miller Trailhead

Pacific Coast Highway

Scenic Trail

Big Sycamore Canyon Trail

Hike #4 Route
Other maintained trails
Bushwhack trail
Steep unmaintained trail

The Great Sand Dune

Campground

1 mile

HIKE 4

Maps:	SMMts, Western Section
Distance:	7½ miles
Elevation:	1400'
Terrain:	Trail and Fireroad
Time:	4 hours
Trailhead:	Ray Miller Trailhead

During the planning and building of the Backbone Trail we used existing trails and fireroads wherever possible. This practice had a positive effect. We had a ready made route for a good part of the trail, particularly in State Park land and much of National Park land. Environmentally we gained by less disturbance of pristine areas. Early on we could see a problem developing in the western end of the trail. La Jolla Valley came into the Park system with a trail system having an outlet through La Jolla Canyon. La Jolla Canyon is a vee-shaped gorge having steep rock sides. The existing trail is narrow and excitingly hanging on to the canyon wall. Hikers only are allowed on the trail. Equestrians were concerned that for them a suitable western trailhead would be far in the future. One consideration was to build a trail on the slope of the Chumash Trail. Many of us envision the 7000-year-old trail as a national treasure. That it should be destroyed is unthinkable.

An equestrian staging area with room to park horse trailers near the Backbone Trail has solved a problem. Ray Miller Trail is indeed a fitting beginning or ending of a trip on the Backbone Trail, and it comes into La Jolla Canyon.

Like all loop trails one may hike clockwise or counterclockwise. Usually it's a toss up, but here I vote for clockwise because toward the hike's end we come south looking at the ocean. Our view develops slowly but majestically. From 1100 feet high on a ridge we start down toward the floor of the canyon — just a great ending for anyone walking or riding the Backbone Trail.

We get to Ray Miller Trailhead by driving west on the Pacific Coast Highway, 22 miles from Malibu Road to La Jolla Canyon. A fee is charged for parking so stop at the sign. Drive about 400 yards up the canyon and park in a paved lot on the left. Restrooms and water are available.

Walk north from the trailhead on the La Jolla Canyon Trail. We will notice a trail on our right. This will be our exit from the hike. We cross La Jolla Creek and sometimes in late winter the water runs high. We will have had an indication of how much water is running when we drove in. About 3/4 mile from the parking lot and another crossing of the stream brings us to the waterfalls. Until the floods of early 1998 we didn't notice the lower waterfall because willow trees hid it from view. The trees took a beating but will recover. Flooding water in a narrow canyon also leaves its mark on the trail. Large rocks are no longer at the stream crossing between the two waterfalls and trail maintenance will keep Rangers and volunteers busy for months to come. We continue up the trail gaining another 250 feet on a steep narrow path. Please use care; people have actually fallen off the edge and rolled into the poison oak. A near level trail continues upstream. From this point on until we get back to the parking lot we won't make any left turns. In other words, turn right at every fork in the trail. We pass a fork in the trail that if taken would put us on the "frying pan" loop. Our next chance to go wrong is when we come near the pond. We'll keep going until reaching the crest of a ridge overlooking Sycamore Canyon, then turn right onto Overlook Trail. True to its name we look left into Sycamore Canyon and right into La Jolla Valley.

A trail on our left is a section of the Backbone Trail. It drops down to the Sycamore Canyon Trail. Up ahead we will see two water tanks, later pass by peak 1221', then Peak 1390', both on our right. About 15 minutes later as we make a sweeping turn left we will notice the Scenic Trail to the right. After a half mile on the Scenic Trail and great views of the ocean open up, we come to the Ray Miller Trail on our right. Two miles later and 1100 feet lower we rejoin the La Jolla Canyon Trail very close to the restroom.

La Jolla Canyon Waterfall

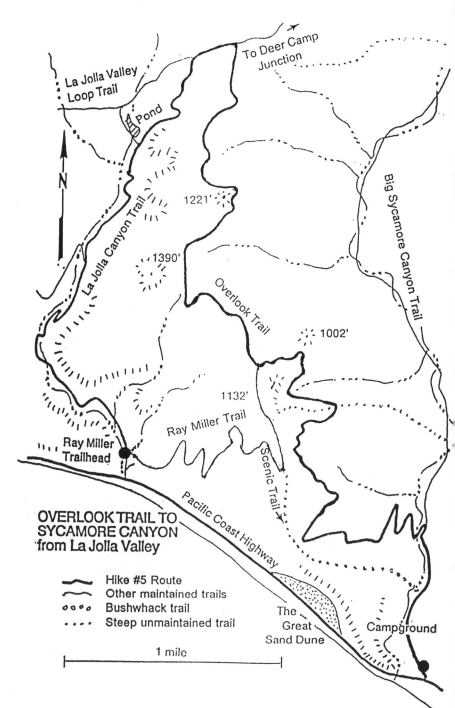

La Jolla Valley Loop Trail

Pond

To Deer Camp Junction

1221'

1390'

N

La Jolla Canyon Trail

Overlook Trail

1002'

Big Sycamore Canyon Trail

1132'

Ray Miller Trail

Ray Miller Trailhead

Scenic Trail

OVERLOOK TRAIL TO SYCAMORE CANYON from La Jolla Valley

Pacific Coast Highway

——— Hike #5 Route
——— Other maintained trails
ooooo Bushwhack trail
····· Steep unmaintained trail

The Great Sand Dune

Campground

1 mile

HIKE 5

SYCAMORE CANYON

from La Jolla Valley
via The Overlook Trail
(shuttle)

Maps:	SMMTS, Western Section
Distance:	9 miles roundtrip
Elevation:	1400' gain and loss
Terrain:	Trail
Time:	3¾ hours
Trailhead:	at Ray Miller trailhead
	La Jolla Canyon (beginning)
	Big Sycamore Cyn (ending)

This trip requires a short car shuttle, because the hike starts at La Jolla Canyon and ends at the Sycamore Canyon Camp-ground. To reach the beginning of the hike, drive west on the Pacific Coast Highway 20 miles from Malibu. Leave a car at Sycamore Canyon, then go past the Great Sand Dune and along the highway another 2 miles from Sycamore Canyon to the La Jolla Valley parking lot.

Walk north from the parking lot going upstream on the La Jolla Canyon Trail. The first 3/4 mile of the walk is gently uphill, then the trail winds through a rocky area under some trees as it crosses the stream between two waterfalls. Immediately after the stream crossing, the trail climbs past the waterfall then gains altitude by going through two switchbacks. In a half mile a trail branches off to the left that would take us to the west end of the upper La Jolla Valley and to Mugu Peak. Today's trip will go into the eastern end of the valley so stay on the main trail.

In about 1/2 mile, another trail branches left and goes along the south shore of a pond. That trail would take us to the La Jolla Valley Walk-in Camp, where we find water and a restroom. Then we could continue and meet the La Jolla Canyon Trail. However, we stay on the La Jolla Canyon Trail and in another 1/2 mile find a succession of trail junctions. At each decision point follow the trail on the right until we are on the Overlook Trail going south. Overlook Trail stays well up on the ridge between La Jolla and Sycamore Canyons and true to its name looks into both canyons. Generally heading south, this trail twists and turns, climbs and dips for 4 miles before making a decisive turn toward Sycamore Canyon and a downhill drop to the trail along the stream. Cross the stream and follow the trail down to the campground and parking area where water and restroom facilities are available.

Bulletin Board at Ray Miller Trailhead

HIKE 6

**POINT MUGU STATE PARK
WALKABOUT**
from La Jolla Valley
(Ray Miller trailhead)(shuttle)
to Sycamore Canyon

Maps:	SMMTS, Western Section
Distance:	26 miles roundtrip
Elevation:	4700' gain and loss
Terrain:	Road and some very steep trail; some stream crossings
Time:	Sunup to sundown
Trailhead:	La Jolla Cyn (beginning) Big Sycamore Cyn (ending)

This is a strenuous hike, some of it on very steep trails. "Walkabout" is a mild term that is deceiving; this is a real hike.

The car shuttle is set up by leaving a car at Sycamore Canyon (the end point of the hike) then going 2 miles west to La Jolla Canyon for the beginning.

Walk downstream toward the ocean from the La Jolla Valley parking lot watching for a trail that crosses the stream and goes up the ridge on the right. The trail goes west, steeply up the point of the ridge toward Mugu Peak. During the 1000' of elevation gain before reaching the trail coming around the south side of the peak, you will have experienced the evolvement of a most spectacular view of the Pacific Ocean imaginable. The trail takes us to the brink of a steep drop to the water below, then continues relentlessly up the mountain.

Upon reaching the trail that contours from the south side of the peak turn left for just a few minutes until finding an indistinct trail on the right. Five minutes on this trail puts us on top of Mugu Peak.

Leave the peak by dropping down a steep trail to the north. Turn right onto the trail that contours around the west side of the peak. This trail makes a big sweeping crossing of the upper part of La Jolla Valley. Generally heading northeast the trail loses some altitude. For the next mile and a half we are on level grade as we go through an open grassland. We cross several tributaries of La

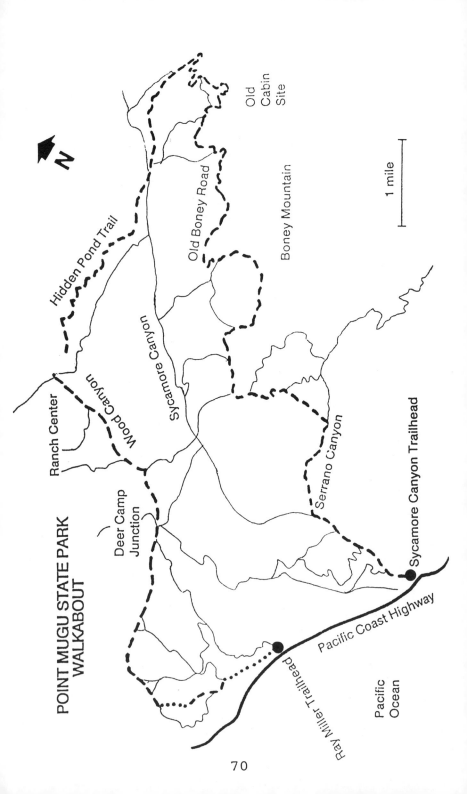

POINT MUGU STATE PARK WALKABOUT

N

Old Cabin Site

Boney Mountain

1 mile

Hidden Pond Trail

Old Boney Road

Sycamore Canyon

Wood Canyon

Ranch Center

Deer Camp Junction

Serrano Canyon

Sycamore Canyon Trailhead

Ray Miller Trailhead

Pacific Coast Highway

Pacific Ocean

Jolla Creek. Two streams are intermittent this far up and may be dry late in the year. Some springs exist farther down the valley. Continue on the trail reaching the Walk-in Camp on the left in a grove of oak trees. Water and restrooms are available.

Continue northeast on the trail for ten minutes, reaching a saddle on the hill. Several trails branch off at this point. Continue ahead going downhill to Deer Camp junction, then turn left. Follow the almost level Wood Canyon Trail, taking one-half hour to reach Ranch Center. Leave Ranch Center by going east on the paved Ranch Center Road until it intersects Hidden Pond Trail near a water tank. Turn north on the trail. Our route climbs to an east-west ridge along the north border of the Park. One might wonder how a pond can exist high on a ridge. Heavy winter rains can add water to a pond, but this isn't reliable. We will see evidence later in the hike of a pipeline between a spring near The Old Cabin Site and the pond. A storm in 1980 broke the pipe so the water now runs down Sycamore Creek. In about 2 miles the Hidden Pond Trail joins the paved road along Sycamore Canyon Creek. Follow this upstream until reaching a trail that turns right just before the road crosses the stream. The trail follows Sycamore Creek uphill reaching Old Boney Road in 1-1/4 miles and gaining 400'. Stop for lunch along the trail.

Turn right on the road and cross the stream going uphill in the shade of oak and bay trees. At the first switchback a trail on our left would take us on a side trip to the waterfall. After viewing the waterfall we return to the road. The road continues gaining altitude as it switches back and forth on the northeast shoulder of the mountain. When we come to a fork, we stay left, on a road. The right fork is Old Boney Road and turns to go up higher on the mountain where we will join it later. About one half mile beyond the fork we reach The Old Cabin Site. This is a good rest stop. The cabin is no longer in existence but the 13' high chimney with fireplace and an outline of the cabin foundation show the location. A memorial to Richard Danielson is located a few hundred feet downslope from the cabin site. Water is available at a spring near the stream. In the last few years the water has taken on a sulphur taste. I don't drink it anymore. This spring was the water source for Hidden Pond.

Continue the hike by following the road past the spring, across the creek and up the hill beyond. After climbing 350' of elevation the road rejoins Old Boney Road, turn left. The Road is at 1800', the highest point of the day, and starts downhill soon. Two trails branch off to the right and join the Sycamore Canyon Trail below. Continue on the road until coming to a junction that would lead to the Danielson Ranch if we turned right; instead, turn left and start to gain 650' as we work our way up a canyon. A large lO' boulder near the junction marks a turning point. Here we may be out two hours since the Old Cabin Site. Turn left to continue on Old Boney Road going up the canyon. we make a big right hand turn as the canyon changes direction.

Old Boney Road follows along the north slope of Boney Mountain. We will notice the Backbone Trail as it joins our trail Backbone Trail hikers are likely to turn right and head for the campground at Danielson Ranch.

We ultimately come to a saddle at the western end of the ridge, looking south into Serrano Valley. Upon reaching this point, turn left and immediately go downhill on a steep road that levels some, making a left turn around a shoulder of the mountain. The road crosses a stream and turns sharply right, then climbs for a few minutes before levelling off on the shoulder of a sloping grassy ridge. Go south down the ridge, heading for a prominent Laurel Sumac tree. Look for a trail to the right of the tree and follow it downhill on the ridge. The trail may be overgrown with grass. If we cannot find the trail, we will stay on the sloping ridge until it levels out. We then turn right and look for a break in the chaparral near the old fence line. A trail here goes west toward the stream dropping quickly into Serrano Canyon shaded with luxuriant vegetation. Look for the best stands of Poison Oak to be seen on the hike.

Serrano Canyon is a solid rock gorge connecting upper Serrano Valley with Sycamore Canyon. The trail is good but has some stream crossings that present a problem when the water is high.

When we reach the Big Sycamore Canyon Trail turn left and have an easy walk to the trailhead.

Upper Sycamore Waterfall

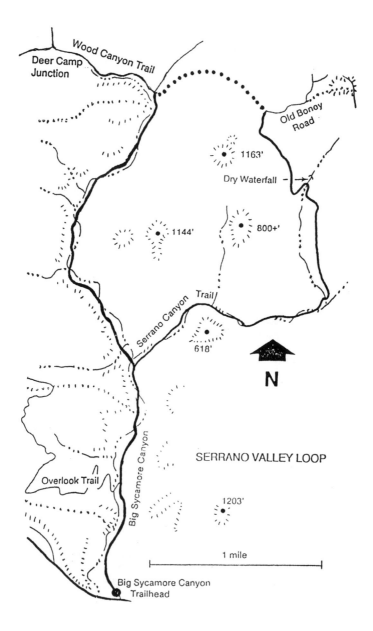

Wood Canyon Trail

Deer Camp
Junction

Old Boney
Road

● 1163'

Dry Waterfall →

● 1144'

● 800+'

Serrano Canyon   Trail

● 618'

N

SERRANO VALLEY LOOP

Overlook Trail

Big Sycamore Canyon

● 1203'

1 mile

Big Sycamore Canyon
Trailhead

HIKE 7

SERRANO VALLEY LOOP

from Sycamore Canyon
Campground

Maps:	SMMTS, Western Section
Distance:	8½ miles roundtrip
Elevation:	1100' gain and loss
Terrain:	Steep trail and road
Time:	3¾ hours
Trailhead:	Sycamore Canyon

This is a moderate trip taking you through some of the most scenic parts of the center of the Park. Big Sycamore Canyon with its large trees, Serrano Canyon with dense foliage, an open field, a ridge, and a large expanse of chaparral present a variety of plant forms.

Reach the trailhead by driving 20 miles west of the Malibu Canyon Road on the Pacific Coast Hwy to Sycamore Canyon. Park at the day parking lot on the left after passing the kiosk.

Walk through the campground and upstream on the Big Sycamore Canyon Trail. A mile and a half after leaving the campground we will pass the Serrano Canyon Trail on the right. That will be the trail that we will come down later. Continue up the gently graded Sycamore Canyon, occasionally crossing the stream. This part of the canyon is wide, and is typical of this outstanding sycamore savannah. We will see deep grass under spreading trees. Keep our eyes open to see deer tracks and on occasion a deer. Look up to see a couple of acorn woodpeckers sitting on Sycamore branches making short flights if you walk up close. Maybe a ground squirrel will run across a log. This natural activity makes this eco-system a vibrant, live and interesting place to visit. One hour after leaving the trailhead we will be near the Wood Canyon Trail junction. Several trails branch out from the main trail in this area; the one that you will be taking is on the right and is a trail, not a road.

Our first view of this trail is shocking after the previous level walking. The trail goes up a steep ridge relentlessly gaining 800 feet before reaching a level area near Old Boney Road. We feel some consolation in the spectacular view of Sycamore Canyon.

Once on the ridge dividing Sycamore and Serrano Canyons, the view opens up considerably. We see the grasslands of Serrano to the southeast and Boney Mountain with its many peaks jutting out to the east. A chaparral plant community dominates the ridge and the slope to the north.

Take the road south downhill into Serrano Valley. This road drops 350', then makes a left turn around a shoulder and goes across an intermittent stream coming down from a prominent rock waterfall. After crossing the stream and making a right turn, the road climbs for a few minutes, leveling off on the shoulder of a grassy ridge that slopes to the south. Walk south on the ridge. Grass grows in the spring, hiding the trail so we watch for a turn to the right. Head for a prominent Sumac tree. Look for the trail to the right of the tree. Nevertheless, do not be concerned if we can't find it — we'll just continue south on the highest part of the downhill sloping ridge. When the ridge levels out, the trail angles to the right and meets the trail that goes down Serrano Canyon. An old fence line divides the grassland from the chaparral. It is near the fence line that we can pick up the well-defined trail into the canyon.

The trail goes through some chaparral, then very quickly enters the canyon environment of shaded trails, pools of cool water, and luxuriant vegetation. Serrano Canyon is a steep-walled, solid rock, water formed gorge, connecting the higher Serrano Valley with the Sycamore Canyon downstream. The footing is good in most places. Some stream crossings might present a problem, depending upon the level of the water. Some low hanging branches can be hazardous, and keep a lookout for Poison Oak.

Upon reaching the Big Sycamore Canyon Trail, turn left and return to the trailhead.

HIKE 8

SERRANO VALLEY LOOP AND OVERLOOK TRAIL
from Sycamore Canyon (loop)

Maps:	SMMTS, Western Section
Distance:	13 miles roundtrip
Elevation:	2100' gain and loss
Terrain:	Road and trail
Time:	5½ hours including lunch
Trailhead:	Sycamore Canyon

This trip is long for a beginning hiker but might be just the challenge we want. The hike takes us through a wide variety of plant communities: grassland, riparian woodland, coastal sage, and chaparral. We follow the map and hiking instructions closely because some trail junctions are obscure.

Begin the hike by driving to the Trailhead at Sycamore Canyon Campground and park at the day parking lot on the left after the kiosk. Sycamore Canyon is on the Pacific Coast Highway 20 miles west of the Malibu Canyon Road.

Walk through the campground keeping to the east side, following the well defined Big Sycamore Canyon Trail as it gently ascends the broad floor of the valley. Several trails come in from the west side. Two trails enter the campground on the west and are hidden from our view. Four-tenths of a mile after leaving the campground the Overlook Trail enters; then three-tenths of a mile farther, a seldom used steep trail from the Overlook comes in. Twenty-five minutes after the start of the hike we will come to the Serrano Canyon Trail. Take the right fork and begin a steady climb on a foot trail. Serrano Canyon is a secluded intimate riparian woodland. The vegetation is luxuriant. This is a large Park with many trails and even with some volunteer help long periods elapse between trimmings. Some of that abundant greenery that we are brushing against may be Poison Oak. Overhead the trees form a closed canopy, making this a shady and delightfully cool canyon. Some low hanging branches may cause a bump on the head and

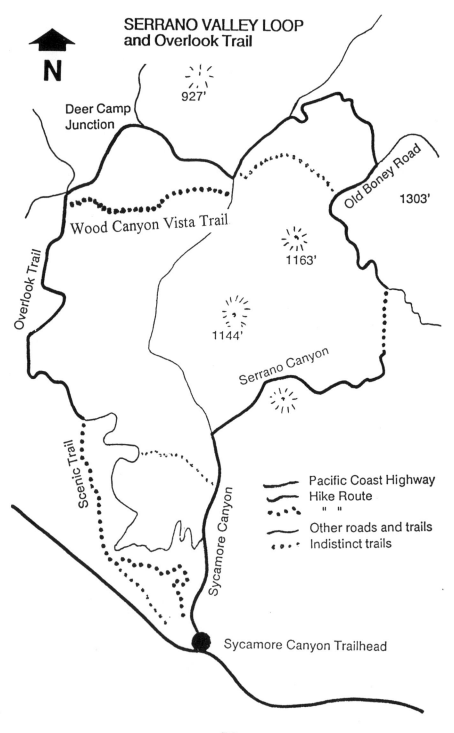

SERRANO VALLEY LOOP
and Overlook Trail

N

927'

Deer Camp
Junction

Old Boney Road

1303'

Wood Canyon Vista Trail

Overlook Trail

1163'

1144'

Serrano Canyon

Scenic Trail

Sycamore Canyon

Pacific Coast Highway
Hike Route
"   "
Other roads and trails
Indistinct trails

Sycamore Canyon Trailhead

some branches over which we must step. The intention is that the trail is not suitable for horses, so they remove only a minimum of trees and branches. This area is truly unspoiled.

Forty minutes after entering Serrano Canyon we will have gradually gained about 300 feet. After crossing a side stream by going down some rock steps, we suddenly leave the stream and its protective environment to climb a chaparral hillside. The trail makes a sharp turn to the right. Actually it is a fork in the trail to the right because many hikers overshoot this turn and have gone up another trail leading into much brush. So make the turn to the right, going through an old fence line to a grassy ridge. Turn left and go north up the ridge through a large grassy area. An old metal building and a metal tank on the hillside are guides. Stay to the left for the easiest going. We will see a Laurel Sumac tree on top of the ridge — head for it. Stop at the Sumac and look around. Serrano Canyon runs east to west, south of us; to the east is a ranch, and the road coming down the slope to the east is the Serrano Road. It goes to the Park property gate through the ranch, then the overgrown continuation of the road passes several hundred feet north of the Sumac. We should head for this road by continuing north on the ridge, then turn left.

Follow this road for nearly a mile as it works its way northwest. It loses some altitude in dropping down to a side stream below a prominent rock waterfall. The trail climbs to the ridge dividing Serrano Canyon and Big Sycamore Canyon. A road junction at the ridge gives us time to rest while we take in some new scenery. Turn right and follow Old Boney Road northeast for about ten minutes. Take a side road on the left that drops steeply down to Sycamore Canyon, losing 700 feet in a little more than one mile. Upon reaching the Big Sycamore Canyon Trail, turn left and walk downstream for 10 minutes until passing the Wood Canyon Trail on the right. This part of the canyon shows its beauty as a sycamore savannah — the best example in the Santa Monica Mountains.

Continue downstream a few hundred yards coming to Wood Canyon Vista Trail. Turn right and climb this segment of the Backbone Trail. We will gain seven hundred feet before reaching the ridge. Upon reaching the ridge separating Sycamore Canyon on the east from LaJolla Valley on the west, turn left on Overlook Trail going south along the ridge.

Time yourself because we will be looking for a not-too-distinct trail on the right in 35 minutes. The Overlook Trail does just what the name implies — it stays high on the mountain presenting views of Sycamore Canyon and LaJolla Valley. We also get a look into Serrano Canyon and of course Boney Mountain beyond. The view of the ocean is special, water as far as the eye can see, and off to the west are the Channel Islands. On a clear day some islands are in view to the south. Mugu Rock isn't in view yet but we will see it later. After 35 minutes on the Overlook Trail and as we come to the saddle north of Peak 1132, Scenic Trail branches off to the south. Take it, and contour around on the west side of the peak. Now we can see Mugu Rock if we look to the west. This rough trail drops down on a ridge to the south, then becomes very steep. Several trails coming up from the campground are in view giving us a selection, after we leave the steep area. By staying to the right, we will come close to the "Great Sand Dune." This sand dune has been formed by the prevailing westerly wind picking up sand from the beach and carrying it up against the mountain. Wind is one natural force that can carry material uphill.

We will have a view of the dune from above by getting off the trail. Now, a short one-half mile, while dropping 400 ft., puts us at the stream crossing in the campground — and the end of the hike.

HIKE 9

RANCH CENTER
via Wood Canyon Trail
Hidden Pond Trail and Big
Sycamore Canyon Trail from
Sycamore Canyon Campground
(loop)

Maps:	SMMTS, Western Section
Distance:	16 miles roundtrip
Elevation:	1200' gain and loss
Terrain:	Trail and road
Time:	6½ hours, incl. lunch
Trailhead:	Sycamore Canyon

This is a long walk covering a large segment of the Park from the ocean to the northern boundary and back. Most of the trails are of moderate grade and good footing. One segment near Ranch Center is steep but we have an easier optional route.

Drive 20 miles west of Malibu Canyon Road on the Pacific Coast Highway to Sycamore Canyon Campground. Park outside the gate and walk through onto the Big Sycamore Canyon Trail.

The trail goes north, almost level as it gently ascends the floor of the valley. A brisk one-hour walk will put us close to the Wood Canyon Trail Junction. Several trails leave the main trail near this point; take the well marked well travelled one on the left.

After crossing Sycamore Creek, our trail follows Wood Creek and enters an area shaded with oaks and sycamores. Hillsides both left and right are chaparral. Grass and flowering plants grow along the floor of the valley. The trail forks at Deer Camp Junction, with the left fork going uphill into LaJolla Valley. We take the right fork and continue the Wood Canyon Trail. Restroom facilities and water are available at Deer Camp Junction. Wood Canyon Trail continues in a gentle climb, shaded most of the way. Ranch Center is the northern terminal of the trail and is on the northern border of the Park. Water is also available there.

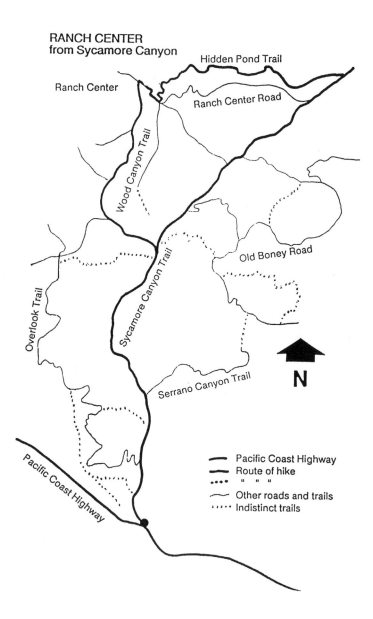

RANCH CENTER
from Sycamore Canyon

Hidden Pond Trail

Ranch Center

Ranch Center Road

Wood Canyon Trail

Overlook Trail

Sycamore Canyon Trail

Old Boney Road

Serrano Canyon Trail

N

Pacific Coast Highway

Pacific Coast Highway
Route of hike
"   "   "
Other roads and trails
Indistinct trails

Leave Ranch Center by going east on the paved Ranch Center Road until it intersects Hidden Pond Trail near a water tank. We go north, angling right as we reach the crest of the ridge. Once we used to leave the Ranch Center and climb directly up the grassy slope to intersect Hidden Pond Trail. This gain of 450' was a good workout but for the environment's sake we don't need another trail. Hidden Pond can be a disappointment — it is sometime dry. The trail winds around some and has short uphill and downhill sections, offering impressive views of Sycamore Canyon and Boney Mountain. Following the trail up the slope is straightforward, but as it drops close to Sycamore Creek, overgrown vegetation presents a route finding problem. Nearing the stream we come down the east edge of a grassy field, then turn left. After paralleling the stream, and crossing it, we join Sycamore Canyon Trail (a paved road at this point). A restroom is available here.

The return trip is downstream on Sycamore Canyon Trail to the parking lot.

Danielson Home in Sycamore Canyon

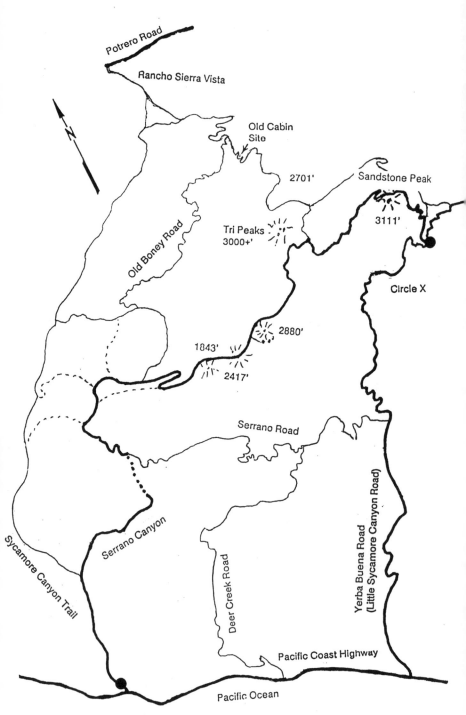

Potrero Road

Rancho Sierra Vista

N

Old Cabin Site

2701'

Sandstone Peak

3111'

Old Boney Road

Tri Peaks 3000+'

Circle X

2880'

1843'

2417'

Serrano Road

Sycamore Canyon Trail

Serrano Canyon

Deer Creek Road

Yerba Buena Road (Little Sycamore Canyon Road)

Pacific Coast Highway

Pacific Ocean

HIKE 10

**SANDSTONE PEAK
FROM SYCAMORE CANYON**
Campground to Circle X Ranch
(shuttle)

Maps:	SMMTS, Western Section
Distance:	11 miles
Elevation:	4000' gain, 2300' loss
Terrain:	Road, trail, and some off-trail bushwhacking
Time:	7 hours including lunch
Trailhead:	Sycamore Cyn (beginning) Circle X Ranch (ending)

This is a strenuous trip and is for only the experienced hiker in a group led by a knowledgeable leader. Finding the route is involved, the uphill bushwhacking is difficult. We'll have hot sun on the ridges and Poison Oak in the canyons.

The car shuttle begins by meeting at the parking lot one mile east of the Circle X Ranch Ranger station. This is on Yerba Buena Road, six and a half miles from the Pacific Coast Highway. If we come in from the other direction, drive west on Mulholland Highway until reaching Little Sycamore Canyon Road; turn right and go 4.4 miles to the parking lot. Yerba Buena Road and Sycamore Canyon Road are the same road. They name it differently at either end. Set up the shuttle by leaving some cars at the Circle X parking lot where the trip ends. Drive to Big Sycamore Canyon Trailhead where the trip begins. We go to the Pacific Coast Highway, turn right and 3 miles later turn right into Sycamore Canyon, and park.

This hike will take us to the top of Sandstone Peak, the highest point in the Santa Monica Mountains at 3111'. We observe an important ritual. We will go from the lowest point to the highest point. To do that we enter the campground, turn left, walk to Big Sycamore Creek and follow it to the ocean, going under the Pacific Coast highway. Wet your feet in an incoming wave and start the hike by going upstream, through the campground and onto Big

Sycamore Canyon Trail. One and a half miles up the trail turn right onto Serrano Canyon Trail.

While we have the opportunity, we will take advantage of the coolness and shade of Serrano Canyon. Because we will soon spend much time on exposed ridges and in dry winds. Look for the poison oak I promised for it is all about us. This is a beautiful place and a Pleasant walk — cherish it. After 30 to 40 minutes on the Serrano Canyon Trail we abruptly pull away from the stream and make a sharp turn to the right. Actually, it is a fork in the trail going uphill to an old fence line and onto a grassy ridge. Now turn left and go north up the ridge through a grassy area. An old metal building and a metal tank on the ridge are route indicators. The trail goes to the left of them and heads for a Laurel Sumac tree on top of the ridge. Continue a couple hundred yards farther, coming upon an old dirt road. Turn left, following the road as it contours along the hillside, then drops down to cross a streambed that features a rock waterfall upstream. The road climbs to the ridge dividing Serrano and Big Sycamore Canyons. At the fork turn right and follow Old Boney Road about a mile coming to a trail on the right. This new trail, completed in 1990, and designated as the Chamberlain Section is part of the "Backbone Trail." It links Point Mugu State Park and the National Park Service's Circle X Ranch.

We take this trail and climb east uphill all the way, passing near a split rock. Before they built the trail, we went cross-country along the ridge, and by tradition went through the split — a tight squeeze. On cool days this is an acceptable lunch spot. Weather protected areas with more shade are found farther along the trail. The trail contours along the north side of Peak 2880, making some turns as it winds through the peaks on Boney Mountain. The trail eases up and enters the "Camp Allen" recreation area. During the Boy Scouts' era of the Circle X Ranch, Camp Allen was location for back country camping. Now water is not available and the campground is not open.

A road leads uphill to the south from the rest area. follow this as it leads to the crest of the ridge overlooking a series of small peaks. Two large water tanks will be in view as we approach the ridge. Our trail branches left. Continue east on the road for about twenty minutes looking for a switchback to our right. When the road next switches left a steep trail on our right goes up some rock steps. This is the route to the top of Sandstone Peak. We should be prepared for a rock scramble.

We have now gone from the lowest point in the Santa Monica Mountains to the highest point — a great feeling. We will want to savor the moment by scanning the horizon. South and west is the Pacific Ocean dotted with some islands that are visible on clear days, the Oxnard Plain is northwest, and the Santa Ynez and Topatopa Mountains beyond, in the near foreground are the many peaks of Boney Mountain. Notice the sheer cliffs on the south side of Sandstone, now look at the rock on which you are sitting. It is not sandstone at all. It is volcanic! Between 13½ and 15½ million years ago a period of volcanic activity in the Santa Monica Mountains resulted in a number of outcrops throughout the range. The highest one being Sandstone Peak, 3111'.

We trace our steps as far as the road at the bottom of the steep trail coming down from the peak. We have the option of returning to the Circle X Ranch by Two routes: (1) The shortest and quickest way is to turn right and go east on the road losing altitude as we hike the two miles to the parking lot. (2) The longest way home is to go west on the road back to Camp Allen. Cross the camp area heading northeast. A road leads east, downhill, from a ridge and soon follows along Carlisle Creek. Continue downstream to Split Rock, a prominent rock along a stream in an oak glen. Cross the stream and find a trail that initially goes southeast as it contours around the shoulder of Sandstone. This Mishe Mokwa Trail leads to a fork and we go right. The trail intersects a road which we follow to our parked cars.

This hike will give us a good workout. We will sleep well.
Remember to get the drivers back to Sycamore Canyon.

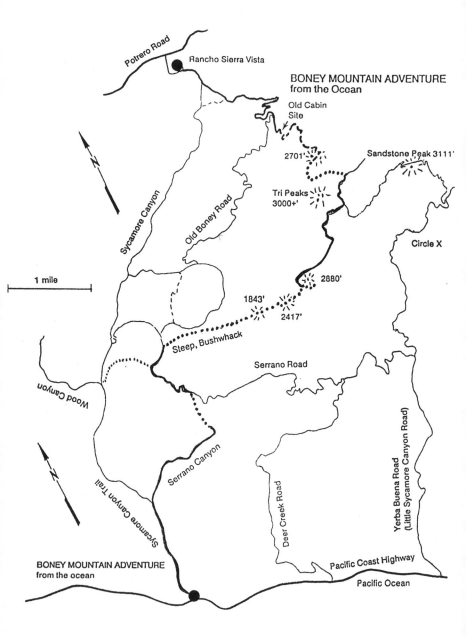

Potrero Road

Rancho Sierra Vista

BONEY MOUNTAIN ADVENTURE
from the Ocean

Old Cabin
Site

2701'

Sandstone Peak 3111'

Sycamore Canyon

Old Boney Road

Tri Peaks
3000+'

Circle X

1 mile

2880'

1843'

2417'

Steep, Bushwhack

Serrano Road

Wood Canyon

Serrano Canyon

Sycamore Canyon Trail

Deer Creek Road

Yerba Buena Road
(Little Sycamore Canyon Road)

BONEY MOUNTAIN ADVENTURE
from the ocean

Pacific Coast Highway

Pacific Ocean

HIKE 11

BONEY MOUNTAIN ADVENTURE FROM THE OCEAN

from Sycamore Canyon to
Rancho Sierra Vista (shuttle)

Maps:	SMMTS, Western Section
Distance:	15 miles
Elevation:	4000' gain, 3250' loss
Terrain:	Road, trail, steep bushwhacking
Time:	8½ hours including lunch
Trailhead:	Sycamore Cyn (beginning) Rancho Sierra Vista (ending)

This trip is for the experienced hiker and is even then best done under competent leadership. The route-finding is involved, some serious uphill chaparral bushwhacking will tax our endurance, and Poison Oak is plentiful along the streams. Also, the sun is hot on the ridges.

Set up the car shuttle by leaving some cars at Rancho Sierra Vista in Newbury Park, where the trip ends, and driving to Sycamore Canyon Trailhead, where the trip begins. We reach Rancho Sierra Vista from the west end of the city of Thousand Oaks. Take the Borchard Road exit from Ventura Freeway, and drive south one and a half miles to Reino Road. Turn left on Reino. Go to Lynn Road, turn right and turn in to the Park at the sign. Drive to the Rancho Sierra Vista parking lot.

To complete the car shuttle to Sycamore Canyon, we leave Rancho Sierra Vista parking lot and turn left. We go west on Potrero Road, and down Long Grade Canyon past the Camarillo State Hospital. Turn left onto Hueneme Road, then another left onto Las Posas Road. Upon reaching the Pacific Coast Highway, go left again and drive to Sycamore Canyon Campground. We reach a parking lot for day hikers on the left just after checking in at the kiosk. Our hike begins here.

Walk through the campground picking up the Big Sycamore Canyon Trail as it gently ascends the broad floor of the valley. Enjoy the less than 100' elevation gain during the first mile because things are about to change. Twenty minutes after leaving the Trailhead, and after two stream crossings, we will come to a fork in the trail — turn right and go up the Serrano Canyon Trail.

Serrano Canyon is heavily shaded near the stream and offers a cool, pleasant walking trail. Expect a few stream crossings in the spring. This adds a small challenge. Poison Oak grows well in this canyon so watch closely. Low-hanging branches over the trail will occasionally become a minor problem. This trail is suitable for hikers only. In 30 to 40 minutes we will leave the riparian woodland atmosphere and almost suddenly find ourselves on a grassy ridge. Turn left at the old fence line and go due north up the ridge for ten minutes. A few isolated Sumacs and a metal water tank dot the ridge. We will join an old road and go left as it contours some, then drops down into a side canyon that displays a prominent dry rock waterfall upstream. The road then climbs to the ridge dividing Serrano and Big Sycamore Canyons. Turn right on the road and follow it as long as it stays on the ridge, maybe five minutes. The road (Old Boney) leaves the ridge, contouring along the north slope. During 1990 we built a segment of the Backbone Trail along the west ridge. This "adventure" became easier. We may elect to use the trail by continuing another half mile along Old Boney Road. I have left the original bushwhacking description in the book for those who want an extra challenge. Leave the road, staying on the ridge as we climb east. After one and a half hours of climbing through chaparral, over several reddish basaltic peaks, and across an old rusty barbed wire fence often, we will come to a prominent split rock. We will cross or join the Backbone Trail when the rock comes into view. Tradition says that the trail goes through the split but it's a tight squeeze and we may not be able mentally to adjust to prolonging such a tradition. This is a good place for a lunch stop.

About a half mile back on the route we passed where a land grant marker is found. Had we been inclined, we could have looked for it. The marker notes a corner of the Guadalasca land grant and the El Conejo land grant. The Mexican government in the 1800's granted these two Ranchos totaling 79,266 acres. Both of these land grants remained intact until recent times. Parts of each now constitute Point Mugu State Park.

Continue climbing east on the ridge. After a stretch of the usual chaparral bushwhacking, we come over a rise and are "on a trail!" Ahead and to the left we see the Backbone Trail and we should head for it. We might elect to continue east on the ridge to the pass overlooking the upper Little Sycamore Canyon. This should take 45 minutes from Split Rock. The view of the south escarpment of Boney Mountain and Sandstone Peak is spectacular. Immense volcanic cliffs dominate Upper Little Sycamore Canyon and the west fork of Arroyo Sequit. Go west back down the trail a few hundred feet then take the right fork as it starts the circle around the peak. The trail twists around some as it winds among the peaks on Boney Mountain. Twenty-five minutes after leaving the Little Sycamore Canyon Overlook, a large split rock is prominent about 100 yards off to the right. Some remnants of a trail from Boy Scout use remain in the area but if we stay on the Backbone Trail until we can see the now deserted Camp Allen we are on course. Hundreds of Boy Scouts camped here in years gone by. Now all evidence of use as a camp is gone, even drinking water that once was piped up the hill from a spring near the grotto.

A real trail doesn't exist that will take us around the east side of Tri Peaks but we head north, climbing some as we contour toward a ridge about thirty minutes away. At this point we usually welcome advice from someone who has hiked this before. A seldom used trail goes east just below the ridge north of us. Once on this trail we go downhill on the ridge that drops down to the northeast toward Peak 2701. After going through a mini forest of Ceanothus and Red Shanks, the trail curls around the south side of the peak and drops sharply for a 1000' elevation loss, going through one of the largest stands of Manzanita in the Santa Monicas. The trail is steep and not maintained, but well defined throughout the descent to the Old Cabin Site. Upon approaching this welcome rest stop, the chaparral changes to Oak trees, Laurel trees, and grass.

The cabin is gone but the thirteen-foot-high fireplace chimney remains and, along with the outline of a foundation, marks the spot where the cabin stood. The Danielson Memorial is a place of respect for the man whose generosity provided a great deal of land to Point Mugu State Park. Downhill and to the left the spring furnishes a strong flow of cool water from a pipe. Horses have tramped about the spring itself and the water doesn't run out of the pipe as it should. I have stopped drinking the water. The water from the spring flows into a stream that runs down the canyon to the northeast and is a tributary of Big Sycamore Creek. So, in a sense, we have hiked from the mouth of Big Sycamore Creek as it entered the ocean and are now seeing the source of one of many tributaries. Stay here as long as time permits. It is only one hour to the end of the hike.

Go downhill from the Old Cabin Site on a road that soon crosses the stream and heads north. In less than ten minutes we will come to Old Boney Road; take the right fork and continue to contour around the shoulder of the mountain before making switchbacks down to the main stream. Cross the stream and continue on the road as it starts a slight grade — resist the temptation to follow the shady trail downstream. In a half mile the road comes to an open meadow. Several trails cross the large field, all leading to the exit road and the parking lot.

"Spring" near the Old Cabin Site

92

HIKE 12

Maps:	SMMTS, Western Section
Distance:	7 miles roundtrip
Elevation:	1500' gain and loss
Terrain:	Road, trail (sometimes rocky and steep) Some optional class 2 off trail
Time:	3 hours
Trailhead:	1½ miles east of the Circle X Ranger Station.

Sandstone Peak and the trails leading to it are on a massive volcanic rock formation called Boney Mountain. If approaching the area by way of Pacific Coast Highway, we drive north on Yerba Buena Road. Five and a half miles uphill on Yerba Buena we will pass the ranger station on our right. Maps and information are available here. Continue one and a-half miles, passing an entrance to a parking lot on the left, to a steep sharp turn of the road. Find a parking area on the left. This is our trailhead. For reassurance we have stopped at the correct spot, we notice a eucalyptus tree across the road. If we come into the area from the east, we would drive west on Mulholland Highway until reaching Little Sycamore Canyon Road on the right. Follow Little Sycamore Canyon Road 4 miles to the Trailhead. A parking area is on the right. It is another 1-1/2 miles to the ranger station. Two other parking areas are along the road, but for today's hike we should concentrate on finding Mishe Mokwa Trailhead. We will notice that driving from the coast on the road it is "Yerba Buena," and going west on the same road it is "Little Sycamore." Somewhere in the middle, I believe the county line, we could expect a name change. Much duality in street and road names exists in Southern California, causing a degree of

Mishe Mokwa Trail

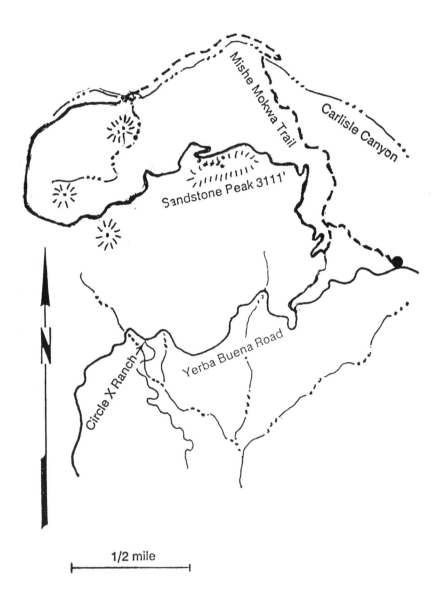

Mishe Mokwa Trail

Carlisle Canyon

Sandstone Peak 3111'

Circle X Ranch

Yerba Buena Road

N

1/2 mile

confusion. Here the name notes the destination of the road itself.

Years ago "Mishe Mokwa Trail" was "Bedsprings Trail" but gained a name change when Boy Scouts arrived. Before "Bedsprings" it was a goat trail when Mr. Hull pastured goats in the back country. A charm of this trail is that in places one thinks "goat trail." I would keep this idea alive. Any major changes would destroy the feel of a back country trail. (Maybe keep the poison oak trimmed back a ways but let us not destroy the basic ruggedness of this remote adventure.)

Initially the trail goes through the chaparral, climbing gently with some level stretches as it works its way around the eastern shoulder of the mountain. Where a side trail comes in on the left, take a moment to stop and look back over the rugged expanse of mountains and canyons. The south slope of this mountain presents a panorama of sunlit chaparral. Look for the different shades of green; maybe not noticeable at first, but soon we can pick out the Red shanks in the chaparral by the light green tinge in spring, turning rusty by fall. The darker green patches could be Holly-leaf Cherry or Laurel Sumac. Near the trail, very close to the ground, can be found a small salmon colored flower called "Poor Man's Weather Glass." During spring and early summer a variety of flowers intensify the beauty of this trail. Look for Golden Yarrow, Wild Buckwheat, Brodiaea, Sticky Leaf Monkey Flower, Popcorn Flower, and Wild Peony.

Continue along the trail as it enters the canyon coming down from the right and ahead. Looking across the canyon we will see the outstanding geological sight "Balanced Rock." This rock is volcanic in origin as is most of the rock in the area. The balancing took place centuries ago. How it has managed to resist the force of earthquakes and other of the elements is something to think about.

The trail becomes shadier as it nears the canyon, dominated by Oak and Laurel trees. Poison Oak becomes common and we see Clematis, Pitcher Sage and Humboldt Lilies occasionally. The trail dips into the canyon at Split Rock. Split Rock is a volcanic breccia, split into three pieces. A pathway large enough to walk through goes between two of the pieces. Bay, Sycamore, and Coast Live Oaks shade the running stream. Plate #8 in my *Wildflowers of the Santa Monica Mountains* book shows this place. Coast Live Oak has a distinctive leaf, it is about 3/4" by 1" and is cupped. If a leaf were placed upside down on water, it would float. We can see another characteristic of the leaf with a magnifying glass. Little tufts of hair are spaced on the upper surface, sort of starbursts. The underside has hairs in the vein axils. Split Rock is a good place to eat lunch.

To continue the hike, go downstream about 100 yards and turn left onto an old roadbed and follow it upstream. As a diversion from the hike, an indistinct trail begins here and goes down stream through poison oak to a rock climbing area at Echo Cliffs. Climbers can also reach Balanced Rock. This route is not easy, but if we are rock climbers consider the extra hike a warmup. Otherwise, it's not recommended.

Return to the hike and go uphill. About 600 yards on the trail look across the stream on the left. An unusual rock formation of massive cliffs are in view. With some imagination a magnificent cliff looks something like a giant slab of Swiss cheese. A wooden bridge crosses a side stream but has burned out. Horehound plants grow here, which we can make into cold remedies either in liquid or candy form. The scientific name is Marrubium vulgare, a name that to me has an intriguing poetic balance. At this point an old trail once went left and upstream. Steep, rocky, and not maintained, the trail is now "closed." Just after crossing the stream make a right turn to continue uphill. When we crest out and head south into a semi-level area, look for two water tanks high on the opposite hill, and to our right. The trail passes below and east of the tanks. We will go through the now unused Boy Scout camping area on our walk toward the water tanks. At the west end of the old camp area notice a trail heading north. We won't take it today unless we would explore the Back Bone Trail as it continues west or if we would climb Tri Peaks. Continue toward the water tanks. After a stiff climb the trail angles left and heads east, level for a few minutes but soon becoming uphill again. At the second switchback look for a trail on the right. This steep trail goes to the top of Sandstone Peak. From this point to the top of the peak and back can be class two rock climbing. Upon close inspection of the rock formation, we find that Sandstone Peak is not sandstone at all, but volcanic rock.

We now have a most spectacular view from this highest point in the Santa Monica Mountains. At 3111', Sandstone Peak commands a 360° panorama of the western end of the mountains. The Pacific Ocean dominates the view of the quadrant in the southwest. To the south we see the islands of Santa Catalina, San Clemente, Santa Barbara, and San Nicholas. On the west are the Channel Islands of Anacapa, Santa Cruz, Santa Rosa, and San Miguel. If we were inclined to name trails we could call this segment The Seven Saints Trail, as it leads to the peak and a viewing spot of the offshore islands. Each island with a San or Santa infers a saintly relationship. Boney Ridge extends westward from the peak for 1½ miles of rugged rock formations.

Oxnard Plain is northwest of our position. This flat land is a giant syncline or downfold of the surface. Material washed down from the surrounding mountains now fills the plain. They have measured the depth of fill including all sediments at 41,000'. Stratigraphically this is a most interesting valley because it is one of the thickest sections of Tertiary, sedimentary rocks in the world.

The mountain range to the north is in the Los Padres National Forest. A significant feature is the Sespe Condor Sanctuary. A program of supplying Condors from the San Diego and Los Angeles Zoos will repopulate the Sanctuary.

Return down the steep trail on the west side of the peak to the road. Follow the road east, then south as it curves around the steep mountainside. Tighten the laces on our boots to prepare for a descent homeward bound. After several switchbacks we will come to the last switchback on the road as it turns right. At this point look for the cutoff trail on the left. The trail takes us uphill for a few hundred yards before dropping down to intercept the Mishe Mokwa Trail. Turn right and reach the parking lot in 10 minutes.

I like this hike. The scenery is gigantic, bordering on the colossal. Balanced Rock is incredible; it cannot stand through the thousands of years of earthquakes, but it stands nonetheless. Even Split Rock has an unusual characteristic. I can convince hikers that walking through the split will dislodge any demon that follows. (We all know that demons will not go where danger to them exists.) Hikers come out of that split laughing and knowing this is a good day.

Of course this hike may be counterclockwise, or clockwise. Depending upon our starting time and hiking speed, we might plan to stop for lunch at Split Rock. This could determine the route.

Shade, or the lack of shade could be a factor in making a lunch-stop decision.

This may be a good time to review some history of the Circle X Ranch, so I'll pick up the story in the 1940's.

The Exchange Club, a Los Angeles service organization, made a search for projects that needed their help. In reviewing most ideas and after investigating many areas, they decided to support a camp so that young people could learn self-reliance by living with nature. After several years of searching for affordable property, the site finding committee found the Crisp Ranch. This property was what they were looking for and the Exchange Club bought it. Most of the 160 acres and the surrounding land was wilderness. Several houses, a barn, a corral, a tennis court, and a windmill, were on the property. The year was 1949; they paid $25,000.

So members could donate money and get an income tax exemption, they formed the nonprofit Circle X Ranch Foundation as a charitable corporation. (The Exchange Club emblem was an encircled C and X, and this translated to Circle X.) A member designed a Circle X ranch brand, which is registered in Sacramento. When escrow closed, the Circle X Foundation bought 120 acres. Boney Ridge Club, bought 40 acres. The Hill House is on the 40 acres.

Circle X Ranch was opened up to all accredited youth organizations, with less than an enthusiastic reception. Eventually the Los Angeles Council of the B.S.A. agreed to maintain the property and operate it. In 1951 the Foundation leased Circle X Ranch to the Boy Scouts of America for 99 years. Annual rental was one dollar.

Happy Hollow became part of Circle X in 1953 when the Hollywood Turf Club donated $23,000 to buy 160 acres. Gifts of land and many purchases increased the holdings. With the purchase of 631 acres in 1954, including Sandstone Peak and Boney Ridge, for $15,000, the Circle X had grown to 1721 acres.

A chaparral fire started in Newbury Park on 7 November 1955, It burned the camping area and all the buildings except the ranger's house. Another fire on 27 December 1956 from the Malibu Creek area burned into the areas missed in 1955, but not any of the new buildings.

Many people were essential in creating Circle X. Throughout

the period of search, acquisition, building, and financing, W. Herbert Allen was totally committed to the project with his energy and money. Without his dedication Circle X would not have become the Scouting training ground that it has. In 1965 a movement began to rename Sandstone Peak to Mt. Allen. A bronze plaque, the one we are looking at if we are on top of the mountain, was cast. They sent a request to rename Sandstone Peak to the Department of Interior. Because of a long-standing policy not to approve a geographic name, which would honor a living person, they did not rename Sandstone Peak. Undaunted, on 23 August 1969, a large assembly of people gathered atop "Mt. Allen" for the formal dedication. The overflow crowd including 400 Scouts representing all fifteen districts of the Council, were below and heard the ceremony by walkie-talkie. So, to a segment of the hiking community Sandstone Peak is Mt. Allen. Of incidental interest, Sandstone Peak is not sandstone. It is volcanic, an igneous rock.

In 1979 the Exchange Club of Los Angeles ceased to function. Circle X Ranch foundation deeded its holdings in the Ranch to the Los Angeles Council of the Boy Scouts of America, and continued as a charitable organization. The Boy Scouts placed the property on the market in 1986. The Mountains Recreation and Conservation Authority bought the Circle X Ranch and assumed management on 1 March 1987. They subsequently sold the property to the National Recreation Area, National Park Service, who have operated the Park since Dedication Day on 6 March 1989.

HIKE 13

SANDSTONE PEAK
from the Circle X Ranch
via Backbone Trail

Maps:	SMMTS, Western Section
Distance:	4 miles roundtrip
Elevation:	1100' gain and loss
Terrain:	Steep dirt road
	Steep trail (class 2) near the summit
Time:	2 hours
Trailhead:	1 mile east of the Circle X Ranger Station

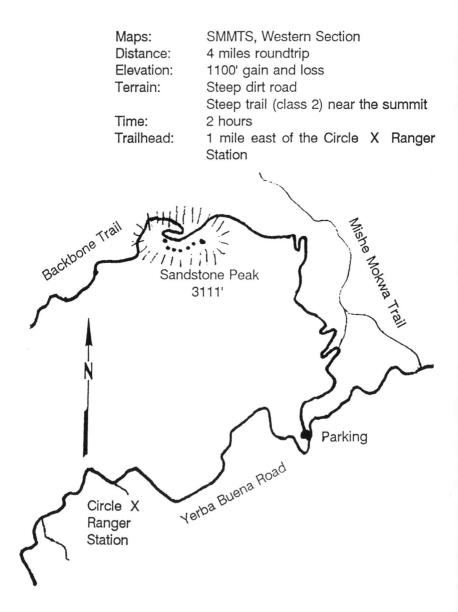

A time may come when we might want to climb Sandstone Peak via the shortest hike and the least elevation gain. I believe this will do it. Expect a steep and rocky trail, great views, and spring wildflowers. **How to get to the trailhead:**

From Malibu, drive west on the Pacific Coast Highway one mile beyond the Ventura County line, and turn inland on Yerba Buena Road. Go north six and a half miles to a parking lot on the left. Our trail goes uphill from the lot. The Ranger Station we passed a mile back is a good source of information and we could have stopped to say "Hello" and ask questions.

We find that it is uphill most of the way. Starting at an elevation of 2050 feet and climbing to 3111 feet in two miles doesn't allow many level sections of trail. As we climb, the scenery takes on a new dimension. Off to our right, deep down in the canyon, Carlisle Creek tumbles its way toward Lake Sherwood. Above Echo Cliffs we can see Balanced Rock although it loses some of its grandeur when below and far away. In time mountains of the Los Padres National Forest come into view north of us. Snow covers the crest of the Los Padres in winter..

As the trail levels off we may note a huge boulder across our path. Early in 1998 this boulder came sliding down onto the trail, uprooting some large trees, partially blocking our way. Hikers have little trouble getting through but this incident reminds us that Mother Nature does not take it kindly when people bulldoze deep cuts into steep hillsides. After our trail crests and starts a slight decline we look left for a trail to the top of Sandstone Peak. It starts as a series of steps cut into the rock and requires us to climb with caution.

When we reach the peak, approach the edge slowly because the south side is a cliff. Sign in on the book if you care to. Notice that a plaque states the peak is Mt. Allen. Everyone knows by now that the peak is volcanic rock, not sandstone. Savor the view for we are on top of our world. If I knew for sure that the seven off-shore islands whose names begin with San or Santa were named for Saints, I would propose naming this short but rugged trail the "Seven Saints Trail." Los Angeles sprawls out east and southeast almost as far as we can see. The Pacific Ocean dominates the south as far as the eye can see.

After we retrace our steps to the main trail we tighten the laces on our boots for a two-mile downhill hike to the parking lot.

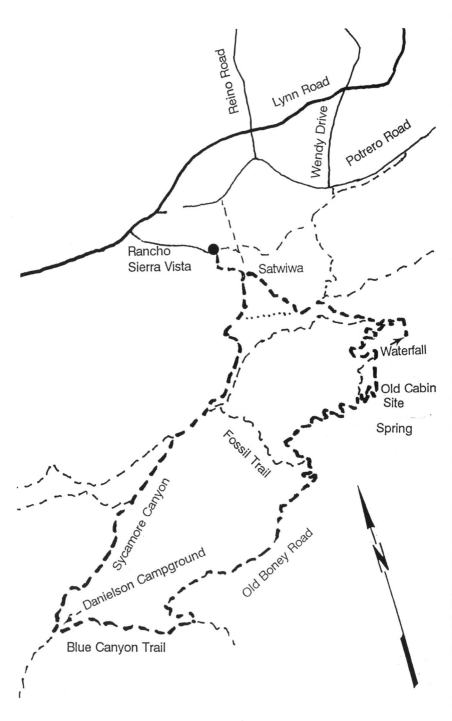

HIKE 14

OLD CABIN SITE
OLD BONEY ROAD
DANIELSON HOME
from Rancho Sierra Vista (loop)

Maps:	SMMTS, Western Section
Distance:	12 miles roundtrip
Elevation:	2100' gain and loss
Terrain:	Road and trail
Time:	5½ hours including lunch
Trailhead:	Potrero Gate

From the Ventura Freeway in the west end of Thousand Oaks turn south on Borchard Road. Follow Borchard 1½ miles until coming to Reino Road then turn left. Drive on Reino to Lynn, turn right. Go to the National Recreation sign. Turn left and drive to the Rancho Sierra Vista parking lot.

Follow the road until coming to a trail that crosses a big field on the left. One-half mile of trail brings us to the beginning of Old Boney Road. Walk on the road uphill for a ways, then downhill and across the stream. The road goes uphill following the stream then makes a hairpin turn to the right. A short side trip from this point takes us to a view of the waterfall. To get there, we go upstream on the path, turning right as we come to a sidestream, then upstream to the waterfalls.

After returning to the hairpin turn continue on the road for about 3/4 mile until coming to a fork. Take the left fork and reach the Old Cabin Site in 10 minutes. Other than a rock fireplace and chimney, the only visible evidence of a cabin is a level area with some rocks, indicating the cabin outline and floor. The slope downhill from the site is grassy with scattered oaks shading the soil. A monument in remembrance of Richard Danielson is downhill from the cabin site. A trail on the upper side of the open area leads to the Boney Mountain Ridge. Today's hike, however, continues on the road, dropping down slightly as it passes the spring then crosses the stream. The road is overgrown to the extent that the term "trail" is appropriate. We might elect to shorten today's hike by five or six miles by turning around here at the Old Cabin Site.

To continue the hike we follow the trail on the right of the chimney, and past the spring.

The next 1/2 mile is up the steep slope on the north side of the stream, gaining 350' altitude before levelling off just before reaching Old Boney Road. Turn left and continue on the road. After 4/10 of a mile a marked trail on the right leads down the slope to the northwest and intersects the Sycamore Canyon Trail. One half mile farther along Old Boney Road another trail leads down the slope, joining the first trail near the bottom of the canyon. We don't take either of these trails unless we want to shorten the hike 3½ - 4 miles. Continue along the road generally in a westward direction but with considerable turning. Most of the grade is downhill, but occasionally some uphill comes along. Two and a quarter miles after the last trail junction, an old road comes up the streambed from the Danielson Home. Near the junction, look for a boulder that must be 10' in diameter — a good landmark.

Turn right and follow the road down to and across the stream. Three hundred yards after the stream crossing, a trail goes uphill on the left. This trail is not distinct and as of now is not marked. Continue on down the road, which can also be indistinct because the winter rains wipe it out. Keep on the west side of the stream, passing by a pond, then down a heavily wooded valley toward the ranch, and through a campground.

Upon reaching the paved road turn right and go upstream. There are restrooms and water one-half mile up the road. Sycamore Canyon is appropriately named. Sycamores dominate the entire valley. Oaks take over on the edges of the valley, and either sage near the coast, or chaparral farther inland predominate on the slopes; but the Sycamores own the valley.

A paved road comes into the Sycamore Canyon Trail on the left about a mile up from the Danielson Home. This is the Ranch Center Road and leads to Wood Canyon. Another 3/4 mile upstream and the Hidden Pond Trail enters on the left. Continue on the road as it gains 300 feet in one mile, then another mile to the trailhead.

OLD CABIN SITE
Upper Sycamore Canyon near Old Boney Road

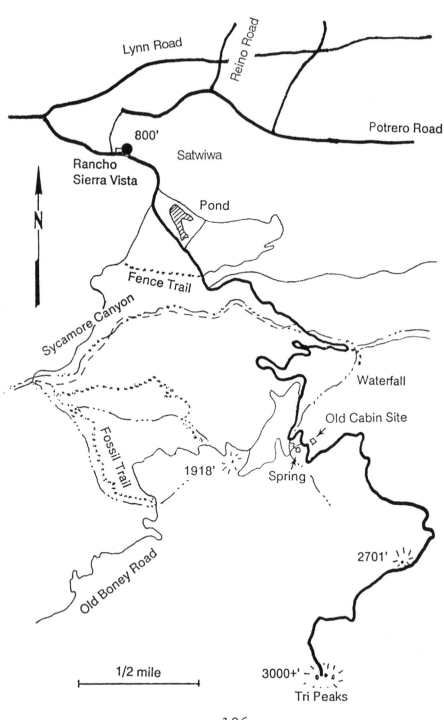

Lynn Road

Reino Road

Potrero Road

800'

Satwiwa

Rancho
Sierra Vista

Pond

Fence Trail

Sycamore Canyon

Waterfall

Old Cabin Site

Fossil Trail

1918'

Spring

Old Boney Road

2701'

1/2 mile

3000+'

Tri Peaks

N

106

HIKE 15

**BONEY MOUNTAIN
VIA THE OLD CABIN SITE**
from Rancho Sierra Vista

Maps:	SMMTS, Western Section
Distance:	12 miles roundtrip
Elevation:	2700' gain and loss
Terrain:	Road, trail, and steep trails
Time:	6 hours
Trailhead:	Potrero Gate

To reach the parking lot at Rancho Sierra Vista Drive on the Ventura Freeway to Newbury Park west of Thousand Oaks. From the freeway turn south on Borchard Road. Stay on Borchard Road until coming to Reino Rd., then turn left. Drive on Reino to Lynn, turn right. Go to the National Recreation sign. Turn left and drive to the Rancho Sierra Vista parking lot.

Upon leaving the parking lot follow the road southeast until coming to a trail on the left. Our trail crosses a wooden bridge and then angles right to cross the meadow. Upon reaching Old Boney Road follow it as we parallel Upper Sycamore Canyon. Below us and on our right we can see a trail down in the canyon. Later, that trail joins our route. Stay on Old Boney Road, cross the stream and continue uphill under the canopy of overarching Oaks and Bay trees. The road shortly makes a hairpin turn to the right. At this point, we may want to take a 15 minute side trip to the waterfall. If so, leave the road and continue upstream on a path a short distance, following the stream that comes down on the right. Expect some boulder hopping up to the base of the falls. The water tumbles and somersaults down a sandstone cliff in about six cascades. Giant Chain Ferns grow on the north side of the wall. Near the stream in shade of the ferns we notice a few Round-leaf Boykinia plants. They are rare in our mountains but do well in shade near running water. A big Leaf Maple once formed a canopy overhead but a fire went across the canyon in 1993 singeing the tree. It has not recovered. This sculptured verdant recess seldom suffers the blast or touch of wind and sun, so retains a sheltered character of its own.

We go back to the hairpin turn and continue up the road. The road makes two sets of switchbacks allowing our first view of the Channel Islands and the Oxnard Plain. After the last switchback from where we can see the ocean, walk about 1/3 mile and notice that Boney Road turns sharply right and continues uphill; go straight ahead, downhill, and in about 1/2 mile arrive at the Old Cabin Site.

The Old Cabin Site is a good place to take a break. This is a grassy slope in an oak grove. All that remains of the cabin is a 13-foot chimney with a fireplace and the remains of a rock foundation of about 12 x 18 feet. The spring is down near the stream. I no longer drink the water. We notice the Danielson Memorial as we leave.

A trail goes south up the hill from the upper side of the site. After a switchback or two the trail heads in an easterly direction climbing along the north shoulder of the mountain. Eventually we turn south and go up a steep ridge toward Peak 2701. In the 50 minutes that it takes us to walk 2 miles and to climb 1200 feet, we go through a beautiful stand of Manzanita mixed with some Ceanothus and Red Shanks. This north side of Boney Mountain is an outstanding chaparral forest.

The trail goes along the ridge and weaves through some Ceanothus and down to a small saddle where the trail crosses another trail — turn right. Continue winding through the chaparral and immediately after breaking out of it into an open area, we will see a rocky ridge with a pinnacle on the right end. The trail goes to the ridge, which affords a limited view of the ocean. Massive rock cliffs flank the canyon on the other side. The trail cuts left at this point and follows along the ridge. We tend to walk along the right edge of the ridge; avoid this as the indistinct trail is twenty feet or so to the left. Within ten minutes we will be on a peak with an outstanding view of Mugu, the ocean, the Channel Islands, and the rest of Boney Mountain.

This can be the turnaround point, or we may explore Boney Mountain by working our way to the southwest. We see several very rugged peaks along the crest, all at 2900' elevation.

Return to the Trailhead by the same route.

SYCAMORE

HIKE 16

Maps:	SMMTS, Western Section
Distance:	6 miles roundtrip
Elevation:	1650' gain and loss
Terrain:	Fireroad
Time:	2 hours 45 minutes
Trailhead:	Leo Carrillo State Beach

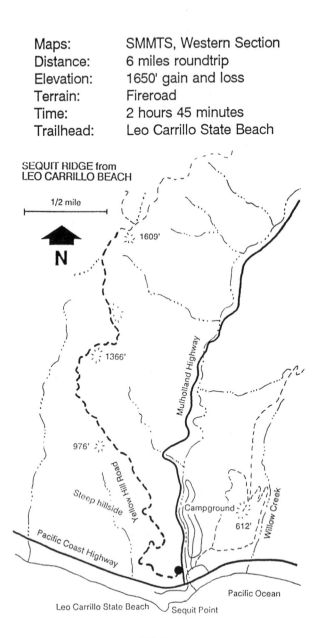

SEQUIT RIDGE from
LEO CARRILLO BEACH

1/2 mile

N

1609'

Mulholland Highway

1366'

976'

Yellow Hill Road

Steep hillside

Campground

Willow Creek

612'

Pacific Coast Highway

Pacific Ocean

Leo Carrillo State Beach   Sequit Point

This hike features outstanding views of the Pacific Ocean and an opportunity to look for Land Grant boundary markers, if any. The western property line of the Topanga-Malibu-Sequit Mexican Land Grant grazing concession coincides with the county line. Topanga-Malibu-Sequit was awarded to Jose Bartolomè Tapia in 1802 or 1804 and confirmed as a grant by Mexico after independence. The United States later confirmed title. A map shows that benchmark 1609 could have been the northwest corner of the property. We can look for features like "a sandstone rock" or "a lone oak" or similar recognizable character of the countryside. I don't know what to look for, maybe a cairn of rocks.

The Yellow Hill Fireroad begins on the west side of Mulholland Highway near the Pacific Coast Highway. Park at Leo Carrillo State Beach or off the Pacific Coast Highway. The Ranger's house and maintenance area are close to the trailhead.

The hike begins on the road heading west paralleling the coast and climbing all the way. After one-third mile the route turns inland and works up a ridge still gaining altitude. Occasionally we might want to stop and look at the ocean. On a clear day the Channel Islands of Anacapa, Santa Cruz, Santa Rosa and San Miguel are visible due west. Santa Barbara Island is small, but is sometimes seen just west of due south.

Initially the hike goes through the Coastal Sage plant community but farther inland changes to Chaparral. On the east side of the ridge a steep hill drops down to Arroyo Sequit. We can see the stream below and a segment of the Riparian Woodland plant community. Now this hike follows Yellow Hill Fireroad out and back.

Peak 1609 is the northwest boundary of the Park and the Land Grant boundary, and is a logical turnaround point for the hike. Outside the Park we will see some homes on private property. We should respect their privacy.

Return the way we came.

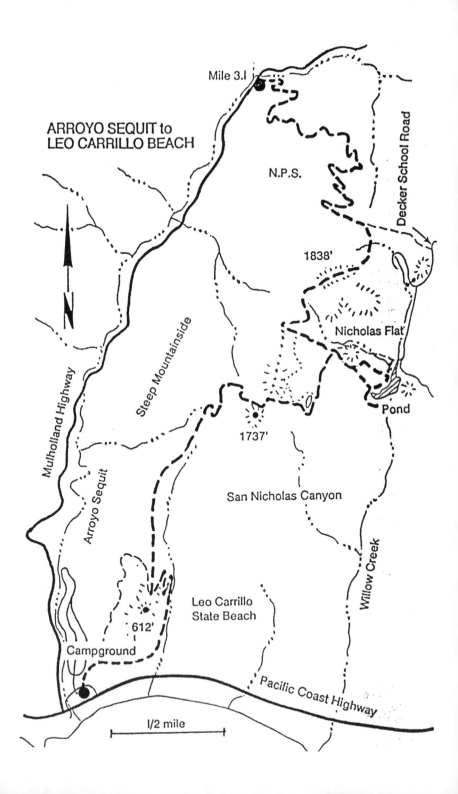

ARROYO SEQUIT to
LEO CARRILLO BEACH

Mile 3.1

N.P.S.

Decker School Road

1838'

Nicholas Flat

Pond

Steep Mountainside

Mulholland Highway

1737'

San Nicholas Canyon

Arroyo Sequit

Willow Creek

Leo Carrillo
State Beach

612'

Campground

Pacific Coast Highway

1/2 mile

HIKE 17

Maps:	SMMTS, Western Section
Distance:	7 miles
Elevation:	1800' gain, 2200' loss
Terrain:	Trail
Time:	3½ hours
Trailhead:	3.1 miles from the west end of Mulholland Highway

Arroyo Sequit has cut a deep channel in the mountains north of Leo Carrillo Beach. This gives us a steep hike on the north facing slope of the mountain onto Nicholas Flat. Usually the hike is one way, using a car shuttle to avoid backtracking on the trail. We set up the shuttle by leaving a car in the Leo Carrillo Beach parking lot and driving 3.1 miles north on Mulholland Highway. Parking space is limited and drivers must take care to find a spot completely off the pavement.

South of the bridge that crosses East Fork of Arroyo Sequit we find an old dirt road leading uphill to the east. Our hike begins here and continues uphill for the next 2 miles. The old road quickly takes on the appearance of a mountain trail because the vegetation has crowded in and taken over Heavy rains sometimes cause small landslides that erode parts of the trail. We pick our way around these areas. As we gain altitude, a panorama develops to the north and northwest, giving us fine views of boney Mountain. Along one section of the trail we can look across to the West Fork of the Sequit and in the spring see a double waterfall.

After about one hour of steady climbing, the trail levels out and then goes downhill a short distance. We look sharply to the right for a trail that branches right and makes a couple of climbing switchbacks, then heads southwest through open grassland, sage and sumac to a saddle. We head in a westerly direction as the trail takes us through overgrown Black Sage. After peaking out at 1838' the trail loses altitude and drops down to an old road. We have an option of continuing south on a trail along a ridge, or turning left to go southeast to the pond. The pond option adds a mile to the hike.

We turn left and go southeast downhill 1/2 mile to Nicholas Flat Pond.

The pond makes a good setting for lunch. A meadowland on one side and an oak grove, backed with clifflike rocks, on the other gives us a choice of sun or shade. Everything doesn't come easy. Some Poison Oak hides out in the shady spots. This entire area supports a variety of plant life, wildflowers grow well in the meadows and under the oaks. The pond offers an environment for Cat-tails, Arrow grass, Pondweed, and other moisture loving plants. A hike here in spring is especially rewarding because the plants are madly competing for moisture before the summer drought. From our lunch spot under the oaks we can take a short walk to the ridge for a good view of Nicholas Canyon and the ocean. After lunch we leave the pond by a trail uphill to the northwest turning left at the first fork. As we approach a large meadow, we continue uphill for a few hundred yards turning right at the ridge. The trail continues west, gains some altitude and enters a chaparral forest.

Continuing, we see Peak 1737 ahead. At the base of the peak and about the time it appears we have a climb ahead of us, look right. A trail branches right and makes a sweeping curve around the north slope of the mountain. We make some switchbacks always losing altitude. For a mile we pass through a dense growth of chaparral, mostly ceanothus. We will vow to come back in March to witness the blooming of this "wild lilac." The ocean comes into view, and we start a long descent down the slope and out onto a broad ridge. A transition from Chaparral to Coastal Sage Scrub takes place as we near the ocean. To the west is Arroyo Sequit Canyon, the point of land at the ocean is Sequit Point. Topanga-Malibu-Sequit Land Grant, first claimed by Jose Bartolomé Tapia in 1802 or 1804, took part of the name from Arroyo Sequit. This land grant extended 22 miles along the Malibu coast from Las Flores Canyon to the Los Angeles-Ventura County line and was kept almost intact until the 1930's. Most of the Nicholas Trail is on the old Land Grant land.

We continue downhill toward the ocean, coming out onto a saddle from which two trails branch, one goes east and contours around the knoll on our right. The other trail takes us around the same knoll, but from the west side. Both trails join near the campground. Upon reaching the parking lot at Leo Carrillo, get the drivers back to the beginning of the hike to pick up their cars.

LEO CARRILLO STATE BEACH AND NEARBY PARK AREAS   35000 Pacific Coast Highway

Leo Carrillo State Park features both the beach and the back-country. The well-known beach extends for 6600 feet and divides into two separate areas by Sequit Point, a rocky bluff. Both the west beach and east beach have restroom and dressing room facilities. The west beach can accommodate overnight campers in 50 campsites, some for tents, some for recreation vehicles — but no hookups. Skindiving, swimming, surfing, fishing, and picnicking is popular.

Two campgrounds are north of the highway. One can accommodate 138 family groups in either tents or recreation vehicles. A restroom and shower building is available but no hookups. A group campground can handle 75 people. It has a restroom and shower.

A nature trail starts at the north end of the campground and makes a loop under the trees and up onto the side of the hill. Also, the streambed makes an interesting hiking area. We must do some rock scrambling and take care to avoid Poison Oak. Nevertheless, exploration along the Sequit is a tradition — the Indians that lived in the village at the stream's mouth used the stream as a corridor for thousands of years.

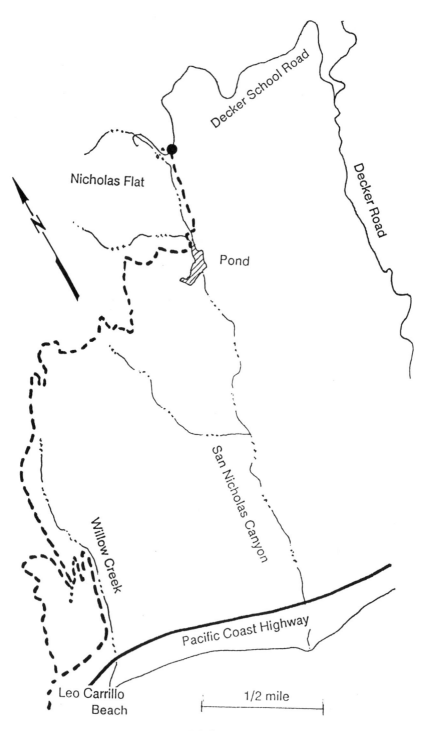

Decker School Road

Decker Road

Nicholas Flat

Pond

San Nicholas Canyon

Willow Creek

Pacific Coast Highway

Leo Carrillo
Beach

1/2 mile

HIKE 18

LEO CARRILLO BEACH

from Nicholas Flat
(shuttle)

Maps:	SMMTS, Western Section
Distance:	4 miles
Elevation:	250' gain, 1750' loss
Terrain:	Trail
Time:	2 hours
Trailhead:	Nicholas Flat

Hiking trails in the Santa Monicas that actually connect the mountains to the sea are rare, and to find a trail that unrolls scene after scene of new discoveries is rare indeed. The hike can be done as a roundtrip from either end, or by using a car shuttle we make it a one-way trip from Nicholas Flat to the seashore. We can set up the shuttle by letting hikers off at the end of Decker School Road. During the half hour that it takes for the drivers to park cars at Leo Carrillo Beach and return to the trailhead, the main group could walk to the lake and wait.

We begin the hike by going around a rustic gate, then along an oak-tree-shaded dirt road. The watercourse to the right invites exploration, but the Poison Oak discourages any careless dash to the streambed. When we come to a crossroad, we'll turn right, cross the stream, and after about 100 yards turn left, staying on a trail that parallels the stream. The trail leads us into a meadow and then to the edge of the lake. A trail curves around the west side of the lake and enters an open oak grove on the south side. Large boulders and rocky cliffs form a scenic backdrop to the lake. A short walk to the ridge offers a view of the steep canyon below.

When the rest of the hikers arrive and everyone is accounted for we leave the pond by a trail that goes uphill to the northwest. At the first fork in the trail, we angle left and continue uphill. In a few hundred yards the trail levels off and forks right (the left fork leads to a levelled spot on a ridge). We continue hiking west, gaining a little more altitude, and enter a chaparral forest. A small group of Sierra Club volunteers built this trail in 1981. A hand-hewn trail is special because the sensitivity of the workers is reflected in the final result. Unique rock formations are left undisturbed, trees that add to the beauty are preserved, and the usual evidence of "overkill" that accompanies the use of power equipment is precluded.

The trail makes a big sweeping curve around the north slope of the mountain, losing altitude all the time. For awhile we pass through a dense growth of chaparral, mostly Ceanothus. We will vow to come back in March to witness the blooming of this "wild lilac." The ocean comes into view, and we start a long descent down the slope and out onto a broad ridge. The vegetation makes a transition from Chaparral to Coastal Sage Scrub. The canyon to the west is Arroyo Sequit, and the point of land at the ocean is Sequit Point. The Topanga-Malibu-Sequit Land Grant, first claimed by Jose Bartolomé Tapia in 1802 or 1804, took part of the name from Arroyo Sequit. This land grant extended 22 miles along the Malibu coast from Las Flores Canyon to the Los Angeles-Ventura County line and was kept almost intact until the 1930's. Most of the Nicholas Flat Trail is on the old Land Grant land.

We continue downhill toward the ocean, coming out onto a saddle from which two trails branch; one goes east and contours around to the ocean, and the other drops down on the west side. Both of these trails meet again on the south side of the hill near the campground, so we can select either one. Another option is to continue south along the ridge to the top of the hill for a special view of the ocean. Whale watching from this point calls for binoculars.

When we reach Leo Carrillo State Beach, we must remember to get the drivers back to the cars at Nicholas Flat. Driving directions to the trailhead from the beach are: Go east on the Pacific Coast Hwy 2½ miles to Decker Road. Turn left and go 2½ more miles to Decker School Road (an obscure road on the left). Turn left and drive 1½ miles to the end of Decker School Road.

NOTE; Nicholas Flat and the area of the trail burned in a fire of October 1985. The plant and animal life have recovered and the Ceanothus has regained its dense forest-like structure. The flowers more than make up the difference and are still a significant part of this hike.

Nicholas Flat Pond

HIKE 19

Maps:	SMMTS, Western Section
Distance:	2½ miles
Elevation:	250' gain and loss
Terrain:	Road and Trail
Time:	1 hour
Trailhead:	34138 Mulholland Highway

Arroyo Sequit Park is 155 acres of open meadows and steep canyons. The Santa Monica Mountains conservancy purchased the land from Dick Mason in 1985 for public recreational use. They have developed the ranch for hiking, picnicking, and wildflower walks. Portable restrooms, picnic tables, parking, and water are available. Future use includes use as an orienteering site, group camping, and as a link for hikes to Malibu Springs, Leo Carrillo State Beach, and Point Mugu State Park. The Park is now administered by the Santa Monica National Recreation Area, NPS.

We drive 6 miles from the Pacific Coast Highway on Mulholland Highway to the entrance at mail box number 34138. Turn right into the driveway and park. The Park is open for day use only. A paved road leads to the ranch house. We can start a loop hike around the property by continuing on the trail south of the house and down into the canyon. This trail is steep. Part of the upper Park and all of the canyon burned in the fire of 1985. Wildflowers dominated the area, but brush has returned.

We are on a one-and-a-half-mile Nature loop that is interpreted by printed information attached to short posts along the trail. Most of the area is chaparral but Coast Live Oaks and Sycamores are found near the streams. Good stands of Poison Oak to keep us alert, are avoidable.

Upon reaching the canyon bottom, we turn left and go upstream. Raging in spring with several small waterfalls, the stream dries up in the summer. During the end of a rain look for a scenic waterfall to our right. The climb out of the gorge is on a well-graded trail but significant enough so that we get some exercise. Upon reaching the top we head west, downhill toward the picnic area. Other trails are available for exploration if our time allows it. Arroyo Sequit Ranch offers great views of the mountains, comfortable hiking, and adventure for all. Several years ago I saw some Western Pond Turtles near the creek at the parking lot, but have not seen them lately.

ARROYO SEQUIT PARK

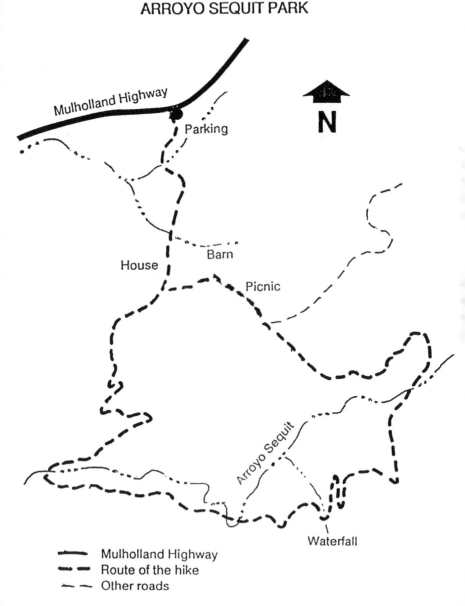

HIKE 20

Maps:	SMMTS, Western Section
Distance:	2½ miles
Elevation:	600' gain and loss
Terrain:	Dirt road and trail
Time:	1½ hours
Trailhead:	Encinal Canyon Road

Charmlee County Regional Park covers 460 acres of rolling meadowland surrounded by rocky ridges and steep mountain slopes. Oak woodlands, ocean views, rocky ridgetops, and fields of wild flowers are features of the Park. The land was acquired by the Los Angeles County Department of Parks and Recreation in 1968 from Charmain and Leonard Swartz. We believe Charmlee was derived from the combined first names.

Facilities include restrooms, drinking water, picnic areas, and a Nature Center. Park is open 8:00 a.m. to sunset daily.

From the Pacific Coast Highway west of Zuma Beach go north (inland) on Encinal Canyon Road about 4 miles to the entrance on the west (left) side. Drive in and park at one of several designated lots. Fee.

We can start our hike at the picnic area by locating the trail on the east side and go south, initially through the oak grove, then up to a rocky outcrop. The main trail skirts the east edge of a meadow and we follow the trail as we pass a couple of oak-sheltered boulder knolls. Any of these spots as well as groves to the east of us make good rest areas. The trail begins to head westerly and we notice a side trail on our left, going to "Ocean Vista" overlooking the Pacific .7 of a mile away and 1250' below. The trail climbs as we head west then north through two switch-backs cresting out near some Eucalyptus trees and a concrete reservoir. A trail takes us northwest to some Oak trees on a knoll — another good lunch spot. From here we take one of several trails northeast along the edge of the meadow until reaching an east-west road, then turn left and go west, uphill.

Several trails and roads become available, but our objective is to stay high and eventually turn north on the ridge that has the watertank. A few hundred yards beyond the watertank we make a turn right and walk down to the Nature Center and the end of the hike.

Many trails criss-cross this Park so we can spend all day exploring.

CHARMLEE PARK

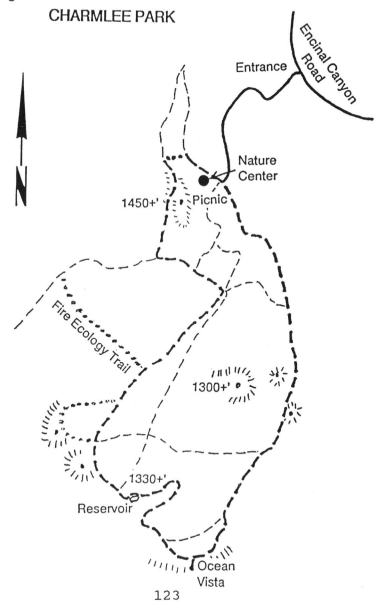

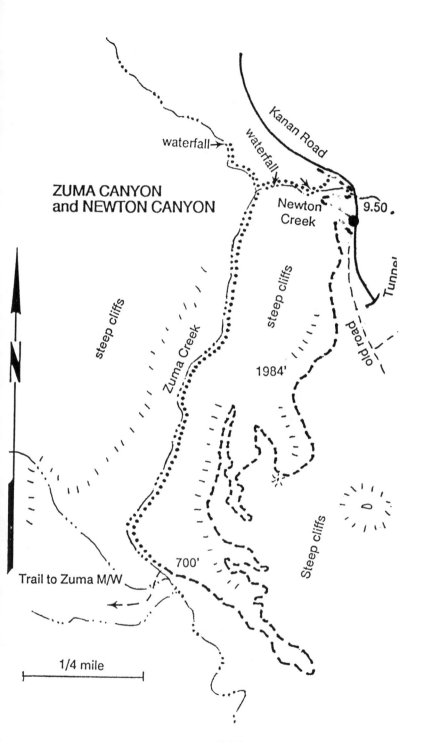

ZUMA CANYON
and NEWTON CANYON

Kanan Road

waterfall

waterfall

Newton
Creek

9.50

Tunnel

old road

steep cliffs

Zuma Creek

steep cliffs

1984'

Steep cliffs

700'

Trail to Zuma M/W

N

1/4 mile

124

HIKE 21

ZUMA CANYON AND
NEWTON CANYON
from Kanan Road (loop)

Maps:	SMMTS, Central Section
Distance:	6 miles roundtrip
Elevation:	1200' gain and loss
Terrain:	Road, trail, streambed boulder hopping, and class 2-3 rock climbing
Time:	4 hours
Trailhead:	Kanan Dume Road

The National Park Service has informed me that portions of this trail cross Park Service land and it has not been approved as a safe public trail.   Once the canyon is in complete public ownership, trails will be constructed for public use.

The National Park Service gives good advice. The dashed line on this map represents a difficult route with little or no main-tenance.   Dotted lines show a general course of rock climbing, bouldering, stream crossing, unmarked adventure in the bottom of a steep gorge. Be prepared for and willing to turn back — and many opportunities to do so will occur. Do not expect to see signs giving route information. Read page 33 for more on rock climbing. This hike presents some class 3 climbs. An experienced leader who has made this trip before is essential.

This section of Zuma Canyon is a most spectacular combination of stark volcanic cliffs, rugged boulder filled stream, and sheltered recesses beside plunging waterfalls. The only way in is on foot and recommended only for the experienced hiker who has rock climbing ability, and even then should join a group being led by someone familiar with the route. Expect some class 2 and 3 rock climbing.

The parking lot at the trailhead is on Kanan Dume Road (County Route N 9) 1.8 miles south of Mulholland Hwy, and is on the west side of the road just north of the southernmost of the three tunnels on Kanan. (Tunnel #1)

Immediately take the steep switchback to the right on the

road up the hill west of the parking area. Twenty years ago when writing the first edition of this book I stated " A vigorous 15 minutes of walking puts us on top of the ridge and at a fork in the road. I just walked this segment in 22½ minutes. The trail has degraded, and of course I am 20 years older. If you miss the right turn and continue to the top of the ridge over the tunnel take this as a signal that this hike is not for you. We go straight ahead and start down from the ridge. Almost immediately there is another branch; we take the one to the right and go downhill. One can rightfully question the term "road" from this point on because small landslides and stream erosion have reduced the route to a trail.

In the next 10 minutes we will have the opportunity to make two more trail decisions, take the right hand route both times. Going downhill continually and flanked on one side by overpowering volcanic cliffs and by a deep canyon on the other, look for a sharp switchback to the left. Stop for a moment to go to the edge and take in the panorama upstream, imposing rugged cliffs on the right, a precipitous abyss at our feet, the hint of refuge in the Sycamore sheltered stream below are all exposed to view. Looking to the south toward the ocean, a small rounded bump is seen above the plain. This is Point Dume. Point Dume is made up of sandstone and mudstone on the north side, and on the ocean side volcanics of 14½ million years of age.

Continue down toward the floor of the canyon and in another 15 minutes the trail we are on crosses one that comes in laterally from the left. Continue on down or take the right hand trail, the difference being that the right hand trail reaches the stream 3/4 mile up from the other. In either event we sit down by the stream upon reaching it, and as a first order of business take the stickers out of our socks. Look for ticks.

Zuma Creek is an amazing stream that rages in spring and trickles in the fall. It plunges and tumbles through a rugged, boulder filled canyon deep in the shade of Sycamore trees. An occasional waterfall that can present a climbing challenge, or Fern covered grottos in the sculptured canyon walls present a continually changing scene in this delightful retreat. Pick your way upstream; sometimes boulder hopping, sometimes crawling between angular rocks as big as a house, but often walking along a pool on hard sandstone. Immense volcanic boulders have tumbled down from the lofty ridges above; some of the gray sandstone exposes the fossils of turritella shells and an occasional pecten; each rock, each turn in the stream, and every pool presents a never ending variety of delight. Do not do this trip alone, not only because of the danger, but because this place should be shared.

I had a phone call one day from a hiker who had the inconvenience of spending a night somewhere in the middle of the canyon. Climbing over boulders in the dark is not recommended. He and I discussed such subjects as starting time, and not being with someone familiar with the route and class 2-3 climbing experience. He did use good judgment by knowing when to stop and wait for morning.

New adventure lies in wait upstream. The gorge cuts deep, and rock walls portend the approach to a waterfall. Thundering after a heavy rain, splashing at other times, the first of a series of falls has hollowed out a gravel lined pool nestled in a sheltered recess graced with moss and ferns.

After negotiating several waterfalls we will notice a major stream coming in on the right (east). This is Newton Canyon and will be the way out, but first we visit "Big Zuma" waterfall. It is 200 yards or so up the canyon in which you have been traveling, and in my opinion is the culmination of the grandeur of this canyon. The waterfall drops 25 feet over a massive ledge, and appears to present an absolute barrier to further travel. For this trip it is the turnaround point.

Go back to Newton Canyon. There are two more waterfalls to see on the way out. The first one cascades some 25 feet over a moss and fern covered rock cliff. When the flow of water allows it, this can be negotiated by approaching the base of the cliff on our left and working up a naturally sculptured stairway cresting out on the stream. Rock climbing ability is needed. Another way up is available by a very steep trail on the left before reaching the waterfall. The next waterfall is 200 or 300 yards farther up. there is no practical way up this waterfall so go back downstream a short distance and climb up the hillside on the north side of the stream. Follow the stream. We will intercept the Backbone Trail and by turning right will soon be back at the parking lot. We do not take this hike in the rain or when the rocks and soil are wet because the climbing becomes class 3-4 and places this hike beyond the scope of this hiking guide.

Waterfall in Zuma Canyon

Zuma Creek Crossing below the big waterfall

HIKE 22

Maps:	SMMTS, Central section
Distance:	1 - 2 miles
Elevation:	200' gain and loss
Terrain:	Trail
Time:	1 hour
Trailhead:	Mulholland Highway at Kanan

Until the 1978 Agoura fire burned the barns, sheds, and farm equipment, Rocky Oaks Ranch was a working cattle ranch. The Santa Monica Mountains National Park Service now manages the property. The Park features a pond, a southern Oak Woodland, Chaparral, areas of Coastal Sage Scrub, and Grassland. Facilities include drinking water, restrooms, picnic tables, an amphitheater, and a trail system. Walkers, bicyclists, and equestrians use the Park. The limited size would lead us to believe that we can't get a good workout. Not so, because of an extensive trail system, it offers exceptional opportunities for wildflower walks, interpretive sessions, picnicking, and family outings.

Reach the trailhead from the Ventura Freeway by going south on Kanan Road to Mulholland Highway. Turn west on Mulholland and then to the right into the parking lot. Going north on Kanan/Dume Road, we reach it from the Pacific Coast Highway to Mulholland, turn west, and then right into the parking lot. Parking is free.

Two trails leave the picnic area and go north, one to the pond, the other (Glade Trail) makes a loop to the east before reaching the pond. They meet near the pond's north end. Follow the trail to the north end of the park and make a sharp turn left on an old road that contours back along the hillside overlooking the pond. In twenty minutes we will find a side trail to our right. This Overlook Trail is for hikers only. It is a short climb including 34 steps to the top of Peak 1850+'. The climb gains a good view of the area. We return to the trail and continue to a junction with several trails. Two trails left allow us an option of going to the pond or directly to the parking lot. The trail west leads to a stream where we can see many wildflowers along the trail above the stream. After a downhill walk turn right and continue to the stream crossing. Look for Watercress in the stream and California Rose along the banks. The trail upstream enters a wooded area with large volcanic boulders near the streamed.

Saddle Rock Ranch at the end of our upstream walk, is our turnaround point. We return the way we came. Follow a trail to the parking lot.

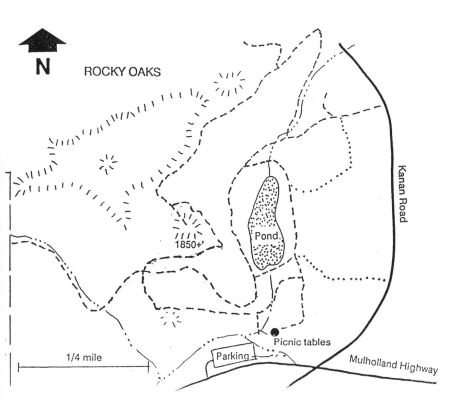

HIKE 23

Maps:	SMMTS, Central Section
Distance:	1/2 mile roundtrip
Elevation:	203' gain and loss
Terrain:	Beach, sand and trail
Time:	1/2 hour
Trailhead:	Westward Beach Road

This isn't going to be an all day hike, but is a "change of pace interlude" for a time when you may need something entirely different from the usual rigor of miles of mountain trail.

Point Dume is a point of land that overlooks the Pacific Ocean. It is located by driving on the Pacific Coast Highway about 1-1/2 miles west of the Kanan Dume Road. Turn south toward the ocean on the access road that takes you to either Zuma Beach or Point Dume Beach; then stay left on Westward Beach Road, driving to the end, and park your car.

Trudge across a couple hundred yards of sand, staying near the cliff on the left. A footpath leads up the cliff, branching several times — stay left for the trail, otherwise you will be doing some steep climbing. A number of trails allow exploration to the top of Point Dume, and also out on the scenic point overlooking the ocean. A steep climbing trail goes down to Dume Cove and to Paradise Cove.

This is an ideal place to watch for the migration of the Gray Whales as they head south to Baja, California, on their annual 10,000 mile roundtrip from Alaska. They usually travel in a pod of two or three or more, surfacing several times, then with their tails in the air, diving deep for a longer period under the water. The migration route is close to shore at Point Dume, and in the winter the probability of seeing some whales is very good.

Besides the Gray Whales, Point Dume provides other interests such as surfers (farther up the beach) riding the challenging waves, active swimmers, relaxed sunbathers, kites flying, people fishing, boats, scuba divers after Pismo clams and other marine life, and surprises.   Plan to spend an hour or two here enjoying this magnificent view.   The sun turns the water into shimmering, sparkling diamonds; and the never-ending splashing of the waves washing ashore makes one reluctant to return to reality.

Geologically, Point Dume consists of three different formations: (1) the trancas Formation consisting of sedimentary sandstone, shale, mudstone, and breccia; (2) the Zuma Volcanics: and (3) Monterey Shale composed of clay shale and siltstone.   The peak and the east slope of Point Dume is Trancas Formation; the rest of the point is Zuma Volcanics; and Monterey shale is prominent in the rest of the area. You may have noticed the layers of Monterey Shale along the cliff where you parked the car. A sample of volcanic rock taken from a spot near the ocean on the southwest side of Point Dume has been dated radiometrically at 14.6 + million years. All three formations are of Miocene age.

ARCHAEOLOGICAL NOTE

About one mile northwest of Point Dume near where Zuma Creek enters the ocean there once was an Indian village. Dating as established by the C-14 method shows that the village was occupied from 5000 years ago until the Spanish Invasion. Several nearby sites, or parts of the same village complex, date 7000 years ago with evidence of occupation until about 3500 years ago.

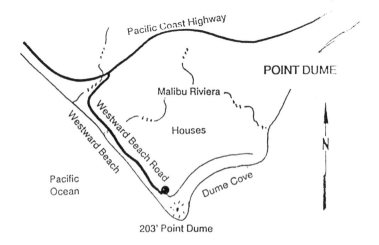

HIKE 24

ZUMA RIDGE TRAIL

(shuttle)

Maps:	SMMTS, Central Section
Distance:	6 miles, one way
Elevation:	800' gain, 2100' loss
Terrain:	Fireroad and trail
Time:	3 hours on the trail
Trailhead:	Ending: Busch Drive
	Beginning: Encinal Cyn Rd

This hike is described as a north to south one-way shuttle. Besides hikers we expect equestrians and bicyclists. If it weren't for the long initial uphill grind a bicycle might be preferred because the trail is actually a well maintained road that flattens out along the ridge.

We set up a car shuttle by driving the Pacific Coast Highway going west of Point Dume and turn inland on Busch Drive. Go to the end and park. This will be the end of the hike. Drive all hikers east on PCH, turn left on Kanan Dume Road, north to Mulholland and turn left. Go nine-tenths of a mile and turn left on Encinal Canyon Road to drive one half mile to park alongside the road.

Zuma Ridge Trail (a dirt road) begins west of the water recycling pool and goes south. For the first quarter mile the climb is a gentle uphill then a slight dip, and here is where the Backbone Trail comes in from Kanan Road. The trail becomes steeper and the next mile gives us a 700' gain. We reach our high point of the hike in about 45 minutes of steady walking, then we begin to lose altitude for the rest of the trip. We do have some ridge knolls to go over but nothing serious. Near the high point Buzzard's Roost Ranch forks left. This is a private road so we continue on the Ridge Trail.

After passing the Buzzard's Roost Ranch junction we can look west and see Trancas Canyon 1400' below. We can't see the bottom of Trancas because the canyon walls are steep and out of our sight. About one hour and twenty minutes after we started the hike, and after a down-ridge elevation drop of 600' in altitude Zuma

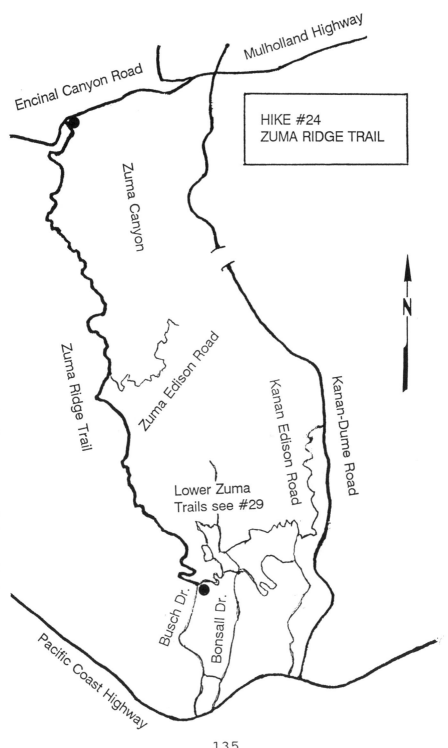

HIKE #24
ZUMA RIDGE TRAIL

Mulholland Highway

Encinal Canyon Road

Zuma Canyon

Zuma Ridge Trail

Zuma Edison Road

Kanan Edison Road

Kanan-Dume Road

N

Lower Zuma
Trails see #29

Busch Dr.

Bonsall Dr.

Pacific Coast Highway

135

Canyon begins to come into full view. I consider this canyon, viewed from this spot to be among the spectacular sights in the Santa Monica Mountains. Although we won't descend into this part of Zuma, a trail does go to the stream and up a trail on the east slope. If you are inclined to do this some other time look for the power lines overhead over the trail. Then a fork on the left will take you 1100' to Zuma Creek. At this point on Zuma Ridge Trail we are almost three and a half miles into our walk, with about two and a half miles to go.

We have been high on a ridge, and with good visibility should identify off shore islands and some features of the coast line. Point Dume is ahead of us and as we approach the end of the hike we can see our cars.

"BALANCE ROCK"
along Zuma Westridge

HIKE 25

CASTRO CREST

from Corral Canyon Road

Maps:	SMMTS, Central Section
Distance:	5 miles
Elevation:	1050' gain and loss
Terrain:	Fireroad and trail
Time:	2½ hours
Trailhead:	Corral Canyon Road

Castro Crest is National Park Service land in upper Solstice Canyon. The area is adjacent to Malibu Creek State Park and has interconnecting trails. The Backbone Trail follows the east-west ridge on Mesa Peak Motorway and Castro Motorway, and as an alternate route, the Backbone Trail follows the trail in Upper Solstice Canyon. The loop trip described here will be on the Backbone Trail.

We reach the roadhead by driving the Pacific Coast Highway to Corral Canyon Road a little over 2 miles west of Malibu Canyon Road. The road marker reads 50.36. Turn north and drive uphill on a paved winding road for about 5½ miles to the end of the pavement and on to a large parking area.

A trail leads down into Solstice Canyon from the west edge of the parking area. After 10 minutes of travel we cross a streambed and walk up to a ridge on the west. An old road comes down the ridge and out to a rise — several service roads still remain from the time the power line was put through the area. The trail temporarily follows the bed of the service road then angles right as the road turns left and goes steeply downhill to a streambed. The trail contours along the slope. As it crosses a stream we can see a 20 foot waterfall (after heavy rain only) upstream.

This entire area was burned in October 1982 during the Dayton Canyon fire — a riot of wildflowers covered the basin five months later. The chaparral will recover in seven or eight years but upper Solstice Canyon will always be a garden. We follow the trail downstream until coming to a fork at the stream junction. We turn

137

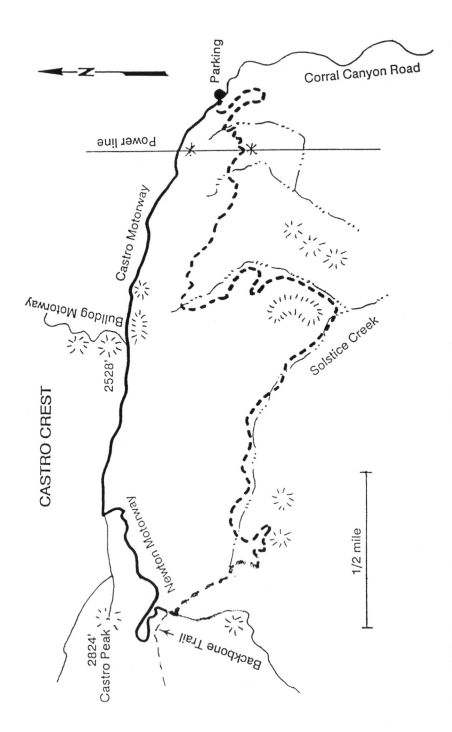

CASTRO CREST

Parking

Corral Canyon Road

Power line

Castro Motorway

Bulldog Motorway

2528'

Solstice Creek

Newton Motorway

1/2 mile

2824'
Castro Peak

Backbone Trail

right and go uphill — a left turn would take us out of the Park and onto private land. The trail stays close to the streambed as it heads west under a cover of Coast Live Oaks. Two-thirds of a mile from the stream junction finds us on some switchbacks going up the slope at the west end of the basin. On reaching the ridge turn right onto a dirt road At a saddle along the Motorway, we will see the continuation of the Backbone Trail heading off to the west. Continue to gain altitude skirting around the south side of Castro Peak until reaching the crest and Castro Peak M/W, and turn right again. The hike along the crest opens up spectacular views on both sides. Look for Hawkweed plants growing out of the cliffs — blooms in June through the summer. Santa Susana Tarweed and Wrights' Buckwheat are found growing in the sandstone outcroppings. They bloom in late summer and fall.

The motorway is a downhill grade to the parking lot.

WILDFLOWER COMMENT

Castro Crest is like an island above the surrounding land. The north slope drops 2000' to Malibu Creek. On the south the immediate elevation change is 1000' as the cliffs drop down to Upper Solstice Valley. Castro Crest drops down both east and west. I think this has something to do with the unusual collections of plants along today's hike. I will discuss a couple of areas and leave the discovery to you. High on the road we find Hawkweed and Wrights' Buckwheat. Silver Lotus and Santa Susana Tarweed are also there. Yerba Santa and Chaparral Pea are plentiful in concentrated zones. Usually plants that are scarce are scattered about into little pockets and this area is no exception. Of all of these plants only one is on the Endangered Species list — the Santa Susana Tarweed. I probably shouldn't mention this but an area a few miles away supports a quarter million or so of the plants. In that area the plants are common, some spreading to six or eight feet in diameter and lasting for many years. To me, Raspberries taste a bit like the tarweed smells. Several years ago a large bush disappeared near Bulldog Motorway during a road improvement program. I miss that plant.

Along the downstream segment in Upper Solstice Canyon we

look for Conchalagua, Woolly Blue-curls, Scarlet Larkspur, Creek Monkey Flower, White Star Lily and Foothill Penstemon. These plants often become prominent after a fire. In 1983 after the fire of the previous winter many thousands of White Star Lilies were in full bloom. We saw them for a year or two and now that vegetation has recovered and shades the ground we see no lilies. They need sunlight to bloom and are waiting for the next fire or someone to build a trail and clear the brush. One can get down to ground level in the chaparral and see flat, arching leaves — but no blossoms.

In open grasslands near the creek we look for Clarkia. Blue-eyed Grass, Golden Stars, California Golden Violet (Johnny-jump-up) Mustard Evening primrose, and Poppy. In shade look for Crimson Pitcher Sage and Milkmaids. Peony, Turkish Rugging, Prickly Phlox, Lomation, and Soap Plant are found in drier areas.

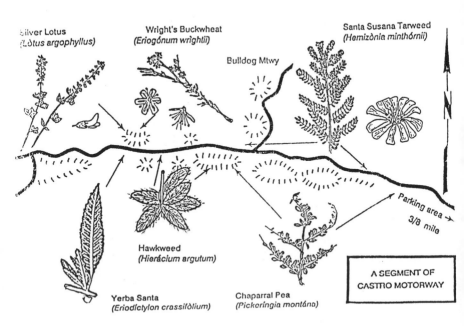

Silver Lotus
(Lotus argophyllus)

Wright's Buckwheat
(Eriogónum wrightii)

Santa Susana Tarweed
(Hemizònia minthórnii)

Bulldog Mtwy

Parking area 3/8 mile

Hawkweed
(Hierácium argutum)

Yerba Santa
(Eriodíctylon crassifólium)

Chaparral Pea
(Pickeríngia montána)

A SEGMENT OF
CASTRO MOTORWAY

GEOLOGICAL COMMENT

Solstice Canyon has an interesting geologic structure. Several faults cross the area, significant of which is the Malibu Bowl Fault downstream of where we will be hiking. Some of the geological features described here are south of the Park property and on private property. Hikers have used the route down the stream for many years, but increased use of the property by owners could cause some restrictions on hikers and equestrians.

Some very important formations are present in the canyon. Most of these can be seen during the usual hike.

First take a look at this diagram to get a feel for the ages we are discussing. The older rocks were formed first, then subsequent layers were built on top until thousands of feet of strata had been built up.

Time in millions of years ago	Periods Epochs	Formations found in Solstice Canyon
	Pleistocene	
3		
	Pliocene	
11		
	Miocene	Volcanics
25		
	Oligocene	Sespe
40		
	Eocene	Llajas?
		Coal Canyon
60	Paleocene	Simi Conglomerate
70	Cretaceous	Tuna Canyon
135		

Starting at the top with the youngest rocks visible and using nomenclature of the stratigraphic succession as used in the publication *Stratigraphic Nomenclature of the Central Santa Monica Mountains* by Yerkes and Campbell, I will briefly describe the formations as we descend the trail.

The parking lot and all of the rock in the immediate vicinity, including the finbacks along the ridge east-southeast, are of a nonmarine sequence named the Sespe Formation. Composed of sandstone, pebbly sandstone, mudstone, and cobbles, Sespe is often reddish colored, but mostly gray here. The 3000 feet of strata dips northeast on a steep angle, in some places 80°. Sespe was formed during late Eocene, Oligocene and early Miocene times, 40-25 mya, when the land was above sea level and an immense flood plain. The first 20 minutes of our hike into the canyon is on Sespe.

400 yards beyond the waterfall and as we drop down into the canyon, we leave the cobbled Sespe Formation and enter the Llajas (?)Formation;, a marine sequence of sandstone, siltstone, and pebbly conglomerate that was laid down during Eocene times, 50-40 mya. Peak 2034' and the rock along the streambed is all on Llajas (?).

The route of the loop hike turns right at the junction with the west fork of the stream, and goes upstream on Llajas Formation. If we elect to go downstream at the junction we will reach the Coal Canyon Formation in about 3/8 mile. Keep in mind that at the present time the land downstream is privately owned, and even though the trail has been used by hikers for many years, future use and development may change the condition of its use. The Coal Canyon Formation is another marine sequence of sandstone, siltstone, and pebbly conglomerate. This formation was laid down during late Paleocene and Eocene times, 60-50 mya. Marine fossils can be seen in many places along the streambed. Layers of mollusks are clearly seen in the large rock slabs.

After crossing about 1/4 mile of Coal Canyon Formation, the stream flows over 100 yards of Simi (?) Conglomerate. This nonmarine formation is characterized by well-rounded polished cobbles and boulders of quartzite, granitic rhyolite, and gneissic conglomerate in coarse-Formation is of Paleocene age, 70-60 mya, and has no fossils.

GEOLOGIC FORMATIONS IN UPPER SOLSTICE CANYON

Downstream of the Simi(?) Formation is found a small exposure of Tuna Canyon Formation, a marine sequence of sandstone, siltstone, and small pebble conglomerate. This sequence is located in a broad triangle not much over 1/4 mile east and west with the south limit at the Malibu Bowl Fault. It is upper Cretaceous in age, 135-70 mya, not exposed at the base in Solstice Canyon and overlaid in part by Conejo Volcanics.

At Baller Motorway the stream crosses a major fault — the east-west trending Malibu Bowl Fault. Conejo Volcanic rock, constituting the upper plate of the fault, is found downstream of this point. The age of the Conejo Volcanics is Middle Miocene, 16-12 mya.

Geologists are not in complete agreement as to nomenclature of the various formations, and the ages are subject to interpretation. I have used Geological Survey Bulletin 1457-E by R.F. Yerkes and R.H. Campbell as a major source of information. A (?) indicates questionable data.

HIKE 26   ESCONDIDO WATERFALL

Maps:	SMMTS, Central Section
Distance:	4 miles roundtrip
Elevation:	600' total
Terrain:	Roadside and trail
Time:	2 hours
Trailhead:	Winding Way and PCH

Escondido in Spanish could be interpreted as "to hide" or hidden. The waterfall certainly is out of sight. I should say *they* because three waterfalls in succession come over a cliff. all three are spectacular waterfalls. Accessability of Upper and Middle Falls is a problem unless one is a rock climber at heart. Today's hike will take us to the foot of the lower falls and I don't encourage further exploration.

Route of the trail has been privately owned for many years and traditionally accessable to hikers and equestrians. Several years ago an owner on upper Via Escondido (a road) objected to travel across his property. Much discussion until the Santa Monica Mountains Conservancy bought some creek bottom land and built a parking lot at Pacific Coast Highway and Winding Way. Both Via Escondido and Winding Way are posted as private roads so as of now we don't drive on them.

Park in the lot on the inland side of Pacific Coast Highway on Winding Way. A bit of history parallels PCH. A remnant of "Old Pacific Highway" runs east-west at the north end of the parking lot. A printed imprint in the cement indicates a date of 17 April 1929. A sign identifies our path to the Falls as "Winding Way Public Hiking and Riding Trail." At the bottom of the sign we see "Private Road." I interpret this oxymoronic statement as "this is the way but keep off the road." At least one person has solved the quandry by scratching out the "Public hiking and Riding Trail" part of the sign. Arrows indicate on which side of the road we should walk. The shoulder of the road is not my preferred trail but in twenty minutes we spot a trail on the left going downhill to the creek. Cross the stream, turn left and head upstream.

Even though we know the best is yet to come we do not hurry. Along the stream we are in the shade of trees. Sycamore, Alder, Walnut and Coast Live Oak grow here. On the immediate sides of the trail we will see a mixed display of flowers well into summer. Look for Canyon Sunflower, White Nightshade, and German Ivy in deep shade. Cliff Aster, Rose, Bush Monkey Flower, Slender Tarweed, Fennel and Bristly Ox-tongue are happier with more sun. Black Sage, Sumac, Toyon, and Bush Mallow are found away from the stream in the chaparral plant community. Two plants to be on the alert for are Poison Oak and Poison Hemlock. Avoid both plants. They grow in partial shade.

We cross the stream four times before arriving at the lower waterfall and we do gain some elevation at a moderate rate. Expect a spectacular waterfall because it is. In summer and fall don't look for a lot of water, but after a few good winter rains Escondido is real. Look high and to our left to notice a stone drape. This is calcium carbonate (limestone) and is formed by evaporation of the water, leaving a growing sheet of stone. The upper waterfall supports a great display of these formations and a few caves besides.

On our return from the waterfall we will notice trails to the stream. Most of them end but at least one will cross the creek and take us high on the hill to the west and allow a good view of the waterfall and canyon. I prefer to return the way I came.

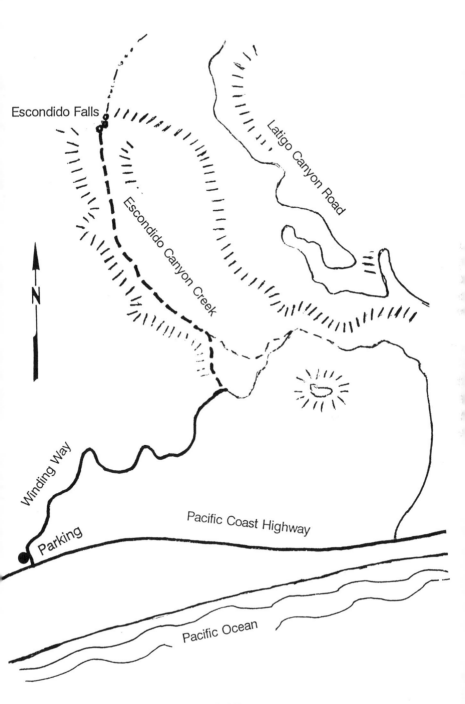

Escondido Falls

Latigo Canyon Road

Escondido Canyon Creek

N

Winding Way

Parking

Pacific Coast Highway

Pacific Ocean

HIKE 27

PETER STRAUSS RANCH
(Lake Enchanto)

Map: SMMTS, Central Section
Distance: Main Loop Trail — 1 mile
Elevation: Main Loop Trail — 175 ft. gain and loss
Terrain: Trail, some steep and narrow
Trailhead: Mulholland Hwy and Troutdale Dr.

AREA FEATURES

The 64 acre Peter Strauss Ranch is partly on steep hillsides and also on level ground west of Triunfo Creek. A stream terrace of sand and gravel has been built as a natural result of heavy runoff during periods of rain. The stream terrace forms a large grassy area surrounded by Oak, Sycamore and introduced Eucalyptus trees. The main building, built in 1923 of local rock, is Park headquarters. A restroom is north of it. A house uphill is residence for the park ranger. An amphitheater of rock and cement was built about 1936. A swimming pool and patio were constructed in 1939. A dam across the creek resulted in Lake Enchanto, but the dam went out during a flood and nature has reclaimed the stream.

An important bit of history is preserved on the property. Northwest of the headquarters building we will find "The Land Grant Oak," a Coast Live Oak that was used as a corner marker for El Paraje de las Virgenes, a Spanish grazing concession granted to Bartolomé Miguel Ortega in 1802.

Peter Strauss Ranch was purchased by the Santa Monica Mountains Conservancy and held until 1987 when bought by the National Park Service who now manage the property. The ranch is known for holding a variety of special events, family recreation, rotating art and sculpture, and walks through wooded areas.

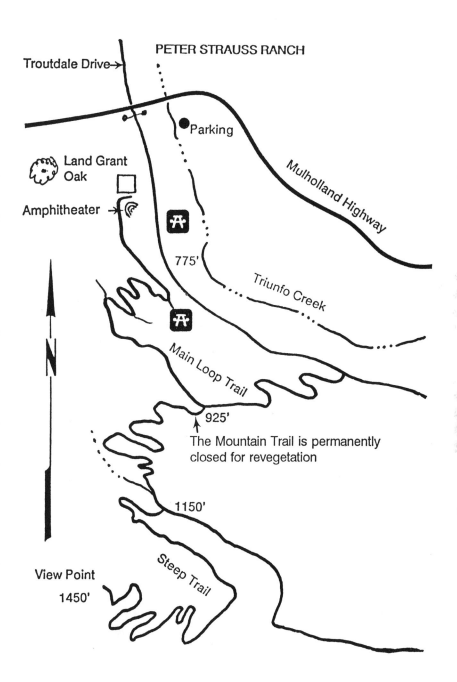

PETER STRAUSS RANCH

Troutdale Drive →

● Parking

Mulholland Highway

Land Grant Oak

Amphitheater →

🏕 775'

🏕

Triunfo Creek

Main Loop Trail

N

925' The Mountain Trail is permanently closed for revegetation

1150'

View Point
1450'

Steep Trail

TRAIL INFORMATION

Peter Strauss Ranch is located at 30000 Mulholland Highway. Drive on Ventura Freeway to Kanan Road and go south 2.8 miles to Troutdale Drive and turn left. At Mulholland Highway again turn left, cross a bridge and turn right into the parking lot. Walk back across the bridge and enter the gate into the ranch. In time, a footbridge will cross Triunfo Creek from the parking lot. Restrooms, drinking water, a play area, and picnicking facilities are available.

A loop trail of about 1 mile is suitable for family groups and offers a diverse plant environment;

Because this park presents a diversity of plant communities and of wildflowers in season, I have used my book *Wildflower Walks of the Santa Monica Mountains* as a source for today's walk. Pass the amphitheater and turn left onto a level trail heading south. Grasses, Pineapple Weed, and Filaree are common underfoot; a Southern Oak Woodland is to the left, and the edge of Chaparral is on the right. Look for Golden Yarrow, Woolly Aster, Foothill Penstemon, Telegraph Weed, Yellow Star Thistle, Phacelia, Bush Monkey Flower, and Horehound off to either side. Coyote Brush, Hollyleaf Redberry, Coffeeberry, and Buckbrush are the shrubs back from the trail. Milkmaids will bloom in February and March here. At the first switchback a spur could take us to a picnic table and swing. Instead, turn right to keep on the trail climbing past Maidenhair, Goldback and Woodferns. We will find Heart-leaved Penstemon, Fuchsia-flowered Gooseberry, Honeysuckle, and Elderberry in the gradual shift from oak woodland to chaparral.

Five more switchbacks take us on a climbing tour through Chaparral of Scrub Oak, Woolly Blue-curls, Mountain Mahogany, and Buckbrush Ceanothus. The trail levels out as it heads southeast. As we make a sharp left turn and cross a dry streambed, look for Flowering Ash, Miner's Lettuce, Man-root, Peony, Purple Nightshade, and Hairy-leaved Ceanothus.

We continue east. Crimson Pitcher Sage, Poison Oak, and Bay Trees are significant plants of the oak woodland as the trail begins to lose altitude. Some steps at the switchbacks make the walking easier. More Hairy-leaved Ceanothus and Coffeeberry shrubs are seen on both sides of the trail. At a fork we turn left and complete the loop on a gentle downhill walk in deep shade.

We can see both species of Ash, Sticky Cinquefoil, Heart-leaved Penstemon, and several species of ferns. Upon reaching the flat area, notice the unique children's play area. Lots of level ground and a structure that can be climbed upon should keep youngsters busy. The remains of the dam that once crossed Triunfo Creek to impound Lake Enchanto is about 50 yards off to our right. The administration building is in view and we have completed the loop.

Poison Oak   Man-root

HIKE 28

AREA FEATURES

Paramount Ranch was a location for filming scenes for hundreds of movies, between 1921 and 1946, while the property was owned by Paramount Studios. Beginning in the early 1950's the ranch also became a site for large recreational events from square dances and hay rides to scout jamborees and rodeos. The National Park Service acquired 326 acres of the ranch in 1979 and has rebuilt the Western Town. Since then the ranch has been open to the public. The Western Town has been made available for occasional filming of commercials, television shows and movies. Hiking and equestrian trails have been built, picnic areas are available, and programs are regularly scheduled for public participation.

The plant communities of Paramount Ranch include: (1) a Riparian Woodland of willows and cat-tails along Medea Creek, (2) a Southern Oak Woodland along part of the Stream Terrace Trail and the picnic area, (3) Grasslands, and (4) Chaparral. The Dayton Canyon fire of October 1982 burned much of the area. Recovery has been natural and little evidence of the fire remains.

TRAIL INFORMATION

Paramount Ranch is south of Agoura Hills. Drive south of Ventura Freeway on Kanan Road 3/4 mile to Cornell Road (Sideway Road) and turn left. Go 2½ miles south on Cornell to the ranch entrance on the right. Two trails are described: Stream Terrace Trail (Medea Creek Trail) and Coyote Canyon Nature Trail. Also a network of trails for your exploration tie in to the Coyote Canyon Trail and go north. These are not described here.

PARAMOUNT RANCH

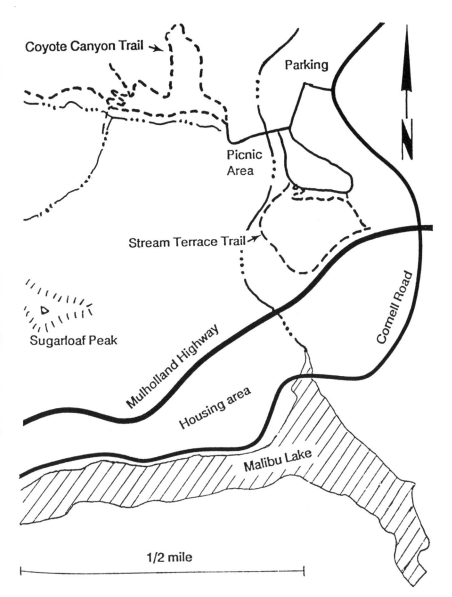

Coyote Canyon Trail

Parking

Picnic Area

Stream Terrace Trail

Sugarloaf Peak

Mulholland Highway

Cornell Road

Housing area

Malibu Lake

N

1/2 mile

(Medea Creek Trail) STREAM TERRACE TRAIL
Distance: 3/4 mile
Walking time: 20 minutes

Begin the walk south of the parking lot in the Oak Woodland on the north side of hill 860'. Go east on a well-graded path that gains altitude gradually. The trail is in the shade of the hill in rich soil and takes us through an area of a variety of plants. At the switchback to the right look for Flowering Ash on the right and Coffeeberry on the left. We will see both of these plants along the route as long as we are shade protected. We continue to climb and as we make a switchback to the left the trail enters an area of some chaparral plants. Scrub Oaks are found on both sides and Hollyleaf Redberry on the right, and more Flowering Ash. Look for Hairy-leaved Ceanothus, Buck-brush, and Greenbark Ceanothus in one area near the trail. Upon reaching a small arroyo we turn right and enter an open area of many chaparral species. Scrub Oak, Chamise, Yucca, and Buck-brush are the dominant shrubs with Western Ragweed, Verbena, Wand Buckwheat, and Woolly Aster filling in some of the spaces. We continue along the arroyo and then turn right to parallel Mulholland Highway through a sparse Chamise slope. The hill — a remnant of a stream terrace deposit laid down during pleistocene times — is characterized by gravel, silt, sand, and clay. This soil differs from the fragmental volcanic rock west of Medea Creek so we have an opportunity of comparing the two.

An indistinct trail branches right making a loop to the hilltop then back down. The south facing slope is dominated by Chamise with some Scrub Oak, Buck-brush, Sawtooth Goldenbush, and spring blooming wildflowers. Toward the top look for Bush Sunflower, Deerweed, Woolly Blue-curls, California Buckwheat, Sagebrush, and on the very top, Vinegar Weed.

As we follow the Stream Terrace Trail down toward the creek, a side trip to the creek and the dredging pond area will produce interesting plants. Look for Mexican Tea, Datura, Nettles, Milk Thistle, Quail Bush, Tree Tobacco, Russian Thistle, Arizona Ash, Horseweed, Horehound, Heliotrope, Bush Mallow, and others. Good stands of Cat-tail grow in the stream and Willow, Rose, and Walnut line the banks.

PAVED LOOP
Distance: 500 yards
Walking time: 5 to 10 minutes

This walk almost does not qualify as a "walk" because it is on pavement. The loop has some things worth while: because of relatively smooth terrain, parents with children in strollers can do this one. Also, those in wheelchairs can make this loop with some uphill work at the east end. A surprising number of wildflowers can be seen along the route. Start at the west end and go counterclockwise. On the right, about where the Stream Terrace Trail begins, look for Wild Gourd *(Calabazilla)*, Goldenbush, Bush Sunflower, and Narrow-leaved Milkweed. For about 150 yards we will be going along a Southern Oak Woodland plant community dominated by Coast Live Oaks. Coffeeberry, Flowering Ash, Honeysuckle, and a variety of spring wildflowers will be the understory. At the eastern end of the pavement look for a trail on the right going up an arroyo. Several Valley Oaks are within view. At the very edge of the pavement and in cracks of the pavement, we find Gumplant, Verbena, Telegraph Weed, Woolly Aster, Wand Chicory, Western Ragweed, Turkey Mullein, Filaree, Narrow-leaved Milkweed, Wand Buckwheat, Black Mustard, Vinegar Weed, Hore-hound, and around the corner — Fuchsia.

COYOTE CANYON NATURE TRAIL
Distance: 3/4 mile
Walking time: 25 minutes

Stop at the bulletin board west of the parking lot to check for new information and a trail guide. Continue walking west and turn right after passing the last building. Coyote Canyon will be in view west of the western town. The trail follows the north bank. A field of Mediterranean Mustard dominates the area on the left. Look for Western Ragweed, Mulefat, Madia, Sawtooth Goldenbush, and Bush Mallow along the trail — all will be in bloom through late summer. Perezia, Honeysuckle, Poison Oak, Bush Sunflower, and Cliff Aster will be seen before we have walked 200 yards. A number of Buckbrush *(Ceanothus cuneatus)* bushes dominate an area of the hillside to our right. The canyon narrows and becomes shadier. Look for Fuchsia, Peony, Purple Nightshade, and across the stream — Hoary-leaved Ceanothus. The trail makes a climbing right turn away from the streambed. We may want to make two exploratory side-trips at this point: (1) turn left and walk about 100' up a side stream to look for Flowering Ash, Small Evening Primrose, Woodfern, Crimson Pitcher Sage, Miner's Lettuce, and Chia. (2) Continue upstream on an old dirt road. Presently not maintained, this trail heads westerly along the north bank of the streambed for about 1/4 mile, then angles northwest and goes up a steep ridge. In the spring of 1983, following the fire of October 1982, Giant Phacelias covered the lower slopes in several areas. These 4' robust plants deposited thousands of seeds to await another fire. Now we will find Telegraph Weed, Sawtooth Goldenbush, California Buckwheat, Giant Rye, Mulefat, Madia, and as we start up the ridge we will be in a chaparral community of Woolly Blue-curls, Chamise, Black Sage, Bigberry Manzanita, Bush Poppy, and Buckbrush.

When we return to the Nature Trail our route is east, slightly uphill on a winding tour overlooking the Western town. Birds' Beak, Blue Dicks, Everlasting, Wild Sweet Pea, Mariposa Lily, and Soap Plant can be seen from the trail. Continue the loop and come out near a grove of introduced Eucalyptus trees. Take time to look at the Western town or cross the grassy area and relax under the trees at a picnic table.

HIKE 29

The National Park Service holds title to most of Zuma Canyon from a few miles north of the Pacific Coast Highway to Encinal Canyon Road. Private inholdings exist throughout the area but trails avoid private property unless easements have been granted.

Zuma Creek drains a large watershed from the central part of the mountains and when the winter rains hit, our trails are damaged. We ask around before planning a hike in early spring. The good news is that wildflowers are everywhere. Streamside trees give shade in the canyon floor and Coastal Sage Scrub and Chaparral cover the hillsides. The area is accessible from Pacific Coast Highway which can be reached from the inland valleys by Kanan Dume Road, or Malibu Creek Road.

TO GET TO LOWER ZUMA TRAILS:

From the Pacific Coast Highway eight-tenths of a mile west of Kanan Dume Road, turn inland on Busch Drive. At Rainsford Place turn right and go to Bonsall Drive. A left on Bonsall takes us to a dirt parking lot within the Santa Monica Mountains National Recreation Area. An open gate gives us pause to think we might be driving into someone's yard. Such is not the case, we are entering National Park Service land. This Bonsall Drive Trailhead gains access to Ocean View Trail, Canyon View Trail, Zuma Canyon Trail, Zuma Loop Trail, and Ridge-Canyon Access Trail. Had we stayed on Busch Drive rather than cutting across to Bonsall we would go directly to Zuma Ridge Canyon Trailhead. The reason I don't go directly from PCH to Bonsall is because the sign is obscure, on a curve and I always miss it. Busch has a stop light. On our way out on Bonsall we must use Rainsford (unless it is flooded) because Bonsall requires a right turn only onto PCH, on a curve.

OCEAN VIEW TRAIL/CANYON VIEW TRAIL LOOP

Map:	SMMTS, Central Section
Distance:	3 miles
Elevation:	700'
Terrain:	Dirt Trail
Time:	2 hours

From the Bonsall Trailhead we hike north on an almost level trail and in five minutes pass the Zuma Loop Trail branching left. We continue a short distance then take the Ocean View Trail branching right. After crossing the stream the trail begins a steady climb on the east slope of Zuma Canyon. We come out of a Sycamore, Walnut, Oak plant community into a Coastal sage community. We can see the ocean and as we climb to the ridge the view indeed dominates the scenery. Depending on the hiking group it could take us one hour to reach the high point, where we intersect Kanan Edison Road and turn left. Almost immediately we see the Canyon View Trail on our left. As we hike downhill an ever-changing view of Zuma greets us at every turn. If we take advantage of view points it could take us forty-five minutes before we reach the canyon floor and the Zuma Canyon Trail. A left turn will take us to the trailhead in fifteen minutes.

ZUMA LOOP TRAIL

Map:	SMMTS, Central Section
Distance:	2 miles
Elevation:	450'
Terrain:	Dirt Trail
Time:	1 hour 15 minutes

If we extend this hike by going to the end (as of 1998) of Zuma Canyon Trail, add 1-1/2 miles for a total 3-1/2 miles round trip.

From the Bonsall trailhead we hike north along the west side of Zuma Creek. In five minutes we pass a trail on our left signed "Zuma Loop Trail" (and after making the loop will return by this trail). But we continue on the Zuma Canyon Trail passing Ocean View Trail on our right and five minutes later pass Canyon View

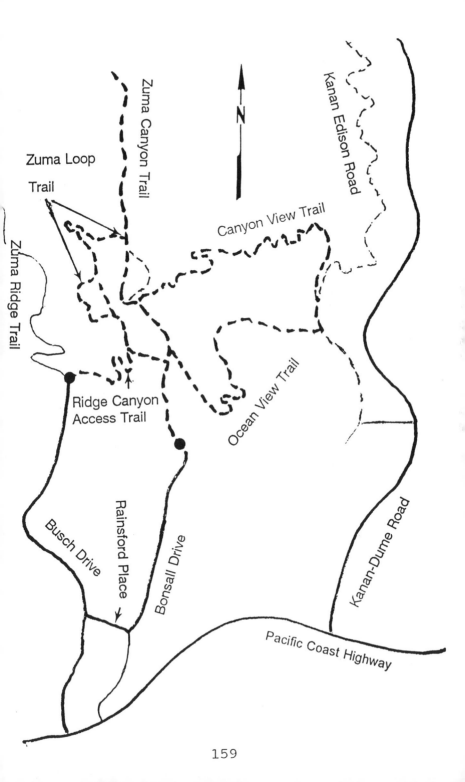

Zuma Canyon Trail

Kanan Edison Road

Zuma Loop
Trail

Zuma Ridge Trail

Canyon View Trail

Ocean View Trail

Ridge Canyon
Access Trail

Busch Drive

Rainsford Place

Bonsall Drive

Kanan-Dume Road

Pacific Coast Highway

Trail on our right. The Scenic Trail angles off to the right to rejoin us five minutes later. We cross the stream and reach a fork in the trail. The right fork continues up the canyon three quarters of a mile to the end, and is an option. The left fork is the Zuma Loop Trail. We go up a side canyon gaining 100 feet in shade. After a left switchback we contour along the hillside and reach a fork in the trail. Either trail is correct, as they join later. We go right if we need another 100 feet of elevation gain, go left if we take a shortcut. It's all downhill from here taking a left at the intersection with the Ridge-Canyon Access Trail. We recognize the Canyon Trail and are soon at the parking lot.

RIDGE-CANYON ACCESS TRAIL

Map:	SMMTS, Central Section
Distance:	2 miles
Elevation:	350'

If we leave from the Bonsall Trailhead it is a short walk upstream to the first fork in the trail, go left. We turn left at the next fork and climb uphill to the Busch Trailhead. Maybe 30 minutes to Busch Trailhead and less coming back down.

Of course many variations of routes are open to us depending on the time and energy we have.

HIKE 30   UPPER ZUMA CANYON TRAIL
(Section of the Backbone Trail)

Maps:	SMMTS, Central Section
Distance:	5½ miles, roundtrip
Elevation:	500'
Terrain:	Trail
Time:	2 hours 15 minutes
Trailhead:	Kanan Road - inland of Tunnel #1

Zuma Canyon is a rugged channel cut into the mountains from Encinal Canyon Road to Zuma Beach. Trails accessing remote areas are almost non-existent. A dirt road along Zuma Ridge gives us great views of the canyon below, and the lone steep and winding trail drops to the stream then climbs 1200' to the east ridge. When power lines were brought across the mountains access roads were constructed — but this was a long time ago and now the roads are trails for the most part.

We will cross Zuma Canyon on a recently built trail in a less dramatic area, but will still see two great waterfalls, and some of the most colorful flowers in the mountains.

The parking lot at the trailhead is on the west side of Kanan-Dume Road 1.8 miles south of Mulholland Highway. Look for the trail on the Zuma Canyon side.

We leave a flat sunlit parking lot and contour along a steep north-facing hillside. As we lose altitude trees give shade and a feeling of seclusion surrounds us. A switchback right brings us closer to Newton Canyon stream. Look for Virgin's Bower and Humboldt Lilies — a transformation to this natural setting happens quickly. After crossing Newton Stream we take a side trip to the top of Upper Newton Waterfall. Across from our viewing point we can see an evergreen shrub — California Barberry. We are not likely to see Barberry plants anywhere else in the Santa Monica Mountains. Look for bright yellow flowers in racemes during mid spring. It is possible to get to the bottom of the falls by continuing along the trail, finding a steep trail on the left to get to the stream.

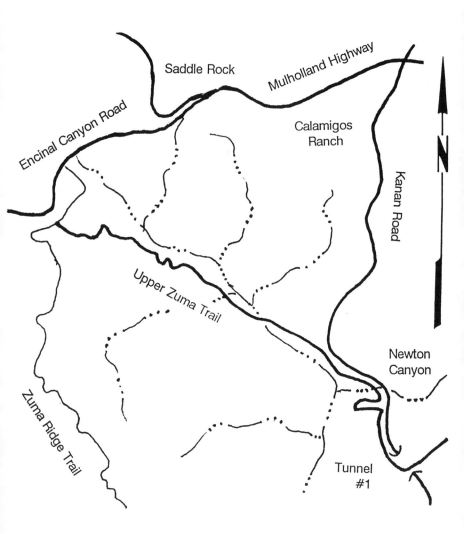

Two more falls are downstream; a 9' middle drop and a 50' lower falls. No trail leads to either.

Back on the trail we hike through a chaparral forest mostly of Ceanothus. We are well above Zuma Creek and will not see Big Zuma Waterfall. But we soon close in on the stream and cross over on a bridge. From the bridge our hike is uphill all the way with a few dips when we come to side ravines. Along one part of the trail coming out of a ravine we make a left turn and look upstream at Upper Zuma Waterfall. Springtime after a good rain is the best time, but even in summer a trickle of water comes down. Our trail ends at the north-south trending Zuma Ridge Trail, a major trail connecting the Backbone Trail to the Pacific Coast side of the mountains.

We turn around and return to Kanan-Dume Road, or if this is a car shuttle we turn right on the Zuma Ridge Trail and in 10 minutes we'll be at our cars. In time a continuation of the Backbone Trail will go into Trancas Canyon.

HIKE 31

DEER LEG TRAIL
and MALIBOU LAKE VISTA TRAIL

Maps:	SMMTS, Central Section
Distance:	3 miles roundtrip
Elevation:	400' gain and loss
Terrain:	Trail and some optional boulder hopping
Time:	2 hours
Trailhead:	Reagan Ranch

This trip introduces us to the northwest sector of the Park allowing us to get high on a hill while walking a gently graded trail.

The trailhead is on the SE corner of the intersection of Cornell Road and Mulholland Highway. Park off the highway and walk into the Park on Yearling Road.

Walk southeast past the building area and get on a trail going past the pond and along the creek. Turn right on the first trail that you come to — the Deer Leg Trail. This will lead onto an oak covered slope. A couple of trails branch right and go uphill. At present, take the second of these trails — the other one is not maintained. Go uphill through an oak woodland. We are now on the Malibou Lake Vista Trail. Enroute we can look east and see the vernal pond and the building area. The trail enters chaparral and turns west just before reaching the ridge for the view of Malibou Lake. This is a turnaround point on this hike. We retrace our steps, then turn right and join Deer Leg Trail going southwest. Follow this as it goes through the picnic area of the Reagan Ranch where the old barbecue pit once stood. The oaks afford good shade, with room enough and rocks enough for a group to stop for lunch.

Continue southeast coming to Udell Creek and a trail intersection. A short side trip can be taken by going downstream to the right. The trail quickly turns to a rock scramble, then to serious rock climbing. Some 8 to 10 foot waterfalls can be seen before the route becomes difficult. Return to the main trail, crossing Udell Creek as we again head southeast. In less than ten minutes the trail leads to a ridge overlooking Century Lake, and Goat Buttes beyond.

Return by going downhill to the northwest and getting on the trail that follows the bottom of the valley back to the building area. This route passes through an extensive stand of Golden Currant. The open fields along this trail provide a wide assortment of spring flowers: the creek bed and shaded areas support ferns, mosses, and Wild Pansy; the dry hillsides display Baby Blue Eyes and many others including Yucca.

Pass the pond that has been drained. We continue to the end of the hike and the trailhead.

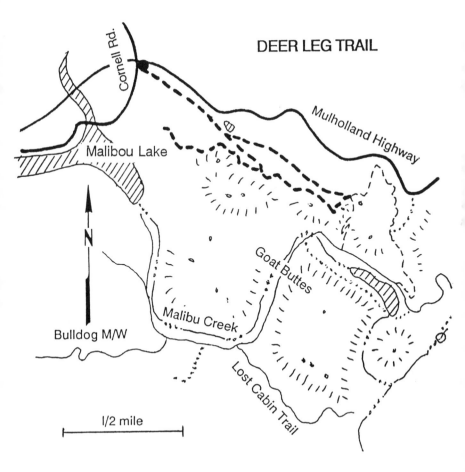

DEER LEG TRAIL

Cornell Rd.

Mulholland Highway

Malibou Lake

N

Goat Buttes

Malibu Creek

Bulldog M/W

Lost Cabin Trail

1/2 mile

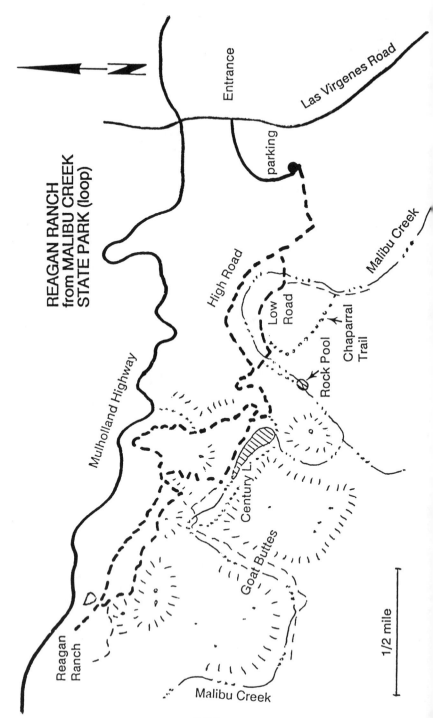

REAGAN RANCH
from MALIBU CREEK
STATE PARK (loop)

Entrance

Las Virgenes Road

parking

Malibu Creek

High Road

Low Road

Chaparral Trail

Rock Pool

Mulholland Highway

Century L.

Goat Buttes

Reagan Ranch

1/2 mile

Malibu Creek

HIKE 32

Maps:	SMMTS, Central Section
Distance:	7 miles roundtrip
Elevation:	500' gain and loss
Terrain:	Trail and Road
Time:	2 hours, 45 minutes
Trailhead:	Malibu Creek State Park

The entrance to Malibu Creek State Park is from Las Virgenes Road, 2/10 of a mile south of Mulholland Highway. A fee is required for parking.

This hike will take us along the floor of the valley, then up a hill and down into a valley known as the Reagan Ranch.

Drive through the gate at the attended entrance and go west on the road into the park. Park in the second lot and start hiking. The first mile is relatively level on a good road. Las Virgenes Creek comes down from the north joining Stokes Creek, which in turn enters Malibu Creek. We will cross Las Virgenes Creek, and in about 5 minutes take a right fork (High Road) along an oak lined lane on the north shore overlooking the creek. Movie sets for "Planet of the Apes" and many other films were built in this area but have been removed so the Park can return to a natural state.

A road comes in from the left after crossing a bridge; keep to the right and start winding uphill. This road tops out in about ten minutes, opening up a view of Century Lake and the Malibu Creek valley to the northwest. Goat buttes on the west of the lake were produced about 15 million years ago under the sea by volcanic action, then later were forced up during the time when the Santa Monica Mountains were formed.

Continue along the road as it starts downhill toward the shore of Century Lake. In a couple hundred yards turn sharply to the right on Lookout Trail. This trail takes us uphill around the south, then the east shoulder of a hill before heading northwest to the ridge overlooking the upper valley. Fifteen minutes after leaving the road we should be on the crest of an oak covered ridge. Turn right and gently drop down an enchanting trail deep in Oaks, Laurel and high Chaparral.

The fire of October 1982 burned the chaparral on this slope, and the recovery is good. The trail is restored to the shaded canopy of trees that it once had.

Look for a clearing on the left; the chances of seeing deer are good. The trail enters a grassy meadow, covered with flowers in spring but very dry in summer and fall. Looking northwest, the grassy strip stretches 3/4 mile and we should see the Park buildings near the far end.

The trail passes a small grove of Coast Live Oaks. An Indian mortar once used in the grinding of acorns, can be seen in a flat sandstone rock. The trail keeps to low ground at the edge of the meadow as it gently climbs northwest. Some Golden Currant bushes are growing on both sides of the trail. The plants bloom in late March and April putting on a rare display. A few hundred yards farther along, the trail nears what was once a pond on the right.

A restroom is available at the turnaround point. Return on the same trail until we have an opportunity to go right and get on the trail paralleling the one we came up on. This trail stays in the shade of Oak trees, passing through the picnic area of the ranch. The remains of an old barbecue pit mark the site of earlier outdoor gatherings. Good lunch stops are found along this stretch of the trail where even a large group can relax in the shade of trees or the sun of open areas.

Cross Udell Creek farther along, then a gentle climb of less than ten minutes places us on a ridge overlooking Century Lake.

At one time we walked downhill on the steep "cat track" toward the Lake but serious erosion required rerouting, and during the spring of 1985 a volunteer Sierra Club crew built the Cage Canyon Trail. At the "overlook" turn left and intersect the trail we came in on, then turn right. In about 100 yards turn right again, onto Cage Canyon Trail, which winds down to Century Road near the lake. Turn left and return on the road by which we entered.

Century
Lake

HIKE 33

Maps:	SMMTS, Central Section
Distance:	3 miles roundtrip
Elevation:	550 feet loss and gain
Terrain:	Trail and Fireroad
Time:	2 hours
Trailhead:	Mulholland Highway

We reach the trailhead by driving 1.2 miles east of Cornell Road on Mulholland highway, and park on the south side off the road. Room for about 10 cars is available off the highway. A narrow trail goes southeast up to a cistern on the ridge. A sloping cement slab catches rainwater and drains it into an underground cistern. No one has explained why the cistern was built or what the plans are for using the water. Matillija Poppies grow on the slopes of the ridge and put on a floral display in late spring to mid-summer.

Cistern Trail follows the ridge top one-half mile to a cross trail. We turn left and descend on the Lookout Trail. Spectacular views of Goat Buttes and Century Lake make a panorama to the west. We will bring a camera next time. We are soon at the lower end of the trail and at Century Lake. In 1901 a dam was built by the Crags Country Club and impounded water for recreational use. Fishing is allowed but not duck hunting. We can extend our hike by walking left along the lake shore to the dam. Drinking water, picnic tables, and a restroom are available.

Walk northwest on the road along the lake. A trail goes through the willows on the left, if we want to take a close look at cat-tails and Wocus. Come back to the road and continue to Cage Canyon where a trail on the right takes us on a steep, winding climb to the trail coming down from Reagan Meadow. At the intersection of the trails, look for Cream Cups, Linanthus, Brown Microseris, and Owl's Clover. March and April are good months for finding flowers.

We are going to turn right and hike back to where we parked, but first let's take a look at a bedrock mortar found under some

Oaks about 200 yards to our left. We go west to a grove of Oak trees and leave the trail to look for the mortar. Indians lived here thousands of years before the Spanish invasion, and lived off the land by hunting and harvesting. Thirty-five hundred, or more, years ago the native Americans discovered that if acorns were ground up and the meal was leached, the water soluble tannin was removed, making the acorns edible. This mortar is now in the shade of Oaks and probably has been for centuries. Several intermittent streams nearby would have been the source of water.

The return trail goes over a low ridge, then contours the south facing slope before crossing a stream and into an Oak woodland. Turn left at the Cistern Trail and climb the ridge.

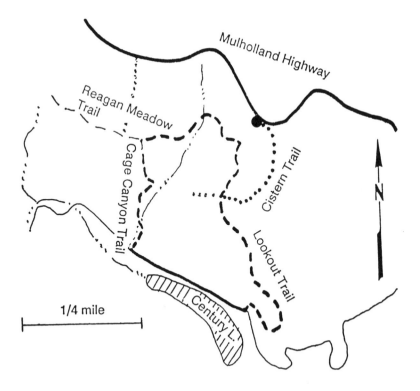

HIKE 34

ROCK POOL

via the Gorge Trail
from Malibu Creek State Park

Maps:	SMMTS, Central Section
Distance:	2-½ miles
Elevation:	150' gain and loss
Terrain:	Road and trail
Time:	1 hour
Trailhead:	Malibu Creek State Park

Enter Malibu Creek State Park from Las Virgenes Road, 2/10 of a mile south of Mulholland Highway. A parking fee is required.

This short, almost level hike on a good trail is almost made to order for those days that your time is limited or you just don't feel like a long hike.

ROCK POOL

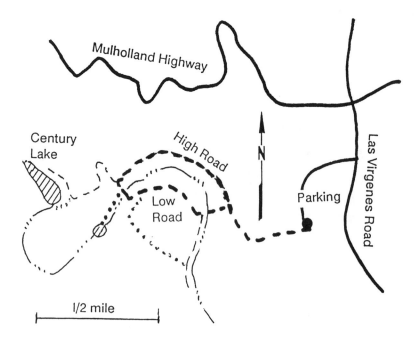

1/2 mile

172

Drive through the main gate to the parking lot. Walk a short way along the road and ford Las Virgenes Creek as it spills across the road on a concrete apron. Usually the water can be measured in inches, but this changes with a good rainstorm. Upon reaching a fork go right and walk along the High Road in the shade of Oak trees that line both sides. This route follows the north side of Malibu Creek until reaching an intersection with a road that crosses the stream on a bridge. Turn left at the intersection. We then turn right before reaching the bridge.

Follow Gorge Trail upstream to Rock Pool. Some years the trail becomes washed out by the winter rains and we must do some easy boulder hopping. Rock Pool is at the mouth of the gorge and both the pool and the gorge contain large volcanic boulders. Volcanic cliffs rise from both sides of the pool forming a spectacular setting. When the water is high the pool presents a barrier to further travel unless we care to get wet. Fish can be seen if we are patient. Expect to be scolded by a Scrub Jay or two for intruding into the gorge. Look high overhead toward the mountain to the southwest for soaring Red-tailed Hawks, and perhaps a Golden Eagle. Rock Pool has been the site of television and movie productions. The Tarzan series and Swiss Family Robinson had many of the outdoor sequences filmed here.

Return to the road, turn right and cross the bridge staying on the road as it goes downstream. At the fork turn left, fording Malibu Creek and continue to the High Road. Turn right, retracing our route back to the parking lot. We may stop at the Visitor's Center just after crossing the bridge.

ARCHAEOLOGICAL COMMENT

Indians lived along Malibu Creek and its tributaries more than 7000 years ago. Several prehistoric village sites and camp areas have been located within Malibu Creek State Park. Some of these areas had been occupied for long periods of time, in one case 2000 years, then died out as a village.

When the Spanish invaded California in the late 1700's, a village named Talopop was found near Las Virgenes Creek. The village survived at least until 1805, when mission records at both San Fernando and San Buenaventura no longer referred to the village. Bartolomé Miguel Ortega received a Spanish land use permit in 1810, for Rancho el Paraje de las Virgenes, a few miles to the west. He had been ranching the land since about 1803, so it is quite possible that the people of Talopop went to work on the ranch. Investigation of the site indicates that people continued to live in the village area for a number of years.

All of the waterways in the Santa Monica Mountains were favored by the Indians as places near which to live. Malibu Creek drains a greater area than any other stream in the mountains. It also is the only antecedent stream — one that cuts completely through the mountain range — and was a convenient transportation network for the Indians.

All of the sites are protected so that only archaeologists under proper permit can excavate. A cultural resource center at the Visitor's Center is worth our time. It normally opens at noon on weekends.

Rock Pool

HIKE 35

Maps:	SMMTS, Central Section
Distance:	6 miles
Elevation:	1500' gain and loss
Terrain:	Steep fireroad
Time:	2 hours 45 minutes
Trailhead:	Tapia Park

Peak 2049 is so named because it is 2049 feet high. Most of the comments that I have heard indicate that an emphasis on the altitude is not misplaced as some uphill stretches are a challenge to one's endurance.

The trailhead is south of Tapia Park on the west side of Las Virgenes-Malibu Canyon Road. The parking lot is south of the bridge. Restrooms are located under pine trees along the trail. Beyond the restrooms look for the trail as it makes a sharp left turn and heads south paralleling the canyon road. In 200 yards make a right turn onto Mesa Peak Motorway at the parking lot south of the bridge. Turn left past the restroom and continue until reaching Mesa Peak Motorway. Turn right to follow the motorway two and a half miles gaining 1500' of elevation.

About a half mile farther along the trail, a road branches right and dead-ends at a gate. (On the return trip we may find ourselves wanting to follow that road because it is downhill.) The north slope of the mountain is very steep, and the trail makes a few switchbacks to gain altitude. At one switchback we cross over the ridge and look down into the Malibu Creek gorge, the only stream to cut completely through the Santa Monica Mountains.

Malibu Canyon has been a transportation corridor since the Indians first lived there. The steep canyon is filled with boulders and is difficult to travel through, but as we are about to find out, travel between the ocean and inland over the mountains is also difficult. The highway through the narrow gorge was built during the early 1950's.

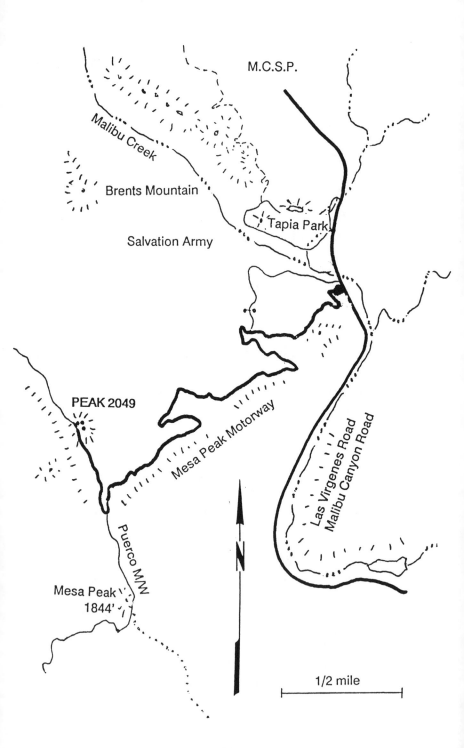

M.C.S.P.

Malibu Creek

Brents Mountain

Tapia Park

Salvation Army

PEAK 2049

Mesa Peak Motorway

Las Virgenes Road
Malibu Canyon Road

Puerco MW

Mesa Peak
1844'

N

1/2 mile

176

The view of Malibu Canyon continues to expand as we gain altitude. The creekbed below is at an elevation of about 300', and long before we reach our destination at 2049' it becomes apparent that Malibu Creek has cut the steepest and deepest gorge in the mountains. Climb here on a clear night for a spectacular view of the shore line and the lights of the city below. A group of us did this at night on New year's Day, 1981, and aside from being chilly after the warmth of exertion, were convinced that being atop Peak 2049' was the place to be.

Before reaching the peak, however, we come to a fork in the road. The left fork drops downhill past Mesa Peak and down through Puerco Canyon ("Pig Canyon") to the Pacific Coast Hwy. The road we have been hiking is Mesa Peak Motorway, and after a right turn at the fork, continues past Peak 2049, and ultimately connects with Castro Motorway and Corral Canyon Road about 2-1/2 miles farther west. One-third mile beyond the road fork, we turn right at a saddle and walk to the top of the peak. We return the way we came.

A persistent notion exists within the hiking community that Mesa Peak M/W should lead to Mesa Peak. This application of logic has caused some confusion when a hiking group doesn't stay together. On at least one occasion a lone hiker ended up at Puerco Beach instead of back at the Tapia Park trailhead. (That hike should be a good car shuttle — if planned.)

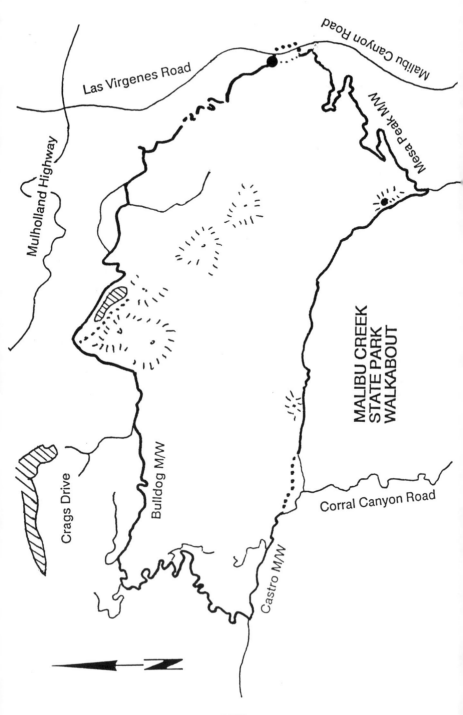

MALIBU CREEK
STATE PARK
WALKABOUT

Malibu Canyon Road

Las Virgenes Road

Mulholland Highway

Mesa Peak M/W

Crags Drive

Bulldog M/W

Castro M/W

Corral Canyon Road

178

HIKE 36

**MALIBU CREEK STATE
PARK WALKABOUT**
from Tapia Park

Maps:	SMMTS, Central Section
Distance:	14½ miles
Elevation:	2000'
Terrain:	Fireroad and trail
Time:	6½ hours
Trailhead:	Tapia Park

This hike takes us on a big loop around the perimeter of the Park, keeping to the ridges where possible. We reach the trailhead by driving on Las Virgenes/Malibu Canyon Road either 4.6 miles north of the Pacific Coast Highway or 4.8 miles south of the Ventura Freeway. The Tapia Park lot is west of the highway.

We begin the hike at the parking lot of Tapia Park and walk south along the highway, crossing over and back because the sidewalk on the bridge over Malibu Creek is on the east side. Crossing Malibu Canyon Road twice and walking along the shoulder is hazardous. We must exercise a good deal of caution when traffic is heavy. Sometimes Malibu Creek can be crossed upstream of the bridge.

The trail begins at the parking lot south of the bridge. Turn left past the restroom and continue until reaching Mesa Peak Motorway. Turn right to follow the motorway two and a half miles gaining 1500' of elevation.

About 2¾ miles from the trailhead, Puerco M/W comes up from the coast and joins Mesa Peak M/W. Continuing on Mesa Peak M/W (which does not pass Mesa Peak) we pass by Peak 2049 on our right. During the next 2½ miles of ridge hiking we walk over an area of turritella fossils, up and down over some little peaks, and to a series of Sespe sandstone pinnacles.

A trail on the right leaves the road and goes along the ridge of rock formations for about 1/2 mile, then intersects Corral Canyon Road. We continue on Corral Canyon Road (or it may be Castro Peak M/W from this point on) for one mile, reaching the intersection with Bulldog M/W, near Peak 2528. Of interest to botanists, Santa Susana Tarweed grows here. This plant blooms in mid-summer with flowers lasting into fall. Considered rare elsewhere, Santa Susana Tarweed is seen along this rocky ridge.

The walk down Bulldog M/W is one that we remember because it is steep and winding — we lose 1800' before reaching level ground again. Several side roads lead to power transmission towers. We continue downstream, around a gate, to the intersection with 20th Century Road. The downhill distance since turning onto Bulldog M/W is about 3½ miles.

After turning right on 20th Century Road we enter the former site of the M.A.S.H. set, (which has been removed) near where the Lost Cabin Trail begins. We continue past Century Lake, and go over a hill to rejoin the stream on the other side at another fork in the road. The left fork, called the High Road, stays left of Malibu Creek. Straight ahead and across the bridge puts us on the low road. They meet again downstream. A short side trip to Rock Pool can be taken by following the Gorge Trail up the north side of the Creek. Before we start down the Low Road, we go to the Visitor's Center in the large while house, then we will take the low road and go downstream to another fork.

The left fork crosses Malibu Creek and joins the High Road, which takes us to the Malibu Creek State Park parking lot.

Upon seeing the parking lot, turn right and follow the road across the bridge. Just after passing a magnificent Valley Oak on the left, look for and take the road on the right that skirts the east side of a large meadow. At the head of the meadow an Oak grove furnishes restrooms and a picnic area. The trail goes to the east of the picnic area and after a short climb heads down into Tapia Park. Cross the park to your car to complete the hike.

Today's hike has been a segment of the "Backbone Trail" system, a hiking and equestrian trail which will eventually stretch from Will Rogers State Historic Park to Point Mugu State park. Our hike has taken us on the primary route and the alternate route, and I'm not sure which is better. And only time may tell which route is primary and which route is alternate.

M.A.S.H. jeep after the fire

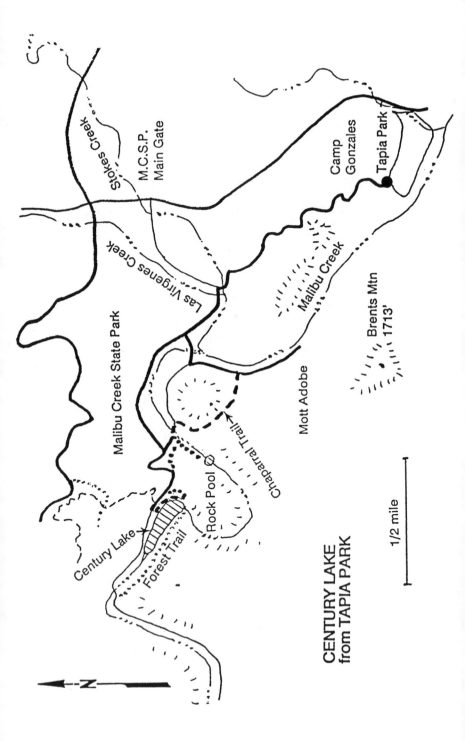

Stokes Creek

M.C.S.P.
Main Gate

Camp
Gonzales

Tapia Park

Las Virgenes Creek

Malibu Creek

Malibu Creek State Park

Brents Mtn
1713'

Mott Adobe

Chaparral Trail

Rock Pool

Century Lake

Forest Trail

N

1/2 mile

CENTURY LAKE
from TAPIA PARK

HIKE 37

CENTURY LAKE

from Tapia Park

Maps: SMMTS, Central Section
Distance: 7 miles roundtrip
Elevation: 1000' gain and loss
Terrain: Trail, road, steep trail
Time: 3 hours
Trailhead: Tapia Park

The Tapia Park to Malibu Creek State Park segment of this trail was built by Sierra Club Volunteers before the Dayton Canyon fire of 1982. I've heard comments to the effect that had they known they could have waited, because trail building through chaparral is hard work. The trail is an important link in the Backbone Trail system and is used a good deal by both hikers and equestrians.

The trail begins near the road in the northwest corner of the Park. Upon entering the main entrance to Tapia Park from Las Virgenes Road, turn right and parallel Las Virgenes a hundred yards or so. At the first opportunity turn left and follow the road about 1/4 mile until it goes downhill and you can see a meadow on the right. Park in the last parking area before the road enters the Salvation Army Camp. A sign on the right identifies the trail as the "Backbone Trail". Walk north as it enters an oak woodland. Watch for a left turn as the trail enters chaparral and goes uphill. After a switchback the trail takes us through a stand of Mountain Mahogany, and soon, after gaining more altitude we can look to our right and see Camp David Gonzales. The rock underfoot to the ridge and beyond is fragmental volcanic breccias that intruded through sandstone about 14 million years ago.

After crossing the saddle, the trail now makes two switchbacks in chaparral before dropping down to a large oak grove at the head of a big meadow. Picnic tables, water, and restrooms are available. Look for Goldback Ferns along the trail. A sequence of the movie "Roots" was filmed at the west end of the grove but all props have been removed so the location is completely restored to nature. The Park Service is in the process of rerouting the trail north of the saddle. The rerouting avoids the steep slope down to the campground, the water, and other conveniences. It also allows for a wider trail.

An old macadam road skirts the edge of the meadow. Part way down the road, a faint trail goes across the ridge on the right, ending at the RV camp. In May we can find Lilac Mariposa Lilies in bloom on the ridge. Continue down the road until we are in the shade of a magnificent Valley Oak. Having read many articles about the plight of Valley Oaks in southern California, this tree is worth observing. In January 1986 ground squirrels were living under the oak and many mounds of dirt were visible. Some oak seedlings were growing. On 13 July 1986, 614 seedlings were growing under the oak, the tallest of which was 23 inches high. Ground squirrels no doubt hid more acorns than they needed or could find, so many acorns sprouted. These seedlings don't survive because the parent tree takes the sunshine, the nutrients, and the water. This process may not occur every year but my guess is that without interference this oak will at least replace itself.

The route continues across Stokes Creek, turns left near the parking lot, and crosses Las Virgenes Creek then makes a wide turn right and heads northwest. At a road junction we continue ahead on the "High Road" which overlooks Malibu Creek on our left. The High Road is shaded by Coast Live Oaks and is an almost level, pleasant walk for about 1/2 mile. At a road junction we turn right and make climbing turns to the top of a low ridge overlooking Century Lake. Century Lake is impounded by a dam built in 1901 by the Crags Country Club who owned the property during the early 1900's. The lake is gradually silting up because of annual run-off and in time could become a marsh. The lake is a haven for wildlife: migrant ducks are often seen, coots are regular inhabitants, and occasionally a heron is seen. Fish live in the lake, and this is a popular place for sons to bring fathers to try their angling skills. The route of this hike takes us to the lake shore then left to near the dam — but not on it. An alternate extra 3/4 mile walk is available if time allows. Instead of turning left at the lake, continue ahead until we cross Malibu Creek on a low concrete bridge, then look left for a trail that follows the base of the mountain west of the lake. The Forest Trail is shady and almost level. It ends at the dam so we retrace our steps. Coast Redwood trees were planted along the trail and some still remain.

A short, steep trail goes uphill from the southeast end of the lake and intersects the road we came in on. We turn right and walk downhill. Before crossing the bridge, we turn right and go a couple hundred yards upstream on a trail and sometimes on rocks, to Rock Pool — a great place for lunch under the Sycamore trees.

After lunch we retrace our steps, turn right and cross over the bridge for a stop at the Visitors Center. Upon leaving the Center turn right and find a trail — the Chaparral Trail — that climbs up the hill behind the house. We gain about 165' of elevation before reaching a narrow saddle and immediately go steeply downhill to Mott Road. Mott Adobe is a short distance downstream and is the ruins of the original building. A stone fireplace is in place and parts of the adobe walls are standing. Fire and water have taken a toll. Look for the simulated bullet holes on the face of the wall — this was used as a prop in a movie.

After turning around at the adobe our route is upstream until we come to the road that crosses Malibu Creek. We then turn right and retrace our steps to the trailhead at Tapia Park. This hike is flexible to the extent that several side trails are available to us and could extend the hike for as many miles as we feel like walking.

HIKE 38

Maps:	SMMTS, Central Section
Distance:	3½ miles
Elevation:	700' gain and loss
Terrain:	Trail
Time:	1½ hours
Trailhead:	Mulholland Highway

Don't be surprised if the sign at the "New Secret Trail" reads "Calabasas - Cold Creek Trail." In 1985 volunteers built the New Secret Trail to replace the "Secret Trail" which the building of a subdivision was displacing. In the tradition of trail building in the Santa Monica Mountains, the volunteers building a trail name the trail, in this case "New Secret Trail." The old trail had been in use for many years when the developer, Steve Harris, being aware of the trail's existence offered an easement for a new trail. The Santa Monica Mountains Trails Council President, Linda Palmer coordinated the project; Ron Webster led the design effort and assembled and led the Sierra Club volunteer crew, Los Angeles County accepted the trail easement, and the Santa Monica Mountains Trails council agreed to maintain the trail. Not only is this a great trail but the cooperation of all people and organizations involved shows what can be done when good people get together.

This hike fulfills a need for a nearby, short but challenging walk. It is not designed as a wildflower walk but we will find a wide variety of plants. We will see the largest holly-leaf cherry found locally and an extensive display of spike moss. The spike moss selects volcanic rock on which to grow. Most other plants find an easier foothold.

We reach the Trailhead by driving west of Topanga Canyon Boulevard on Mulholland Drive/Highway 4.1 miles. A mileage sign across Mulholland from the trailhead reads mile 27.53. Park on the east side of Mulholland Highway.

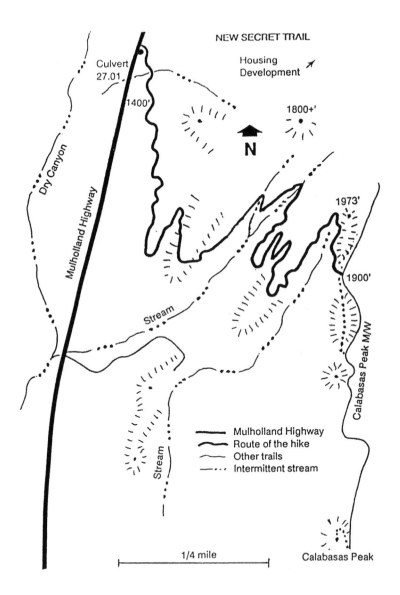

NEW SECRET TRAIL

Housing
Development

Culvert
27.01

1400'

1800+'

Dry Canyon

Mulholland Highway

N

1973'

1900'

Stream

Calabasas Peak M/W

Stream

Mulholland Highway
Route of the hike
Other trails
Intermittent stream

1/4 mile

Calabasas Peak

The trail connects paved Mulholland with Calabasas Motorway (a dirt road on the ridge). We start with some uphill, going through a sage plant community of sumac, buckwheat, purple sage, and sugar bush. For the first ten minutes of the hike the trail winds in and out but parallels Mulholland. We go through a shaded scrub oak forest and cross on intermittent stream. We will find some poison oak near the trail before turning left. Look left as we hike east toward Calabasas Motorway and notice spike moss growing in the volcanic rock. This plant isn't rare but it is the only local species of a family of more than 700 worldwide. This moss prefers sunny slopes and volcanic rock. The technical name is *Selaginella biglovii.*

We see marine fossils in the sandstone formations along the trail. On a steep switchback area only a few minutes from reaching Calabasas Motorway, look for a large holly-leaf cherry tree on the left side of the trail. Several large trunks sprout from a root crown and form a tree with a 30' spread and about 25' high.

The variety of plant communities en route includes Coastal Sage Scrub, Southern Oak Woodland, Grassland, Riparian Woodland, Chaparral, and Cliffs. We will be in deep shade at times and exposed to sun and wind at others.

Toward Calabasas Ridge the trail makes several climbing switchbacks and works along some massive sandstone slabs. New Secret Trail intersects Calabasas Peak Motorway, opening opportunities of exploring the ridge in either direction or of climbing Calabasas Peak. For this hike we turn around at the ridge and return the way we came.

HIKE 39

CALABASAS PEAK

Maps:	SMMTS, Central Section
Distance:	4 miles roundtrip
Elevation:	950' gain and loss
Terrain:	Fireroad and short, steep trail
Time:	1½ hours
Trailhead:	Stunt Road

Reach the trailhead by going west from Woodland Hills on Mulholland Highway to Stunt Road. Turn left and go one mile, parking off the pavement on the right.

Hike up the fireroad to the north. This is steep and rocky giving us an excuse to stop and look around. Cold Creek has its source up the canyon to the south. The porous sandstone stores water from the winter rains, supplying several perpetual springs with clear water. The 530- acre Murphy Ranch which includes the springs and the upper part of Cold Creek was presented to the Nature Conservancy by Kathleen Murphy. The year round stream turns west near where we parked and enters Malibu Creek downstream from Tapia Park.

Continue uphill on the fireroad. Large slabs of sandstone were tilted on edge when the Santa Monica Mountains were being formed and have weathered to grotesque slanted outcroppings. Upon reaching the saddle we are on "Fossil Ridge." The road to the right drops down through Red Rock Canyon to Old Topanga Road. On a day when we want to add 3 or 4 miles to the hike, we can go down into Red Rock Canyon as far as the road, then turn around to climb back. On this segment the loss and gain is 350 feet. Now back to the ridge. Stay on the Calabasas Peak Motorway as it continues the climb. Look west to find the profile of "Lady Face Mountain" on the horizon, about 10 miles away. The road switches back making a climb around the south, then east, shoulder of Calabasas Peak before heading north, slightly downhill to a saddle.

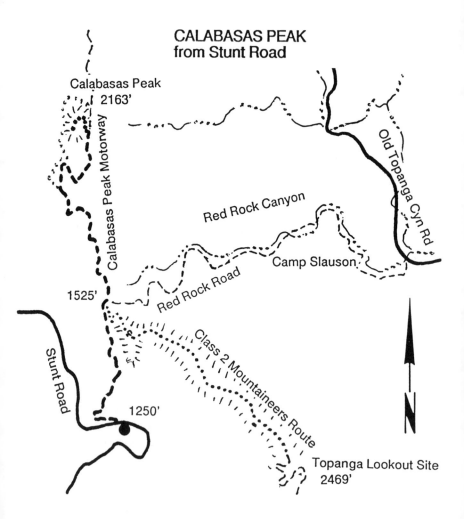

CALABASAS PEAK
from Stunt Road

Calabasas Peak
2163'

Calabasas Peak Motorway

Old Topanga Cyn Rd

Red Rock Canyon

Camp Slauson

1525'

Red Rock Road

Class 2 Mountaineers Route

Stunt Road

1250'

N

Topanga Lookout Site
2469'

190

Upon reaching the saddle leave the road and walk along the bulldozer-eroded area on the left as the trail climbs the bank, then makes a sweeping turn left going steeply uphill. Find a trail through the chaparral to the top of Calabasas Peak. Return the way we came, or as an alternate, continue north on the road and come off the firebreak from the peak. A few hundred feet along the road and just as we begin to see around the north side of Calabasas Peak, a trail goes west contouring around the peak, rejoining the road below the switchback. This trail doesn't get much use and the chaparral reclaims its own territory with a vengeance, so expect some brush. It would be wise to wear goggles and gloves because each year the old trail becomes more overgrown.

"Marmot Rock" near Calabasas Motorway

HIKE 40

STUNT HIGH TRAIL

Maps:	SMMTS, Central Section
Distance:	4 miles
Elevation:	950' gain and loss
Time:	2½ hours
Trailhead:	Stunt Road

Stunt High Trail is special for several reasons. The variety of plant communities is unsurpassed, the trail takes us along Cold Creek through a beautiful Riparian Woodland, then uphill and across some sloping grassland into an Oak Woodland. The upper trail winds through a magnificent stand of Chaparral. Wild animals frequent the Cold Creek watershed. One of the few mountain lions remaining in the mountains is seldom seen, but is known to live in the canyon.

The trail intersects Stunt Road in 3 places; limited off-road parking is available at each place. I will describe the hike that starts at the lower end, makes a roundtrip, and uses the same route back.

From Mulholland Highway, drive 1 mile up Stunt Road to the main parking area on the right. The trail begins at the east end of the lot. We go around the gate and downhill to Cold Creek, following the old road. The trail crosses the creek then follows downstream on the left bank. We look for ferns in the shade along the stream. About 1/2 mile downstream we branch left at a large rock containing bedrock mortars, and start uphill. To continue downstream would take us onto private property and close to homes, so we must use care and not miss the left turn.

The route leaves Cold Creek and goes uphill through the oaks, then on across a meadow. We parallel an intermittent stream to our right and are out of sight of a large intermittent stream to the left. Spring is the most colorful time to be here — a wide variety of flowers will be found in the oak woodland and in the meadow. We turn left near the top of the meadow.

The Stunt Ranch buildings burned in the 1993 fire. The new building area is not on the route of the hike and should be avoided.

After turning left at the top of the meadow, the trail gains

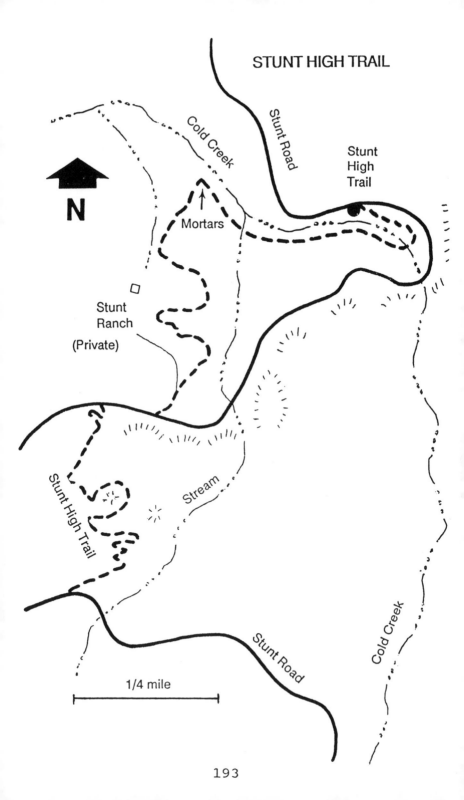

STUNT HIGH TRAIL

N

Stunt Road

Cold Creek

Stunt High Trail

Mortars

Stunt Ranch

(Private)

Stunt High Trail

Stream

Cold Creek

Stunt Road

1/4 mile

altitude and climbs into a chaparral forest. After a couple of switchbacks the trail intersects the Stunt Ranch entrance road. We cross the road and walk on a trail to Stunt Road, then turn right and walk uphill along the road about 400 yards. A parking lot has been graded along Stunt Road near the ranch entrance road. It is expected that this lot will be used by people attending naturalist activities.

After the short walk along Stunt Road we look for the continuation of the trail on the south side. The entry to the trail is through a riparian plant community of Ferns, Poison Oak, and Oaks. After a couple of quick switchbacks we enter a forest of Chaparral — a mixture of Ceanothus, Chamise, Scrub Oak, and Redshank. The trail passes some sandstone formations including one in the shape of a seal called "Seal Rock." The trail turns often and is of a gentle grade even when ascending the steep hillside; before reaching the road and the end of the trail.

The Santa Monica Mountains Backbone Trail comes down the north slope of Saddle Peak. We can access the Backbone Trail by walking a few hundred feet downhill on Stunt Road to a trail on the left. This .3-mile long trail leads to an intersection. We may then turn right to go west, or left to go east on the Backbone Trail.

We turn around at Stunt Road to retrace our steps. Car shuttle options can add variations to this hike. The return hike offers beautiful views of the Cold Creek watershed and Stunt Ranch. The high ridge east of us looks down upon Hondo Canyon and the Topanga watershed beyond. Calabasas Peak and its massive tilted sandstone outcroppings is on the north. Malibu Creek is several miles west.

The land over which the trail has been built was operated as ranches into the 1970's. The Stunt Ranch was homesteaded in the late 1800's. The Murphy Ranch was purchased in 1909. Kathleen Murphy donated her 530-acre ranch to the Nature Conservancy who developed it as the Ida Haines Murphy Preserve (Cold Creek Canyon Preserve), an outstanding pristine area. The Mountains Restoration Trust—a nonprofit land trust dedicated to preserving public access opportunities in the Santa Monica Mountains — has assumed responsibility for management and preservation of the Preserve. The Stunt Ranch was purchased by the Santa Monica Mountains Conservancy, and, a part is now owned by the University of California, Los Angeles, for environmental studies.

HIKE 41

MURPHY PRESERVE
(Upper Cold Creek Trail)
from Stunt Road

Maps:	SMMTS, Central Section
Distance:	3 miles
Elevation:	500' loss and gain
Terrain:	Trail
Time:	2 hours
Trailhead:	Stunt Road

The 530-acre Cold Creek Canyon Preserve was a gift to the Nature Conservancy made by Kathleen Murphy. The Murphy Ranch will preserve a part of the Santa Monica Mountains in its wild state for all time to come.

A written permit is required for entry. Apply by calling The Mountains Restoration Trust.

The entry to the Preserve is reached by driving 3.38 miles on Stunt Road from Mulholland Highway.

The trail into the area follows the old driveway to the Murphy home. The entire area burned in 1970, and again in 1993, but the chaparral has reclaimed the area effectively. The trail is well maintained, a major task because the chaparral is vigorous and has been growing well since the fire.

The outstanding feature of the trail is the variety of plant life. I will comment on some of the plants to be found but leave it to you to spot them along the trail. Chamise and its close relative Red Shanks are both plentiful here, Chamise blooming in May, the Red Shanks in August. California Buckwheat starts blooming in May, lasting well into summer. By looking closely at the flower you can find the Ambush bug, an insect with clawlike pinchers simulating the small Buckwheat flower, waiting for an unwary fly to land and be captured.

Two types of Manzanita are found in the Santa Monica Mountains; both are plentiful along the trail. Eastwood Manzanita sprouts from the root crown after a fire so it can be identified by looking for the old burned branches with new growth all around.

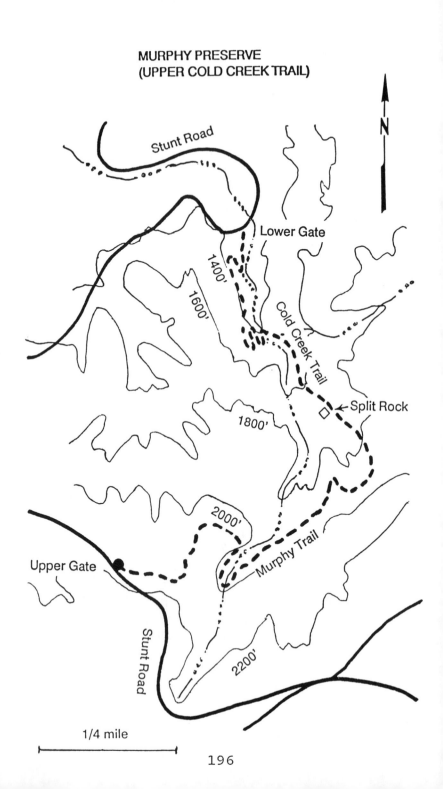

MURPHY PRESERVE
(UPPER COLD CREEK TRAIL)

N

Stunt Road

Lower Gate

1400'

1600'

Cold Creek Trail

1800'

Split Rock

2000'

Murphy Trail

Upper Gate

Stunt Road

2200'

1/4 mile

The leaves have a sticky feel. The Bigberry Manzanita does not root crown but grows only from seeds.

Two types of Sumac bushes are found along the trail: The Sugar Bush and Laurel Sumac. They are somewhat similar in appearance but can be distinguished by their leaves. The Sugar Bush has thick shiny, waxy leaves that fold like a taco and are pointed at one end; the leaves of the Laurel Sumac are longer, pointed, have smooth edges, and some fold. A close relative, the Lemonade Berry, is not found in the preserve but can be found closer to the ocean. It has a flatter, oval shaped leaf. Another prominent member of the Sumac Family is Poison Oak. It is evident throughout the area.

Ceanothus is an important chaparral plant found in the preserve and is represented by several species. *Ceanothus megacarpus,,* or Big Pod, has white blossoms. It blooms in January-February and sets relatively large seed capsules by May; Redheart (greenbark), *Ceanothus spinosus,* has pale blue or white blossoms, a small seed capsule, and the leaves are larger and shinier, but thinner than the Big Pod Ceanothus. Hairy Ceanothus has larger leaves that are shiny on top and dull underneath; and the Chaparral White Thorn, *Ceanothus leucodermis,* is wicked. There are but a few places in the Santa Monicas where it is found.

Farther down the trail we will pass by an old pick-up truck, burned in 1970 and rusted; proof that this trail was once a road.

The trail quickly drops down to an area of dense vegetation. Woodwardia and Bracken ferns are plentiful; Bay trees and large Oaks shade the trail and the canyon; a bed of iris, introduced in the 1950's is crowding out the native plants in the marshy spot below the spring. The massive layers of sandstone that form this mountainside absorb the water from the winter rains and release it throughout the year.

A large split sandstone rock near the spring was used as the walls of a cabin. Notches cut into the rock show where the beams were. The foundation of the main ranch house which burned in the fire of 1970 is farther up the hill.

Travel downstream becomes difficult beyond the cabin site because storms have damaged the trail. This is the turnaround point of the hike, so return by the same trail to the entrance.

The trail downstream was rerouted in 1985 to make the route passable. It is steep and is still subject to landslide activity. I'll describe the route below the split sandstone rock: From this point to the lower gate we add 1 mile each way and 400' loss of altitude. The lower gate is locked so some arrangement needs to be made in advance if we intend to leave the Preserve at the lower gate. As of 1998 a landslide damaged the trail again. The Mountains Restoration Trust will advise us of trail conditions.

From the split rock we drop down on a steep section of the trail. The north facing slope is deep in shade and supports the growth of Bay Trees, Snowberry, Crimson Pitcher Sage, Woodferns, and Humboldt Lilies. We cross a marshy area near a community of Yellow Flag, then get near the creek on the left. A couple of Bigleaf Maples can be seen from the trail.

After another steep section of trail we cross a small wooden footbridge. On the right we see a small waterfall that displays a calcium carbonate buildup. Nearby, Venus-hair fern grows on the side of a cliff. The trail eases up a bit, then continues downhill and crosses the creek, then soon makes some switchbacks going uphill to avoid a steep landslide area. The trail soon leads downhill and after some steep parts, comes to a branch. Turn right and go upstream to a waterfall and Stream Orchids; turn left and go to the lower gate.

Some shell fossils are in the sandstone rocks on the property. Examples may be seen near the display board at the entrance. This Fernwood Member of the Topanga Canyon Formation was deposited during the middle Miocene epoch when the land was under a shallow sea.

HIKE 42   SADDLE CREEK TRAIL

Maps:	SMMTS, Central Section
Distance:	3.2 miles
Elevation:	1600' loss, 400' gain
Terrain:	Trail
Time:	1¾ hours one way

Saddle Creek Trail is a segment of the Backbone Trail. Built in 1987 by crews of California Conservation Corps and Los Angeles Conservation Corps, the trail had been flagged (route determined and marked with flags) in 1986.   Prior to trail construction and going back to the 1970's, a small group of us hiked the entire trail every year. This particular segment demanded that we wear goggles, gloves, and other protection to get through the chaparral. The trail is now a pure delight.   The north and west shoulders of Saddle Peak are steep, rugged, chaparral covered slopes offering views of a large expanse of the Malibu Creek watershed.

I will describe the hike as a one way trip requiring a car shuttle. The beginning trailhead is on Stunt Road 2.8 miles from Mulholland Highway; the ending trailhead is on Piuma Road 1.4 miles from Malibu Creek Road. Park a car at the ending trailhead near the first switchback on Piuma Road. Drive back down Piuma Road to Cold Creek Road, turn right and go to Mulholland, turn right and go to Stunt Road. Follow Stunt Road 2.8 miles and park on the left opposite a gate with sign "Backbone Trail." Follow a trail going west that will intersect the Backbone Trail in 3/8 mile. Initially the Backbone Trail neither gains or loses much altitude as it winds westerly, but soon it begins a gentle downhill character, losing about 500 feet per mile, with an occasional short uphill section.

Saddle Creek Ranch is a short distance north of the trail — far enough away that the dogs don't bark when we walk along. For the rest of the hike we don't come close to habitation until the end. After leaving the Saddle Creek watershed the trail crosses a ridge and heads west crossing a meadow before making some switchbacks down the upper part of an intermittent stream that eventually joins Cold Creek.

The trail contours around the north side of a mountain in dense shade before coming to a western exposure and the beginning of a series of switchbacks, dropping us 800 feet on a constant downhill grade. We cross Dark Creek in the shade of a number of White Alders and climb a 100-foot-high chaparral ridge before the last downhill walk to the end of the hike.

Approval to build this trail came about in an unusual manner. A new Superintendent of the State of California, Department of Parks and Recreation, Angeles District, Bud Getty, agreed to a serious hike through chaparral. The group of us on the hike that day were totally dedicated to building the Backbone Trail and believed the Saddle Creek segment was a must. We had a long hard day thrashing through chaparral and over rocks, wearing gloves and goggles, when sometime in the heat of the afternoon on 17 June 1985, "Bud" Getty remarked that "This would be a lot more fun if we had a trail here." We had previously tried for an approval without much success so one of us asked, "Would you approve it?" "You bet." And we got our trail.

SADDLE CREEK TRAIL

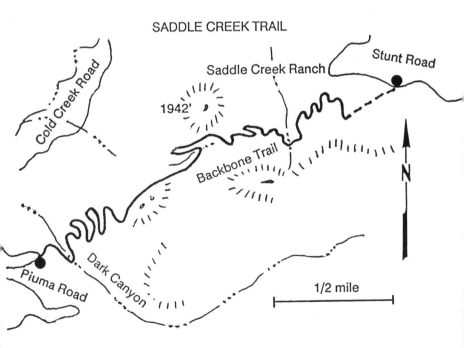

HIKE 43 SADDLE PEAK TRAIL

Maps:	SMMTS, Central Section
Distance:	5 miles roundtrip
Elevation:	1000' (if we go to the peak)
Terrain:	Trail
Time:	2¾ hours
Trailhead:	Top of Stunt Road

Three roads come together, in a saddle east of Saddle Peak. Stunt Road, Schueren Road and Saddle Peak Road all originate at this point. A convenient off-the-road parking area can handle at least a dozen cars, and if we were to organize the parking, maybe twenty. As an aside from hiking, people have been known to drive up here on a quiet night just to look at the lights below.

Our hike starts by walking west, slightly downhill on Stunt Road for 200 yards. The Saddle Peak segment of the Backbone Trail angles left leaving Stunt Road and continues to a ridge crossing over to the south side. We continue almost level until we see a large water tank ahead. Go around the tank to follow an uphill trail to a level area and a fork in the trail. We take the right fork to continue on the trail or we can take the left fork and go to the top of Saddle Peak East. At 2800 feet Saddle Peak is the highest point in the eastern or central part of the Santa Monica Mountains. If timed right, a peak climb on a full moon night will not only reward us with magnificent views of the cities' bright lights but also of the moon coming up from the eastern horizon. On top the peak is flat and open. On the sides hundreds of Spanish Broom bushes, some ten feet high, effectively control the erosion. Come here in April, May, June and maybe July for a real treat of sight and smell. The volunteer trail crew of the Sierra Club hosted a Summit dedication at 12 noon on 8 December 1990.

To continue the hike we start downhill passing through a stand of Chaparral Pea (in the same family as Spanish Broom) also about 10 feet high and blooms in May. A slab of rock several hundred feet long is on our left until the trail makes a switchback right and threads down through "Gateway Rock." We could stop in the protection of immense boulders in preparation for the downhill stretch ahead of us. A north-south land corridor about 300 yards wide was available for trail use coming down the north side of the slope. We notice it took sixteen switchbacks to stay within the land ownership boundary, but the trail is unique and does get us down the hill. We will have descended about 750 feet from the peak when we level out.

From here to joining the Saddle Creek segment, the trail is almost level. We pass a Eucalyptus tree on our right and make a left turn to go west. In ten minutes we intersect the Saddle Creek segment and turn around to return the way we came.

If we turn right at the intersection it is 3/8 of a mile to Stunt Road, if we want to walk back to our car along the road. A left turn at the intersection would put us on Saddle Creek segment with 3.2 miles to go to Piuma Road. Each Sunday in November the Sierra Club leads hikes on the Backbone Trail. Check the schedule for this one.

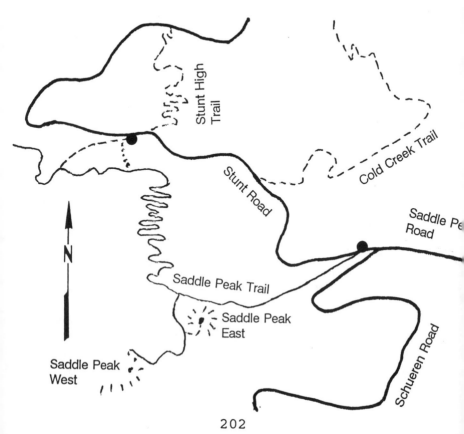

HIKE 44 PIUMA RIDGE TRAIL

Maps:	SMMTS, Central Section
Distance:	4 miles roundtrip
Elevation:	300'
Terrain:	Trail
Time:	2 hours
Trailhead:	Tapia Park

This two-mile trail segment parallels lower Piuma Road from its junction with Malibu Canyon Road to Piuma's first U-turn. Piuma Ridge Trail is often used as a continuation of a Saddle Peak, Saddle Creek hike — backpackers can camp at Malibu Creek State Park, get a drink of water and even take a shower.

Get to Tapia Park Trailhead by going about half way between the Pacific Coast Highway and the Ventura Freeway on Las Virgenes/Malibu Creek Road. We walk across the road carefully. No crosswalk, no sign or other device will aid us. When Malibu Creek is low we can walk along the stream using the bridge as an underpass. The west end of the trail has an annual problem of being washed out by Malibu Creek overflowing so we usually get on the shoulder of Piuma Road until the creek heads south. Once the trail gets above the creek and leaves it we find ourselves crossing a small meadow headed for a wooded area. After crossing a driveway to a house on the right, we are in a pristine area. We will see houses near the road but after the first switchback we are remote from the rest of the world. Bay trees replace the oaks during a stretch of trail. We gain most of the 300 feet during the first half of the hike, then a relatively level trail takes us through a chaparral forest to the bend in Piuma Road. This is our turnaround point, or if we want to see Dark Canyon, cross the road and continue one half mile on the Saddle Creek Trail. Dark Canyon is the only place along the Backbone Trail where we are likely to see native grapes. A turnaround at this point will make this a five-mile hike of maybe three leisurely hours.

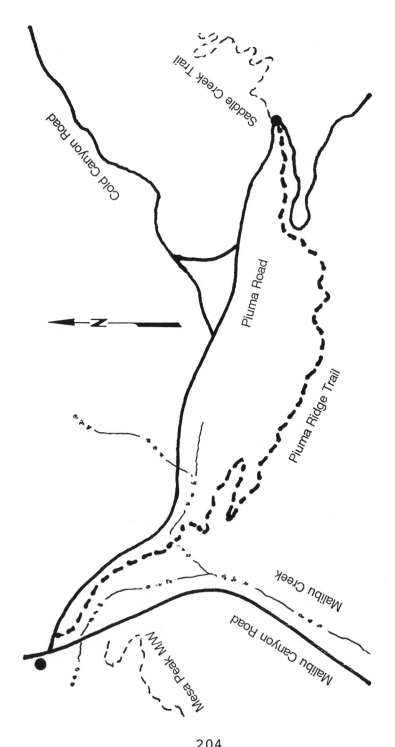

Cold Canyon Road

Saddle Creek Trail

Piuma Road

Piuma Ridge Trail

Malibu Creek

Malibu Canyon Road

Mesa Peak M/W

N

HIKE 45 TOPANGA LOOKOUT SITE

Maps:	SMMTS, Central Section
Distance:	3 miles
Elevation	350' gain and loss
Terrain:	Fireroad
Time:	1½ hours
Trailhead:	Saddle Peak Road and Stunt Road

AREA FEATURES

Topanga Ridge divides the Malibu and Topanga watersheds. Today's walk will be at the 2400 foot level, at first below the ridge, then along it to a high point where a lookout tower stood for many years before it was removed in the 1970s. The site is owned by the Mountains Restoration Trust and the access road is privately owned. Primarily a Chaparral plant community, the ridge does support some Coastal Sage Scrub plants. A fire swept uphill in 1970 and left only the burned trunks of bushes and trees. Recovery has been complete with only a few burned stumps still visible. This is a walk and is focused on the plants that grow here.

TRAIL INFORMATION

Park off the road at the junction of Stunt Road and Saddle Peak roads at the crest of the mountains. The trail is a fireroad leading to the site of the fire lookout. The road is paved for about 500 yards at which point it forks, with the right fork going uphill to a telephone relay tower.

Because the road is paved part way and the grade is reasonably gentle, this walk can be used by those in wheelchairs. When the pavement ends the road becomes rough but it is hard ground and rock, but passable. Parents with children in strollers might have a problem because the wheels are small.

The first part of the walk is high on the north facing slope of the mountain and although classified as chaparral, the vegetation includes Bay Trees, Coast Live Oaks, Canyon Sunflower, Heart-

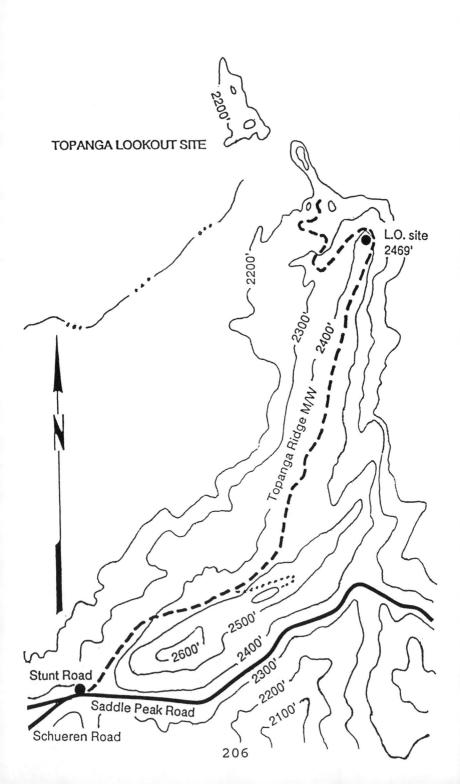

TOPANGA LOOKOUT SITE

2200'

N

L.O. site
2469'

2200'

2300'

2400'

Topanga Ridge M/W

2500'

2600'

2400'

2300'

2200'

2100'

Stunt Road

Saddle Peak Road

Schueren Road

leaved Penstemon, and some Grassland plants. Toyon with red berries from November until late winter, Scrub Oak with small but many acorns, Russian Thistles and other small shrubs dominate the first part of the walk. Look for Giant Rye, Hairyleaf Ceanothus, Saw-toothed Goldenbush, Bush Lupine, Phacelia, Cliff Aster, and Honeysuckle. When the trail forks, we go straight ahead onto a hard dirt road.

Geologically most of the rock along the route is sandstone and pebble cobble conglomerate. We will see some immense slabs, usually sloping steeply toward the northwest. Several intrusive sills and dikes of volcanic diabase in the form of weathered spheroidal blocks will be seen in the road and in roadcuts. This volcanic diabase is called "Onion Rock" because it exfoliates as it weathers. Some of this will be found in a roadcut after the route reaches a saddle and makes a definite turn toward north. Wand Buckwheat is the dominant plant on the face of the roadcut.

Later we will cross an area where the pavement of the road shows the distinctive diabase pattern and we have an opportunity to see it up close as we walk.

California Buckwheat, Chaparral Currant, Bush Senecio, Bigberry Manzanita, Two-tone Everlasting, Telegraph Weed, and Laurel Sumac will be seen all along this stretch of the road. The lookout site is surrounded by alien Pine Trees. These rarely reproduce in the Santa Monica Mountains, but once established, some species are able to live many years. The lookout site isn't the neatest spot in the mountains. The broken bottle evidence indicates that the spot has been popular as a rendezvous for beer drinkers and careless picnickers.

The road continues around the eastern side of the old lookout, dropping rather steeply. Look for more diabase "Onion Rock" in the roadcut. Bush Poppy, Hollyleaf Cherry, Red Shanks, Hairy-leaved Ceanothus, and Mountain Mahogany are found on the north facing slope alongside the road. Plummer's Baccharis is found in the saddle where we can look into Old Topanga Canyon watershed. The road ends at a sandstone knoll and we can look back to see the large tilted sandstone slabs. A rock scramble trail goes down the ridge northwest from the end of the road, but we won't hike the ridge on this walk and will turnaround to return the way we came.

HIKE 46

**HENRY RIDGE CROSSING,
HONDO CANYON, and
FOSSIL TRAIL.**
(all segments of the Backbone Trail)
from Dead Horse Trailhead TSP

Maps:	SMMTS, East
	SMMTS, Central
Distance:	11 miles roundtrip
Elevation:	2625' gain and loss
Terrain:	Trail
Time:	5½ hours
Trailhead:	Dead Horse Trailhead

These three segments of the Backbone Trail are presented as one hike, but we may choose to do the sections separately depending upon the time available, and places to park. Dead Horse Trailhead is reliable, paved, and large enough for 25 or so cars. Further, if we go west and return it gives us a 1600' climb out of Hondo early in the hike rather than later. Also to note is that the two parking areas on Saddle Peak Road are not always available. Parts of the one at the top of Hondo are always used to dump landslide rock and dirt, and the parking area at the top of Stunt is sometimes a Command Post for road repair teams. Also, I prefer to hike with the sun at my back.

We begin the hike by turning east onto Entrada Road, one half mile north of the town of Topanga. Go 200 yards and turn left into the lot. Pay to park. Hike north past the restrooms to take a narrow trail down hill, turn left and with care cross Topanga Canyon Boulevard to Greenleaf Canyon Road. Turn left onto a "use" trail and hike west up a ridge. This section of trail has not been built but is usually passable. We avoid taking a branching trail to the left — this is a nature trail used by grade school students. Upon reaching Henry Ridge turn left for a short downhill walk, then right for ten minutes to Old Topanga Canyon Road. Cross the road to continue on the Backbone Trail. We soon start a three-mile uphill hike with some level respites.

We reach a ridge and on our right is Hondo Canyon. To our left we will have a north-facing slope of chaparral. As we close in on Hondo Creek, oaks become prominent and the shade is welcome. Later on when we get near the stream a grove of Bay trees surrounds us. Hondo Canyon burned in 1993. A chaparral forest consisting mainly of Big-pod Ceanothus covered the upper part of the canyon. Because it does not rootcrown sprout after a fire, Big-pod Ceanothus relies upon seeds to replant the burned plants. This is happening, but in the meantime ten-foot-high Bush Poppies by the thousands have covered the area. Poppy seeds have lain in the soil for many years — probably since some unknown previous fire — and are now furnishing pioneer plants that protect the soil from erosion. Fifteen years may intervene before the Big-pod Ceanothus overtakes and crowds out the Bush Poppies to completely restore the chaparral forest. For a few years I will walk the trail every spring to marvel Mother Nature's solution to a fire.

Upon reaching Saddle Peak Road we notice the Fossil Trail on our right. It climbs some, paralleling the road and opens up our first views of the Pacific Ocean. Look for fossils of shellfish on the rocks alongside the trail. In less than twenty minutes we will reach a parking area at the juncture of three roads: Saddle Peak, Schueren, and Stunt. Return the way we came unless we've elected a car shuttle.

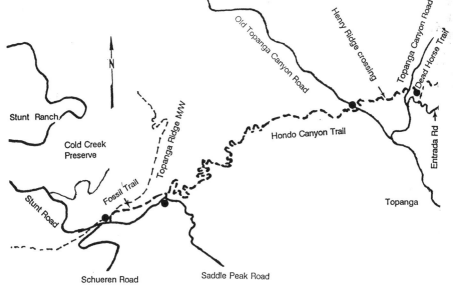

HIKE 47

CALABASAS PEAK

from Woodland hills
via Summit-to-Summit Motorway

Maps:	SMMTS, Central Section
	and Eastern Section
Distance:	9 miles
Elevation:	1750' gain and loss
Terrain:	Trail and fireroad
Time:	4 hours
Trailhead:	Top of Topanga

Find the beginning of the hike by going to the top of Topanga Canyon Boulevard and park off the road on the northeast side. Cross the road to hike on the Summit-to-Summit Motorway. After a steep climb on pavement and a left turn near a water tank the road levels off. On our left note a broad valley that has been preserved from development by concerted action by the people of Topanga and others. This Summit Valley Ed Edelman Park is under the guidance of the Santa Monica Mountains Conservancy. Some trails are already built, and plans for more public use are programmed for the future.

Our trail takes on a decisive southwest direction, losing some altitude. We watch for a water tank and a housing development ahead, and turn left to continue past civilization. We will stay on the Summit-to-Summit motorway for about four and a half miles before we reach Calabasas Peak. In the meantime we have several opportunities to take a wrong road. About one and a half miles from the start, a paved road comes up hill from our right. We aren't likely to turn to go down that road now, but on our return it is inviting — don't do it. We have had people wonder what went wrong and knock on doors to find a way out. Continuing on a few hundred yards, we will pass two roads on our left. One goes to a small community of Glenview, the other to Henry Ridge. We don't take either road but make a sweeping turn right. We leave the pavement and continue west on a dirt road..

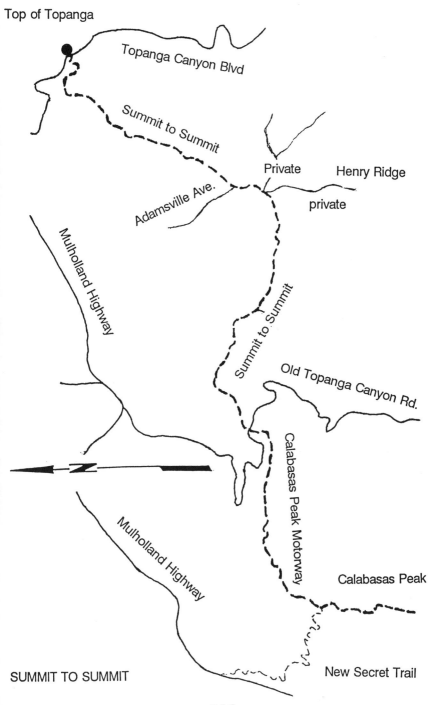

Top of Topanga

Topanga Canyon Blvd

Summit to Summit

Private   Henry Ridge

private

Adamsville Ave.

Mulholland Highway

Summit to Summit

Old Topanga Canyon Rd.

Calabasas Peak Motorway

Mulholland Highway

Calabasas Peak

SUMMIT TO SUMMIT

New Secret Trail

When we have hiked nearly three miles our road is on a west trending ridge. We will cross Old Topanga Canyon Road at its high point and continue west going around a fireroad gate, then uphill. A private road leading to Deer Creek Ranch branches left and should be avoided.

The next segment of the hike is about 2 miles long and gains 550 feet in a series of uphill climbs interspersed with level stretches. The route stays well up on the ridge as it makes a lefthand sweep from a west to south heading. Nearing Calabasas Peak we will lose some altitude, then make a left turn and gain 200 feet going around a shoulder to the right and up a grade with the peak on the right. When the roadcut dwindles, cut back to the right and walk along the trail that goes up a bulldozed area to the peak. A break in the chaparral near the top indicates where the trail goes through. A steep, but short, climb puts us on top. At 2163' Calabasas Peak overlooks everything close by. Only the east-west backbone to the south, dominated by Saddle Peak, is higher. The view one mile west is of Stokes Canyon and Stokes Ridge. Beyond is Malibu Creek State Park distinguished by the volcanic Goat Buttes. Climb this at night to see the lights of the Thousand Oaks area and the Ventura Freeway.

Return on the same road we came; cross Old Topanga Canyon Blvd. and continue east. Upon reaching a 4-road intersection, stay left going uphill on pavement, reaching another road fork after leveling out on the ridge. The left fork goes to Adamsville Avenue; we want to turn right onto a dirt road. Angle right again unless we want to take a short diversion to an overlook. In ten minutes we come to the gate with the bypass. We pass the water tank, turn right and in five minutes will pass two more water tanks. Then we go downhill on a paved road.

HIKE 48

RED ROCK CANYON PARK

Maps:	SMMTS, Central
	SMMTS, East
Distance:	3½ miles roundtrip
Elevation:	600'
Terrain:	Road and trail
Time:	2 hours
Trailhead:	Parking area off Old Topanga Canyon
	Road and Red Rock Road

Reach Red Rock Road by going two miles north of Topanga Post Office on Old Topanga Canyon Road. Turn left on Red Rock Road and park on a dirt area on the right. We will walk two-thirds of a mile on a narrow, winding road through a residential area before reaching the gate to the Park. We do not plan to drive or park on Red Rock Road other than the small lot off Old Topanga. A stream comes through the canyon from the west. We use this as a general guide.

Upon reaching the locked gate go around and into the Park. We have already come through a rock gorge and quickly separated ourselves from civilization. We pass an occupied house on our left and are headed west, uphill on a road. I like this as a conditioning hike because we get a good warm-up period walking on flat ground then a mile and a quarter of uphill gaining 600 feet. On the return we have ample opportunity to cool down.

Red Rock Canyon is in the shade of Oaks and Sycamores along the stream, and later as the route pulls away from the stream, chaparral plants dominate. This gives us a wide variety of wildflowers in season. I recommend this canyon as a wildflower walk because of the variety of plants.

Red Rock Canyon was once Camp Slauson, a weekend camping area for Boy Scouts. Caves, rock walls, trails, and flat camping areas all leave evidence of the use. Until a few years ago a pay telephone stood under the trees. From my many years of Boy Scout camping I don't recall writing letters, but to phone out would have been luxury. Several lateral trails leave the stream and would take us up on the hillsides for good views of the canyon.

At the high point of the hike a look west is into the Cold Creek watershed. Mulholland runs north to south making a turn west where Stunt Road branches off to go south toward Saddle Peak. A left turn from here would take us to Stunt Road. A right turn would take us past Calabasas Peak and eventually to a crossing of Old Topanga Canyon Road about two miles up the road from the start of our hike.

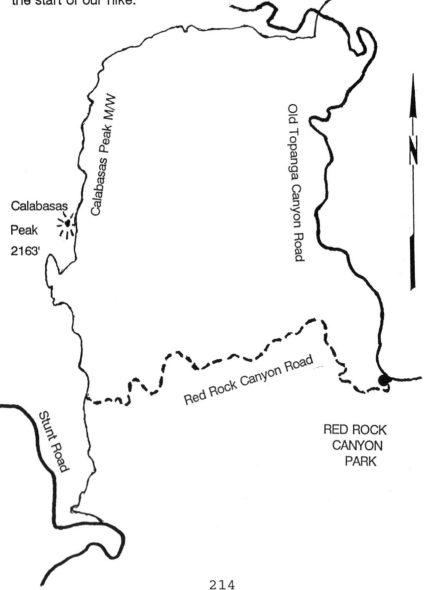

Calabasas
Peak
2163'

Calabasas Peak M/W

Old Topanga Canyon Road

Red Rock Canyon Road

Stunt Road

RED ROCK
CANYON
PARK

HIKE 49

Maps: SMMTS, East
Distance: 4 miles
Elevation: 850' gain and loss
Terrain: Road and Trail
             (some steep)
Time: 1¾ hours
Trailhead: Old Topanga Cyn Rd

Topanga Meadows presents an opportunity to explore. There are many trails in the area — some that are known to have been used by the Indians for centuries. Exploring the several streams leading down to Old Topanga Canyon Creek is interesting, and the meadows lend themselves to independent investigation. This hike can take an hour, or it can last all day, depending on how much you want to see. You need to recognize Poison Oak when you see it as there's a lot of it here.

The trailhead is one-third mile north of highway 27 on Old Topanga Canyon Road, a few hundred feet beyond the bridge. Park on the west side of the road and walk down to the stream and cross it to the trail on the other side. The Backbone Trail goes through here and we follow it for a while.

Turn right at the west bank after crossing the stream and follow the trail as it goes through a California Rose briar patch, making a sweeping left turn as it heads up to an intermittent side stream. The trail crosses one of the streams coming down from the west; a cement apron has been built here to control erosion, as the trail once was a road. Another trail comes down from a meadow to the right. Continue ahead as we leave the stream and turn right going steeply uphill along the edge of a meadow. Upon reaching an unmaintained old road, (now a trail) continue ahead (east). Our trail is almost level for a few hundred yards as we turn left and enter a Southern Oak Woodland. Old Topanga Creek is on the right but out of sight. This section of the hike gives us an

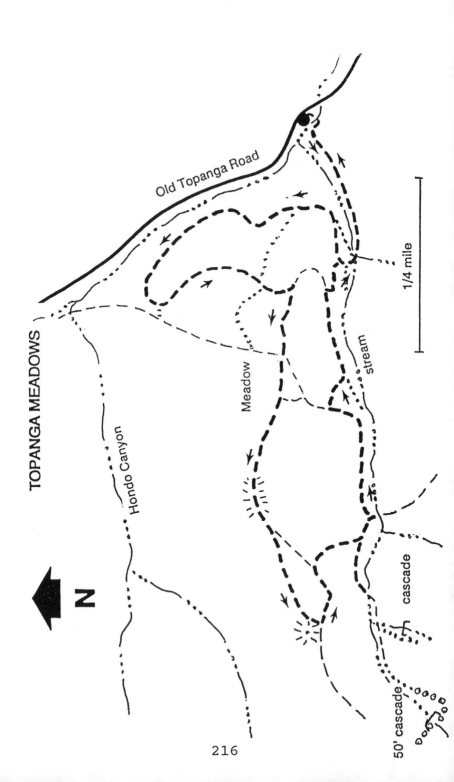

TOPANGA MEADOWS

Old Topanga Road

1/4 mile

Meadow

stream

Hondo Canyon

N

cascade

50' cascade

216

opportunity to see wildflowers and ferns that grow in oak groves. Spring is the best time for viewing but some plants will be in bloom at all times of the year. Look for Milkmaids, Crimson Pitcher Sage, Sweet Cicely, Miner's lettuce, California Buttercup, and more. We continue the loop of this segment and gain some elevation. Several trails will lead us west, uphill, all of which will lead us up to the ridge. The route shown on the map is well used. We turn west and go uphill on the edge of a large sloping meadow. Just before cresting out we see an oak grove on the left that has sandstone rocks that invite a rest stop, or a lunch stop. Farther west along the grassy ridge look for Golden Stars and Mariposa Lilies in the spring.

The arrows on the map indicate the route that can be taken to get an overview of the area. We will get better trail maintenance as time goes on, but until our volunteer organization expands (and we are growing) we will "rough it" some. We will see the Backbone Trail come up the hill when we are on the ridge. The Backbone Trail continues west over the ridge and into Hondo Canyon. Today we will turn left and go downhill on the Backbone Trail for about four hundred yards looking for a trail on the right, going up a side stream through a delightful forest of Coast live oaks, Sycamore trees and California Bays. The trail is not all that easy to walk through and we note that the map indicates that the trail we are now on goes from "route of hike" to "other trails" to "indistinct trail" and finally to "bushwhack." At present we can get to the foot of the first cascade with some rock scrambling, but no further. The "bushwhack" beyond that point is unnerving to say the least. I got a telephone call from a young man who had taken his new girl friend on this hike expecting to get to the 50-foot cascade. After getting scratched up by the brush and not getting to the cascade his lady was less than impressed with the outing. Bushwhacking means "goggles, gloves, long sleeves, etc." Somehow it was my fault that the day had not gone well.

Take this hike in the spring and see a beautiful display of flowers. Look for Humboldt Lilies, Chocolate Lilies, Monkey Flowers, Chinese Houses, Blue-eyed Grass, Roses, Paint-brushes, Golden Stars, and more.

HIKE 50

Maps:	Roadmap
Distance:	12.2 miles one way
Elevation:	600' gain, 1500' loss
Terrain:	Highway
Time:	Don't walk this one; go by bicycle or car.
Trailhead:	Ventura Blvd and Topanga Cyn Blvd.

This drive is designed to give a geological view of the Central Santa Monica Mountains by traversing the range north to south on State Highway 27. Several stops are needed to see the features described. Unfortunately some "no parking" areas are in conflict with this plan, so some walking is required.

The trip begins in the San Fernando Valley on State Highway 27 near the Ventura Freeway. The mileage log starts as you leave Ventura Blvd. so set your odometer at zero if you can, otherwise keep a record. You will start at the top of the geological formations and take a journey through time, seeing the youngest rocks in the valley and oldest rocks near the coast.

mile 0.0 Ventura Blvd. Go south on Topanga Canyon Blvd. Pass Mulholland Drive and start up a slight grade as the road heads for the mountains.

mile 1.5 A large roadcut on the left just beyond Cezanne Avenue displays tilted layers of Modelo shale and sandstone. The Modelo Formation is largely composed of diatomite and clay shale formed 8-12 million years ago when the land was under a deep sea. Layers of this formation can be seen in roadcuts all the way to the summit.

mile 2.9 Summit. Park in the area to the left then cross the highway to inspect the shale at close range. The "Summit-to-Summit" Motorway begins here, goes west, and is a major access trail into the area as far as Old Topanga Road.

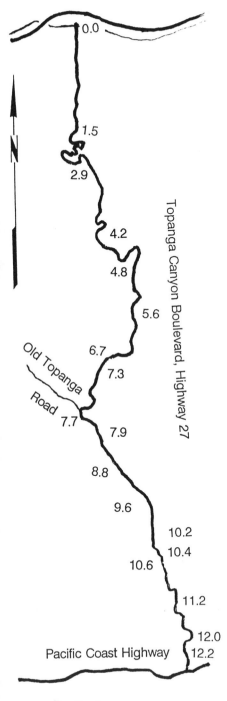

mile **4.2** Stop and park just beyond Entrado Road. Across the road on the left is a loop of the old road. Walk around the loop and look for the contact area between the Modelo Formation and the Topanga Group. The actual contact here is an angular unconformity; that is, a part of the underlying formation is missing. What shows is Modelo shale on its base of pebbly sandstone and conglomerate, overlying the Calabasas Formation of the Topanga Group.

mile **4.8** Beyond road marker 7.50 the road makes a sharp turn to the right as it crosses a branch of Topanga Creek. A dark brown outcropping of volcanic basalt is on the right and a few hundred yards down the road a basalt pinnacle can be seen on the left. The volcanic activity in the Santa Monica Mountains began about 15½ mya

This activity lasted for 2 million years.

mile 5.6   Bridge across Garapito Creek Some rock slides are in this area on the east side of Topanga Creek. The Calabasas Formation of sand-stone is hard and weather resistant, but when the strata dips to the west as it does here, the slides can occur along the plane of the rock layers. Over the centuries Topanga Creek has cut away at the lower edge of the bedding plane and with a little help from builders doing the same, a good rain can trigger a slide.

Cheney Drive follows up Garapito Creek and leads to an entrance to Topanga State Park.

mile 6.7   The sandstone cliffs on the right side of the stream are layered almost horizontally and indicate good resistance to weather-ing. Volcanic rock appears on the left of the road and continues in view to Entrada Road. Many rock walls have been built because of its availability.

mile 7.3   Entrada Road on the left leads to the Trippet Ranger Station at the entrance to Topanga State Park. The sandstone from here down to the business section of the town of Topanga is the Cold Creek member of the Topanga Canyon Formation.

mile 7.7   Intersection with Old Topanga Road, Topanga Post Office, and business buildings.

mile 7.9   Bridge. Marine fossils have been found in the Cold Creek member sandstone in this area, dated as early or middle Miocene. Just beyond the bridge is an east-west division of the Cold Creek member above and the Fernwood member below, both of the Topanga Canyon Formation. This Fernwood, brackish water sandstone forms the cliffs on the east side of the stream to about the 1100 foot level, and on the west of the stream goes to the top of the ridge beyond Fernwood. The dip of the strata is generally east, accounting for the stability and steepness of the cliffs on the east side of the stream.

mile 8.8   The steep bank on the right is composed of dark intrusive rock (diabase) that weathers out and occasionally rolls down onto the road. On the left is a limited area of Sespe sandstone (Oligocene epoch). This is pebbly, and a nonmarine formation that is quite often red colored. Visually above the Sespe Formation is a fault separating the Sespe from the light brown Topanga Formation. The fault is almost vertical and is near the base of the Topanga sandstone cliffs.   Actually, the Sespe and Topanga sandstone lie side by side.   There is a layer of white colored fresh-water limestone in the lower Sespe Formation.   Also notice the prominent thick dikes in the roadcut.

mile 9.6   We abruptly leave the black intrusive rock on both sides of the road and enter a steep walled canyon made up of the Coal Canyon Formation.   This cliff-forming rock is mostly pebble-cobble conglomerate and siltstone.   Formed in a shallow, tropical sea during Paleocene and Eocene epochs (40-70 mya) it contains marine fossils.   The layers are tilted and massive.   At mile 9.8 a small canyon and roadcut on the right affords a close view.   During times of heavy rain the cascades of water coming down the east escarpment present a spectacular view for this normally dry cliff.   Falling rocks and landslides, along with washed-out roads, accompany the heavy storms so one must temper a desire to see this event with caution.

mile 10.2   The east wall shows a division of the Coal Canyon Formation above and the Tuna Canyon Formation (Upper Cretaceous, 70 mya+) below.   The Tuna Canyon Formation is made up of beds of coarse-grained sandstone and minor conglomerate deposits.   The Tuna Canyon thrust fault is discernable on the east wall and can be seen again dipping steeply to the south at a roadcut at mile 11.4.

mile 10.4   Bridge.

mile 10.6   The thrust fault can be seen on the west wall of the canyon.

mile 11.2   Roadcut.   South of here for the next .8 mile the Coal Canyon conglomerate dominates the east wall again.   The Tuna Canyon Formation is found on the west of the road.   The canyon soon broadens, and landslide activity covers most of the base rock.

mile 12.0   Tuna Canyon Formation rock forms the base to the coast even though much of it is covered over with alluvium.

mile 12.2   Pacific Coast Highway.

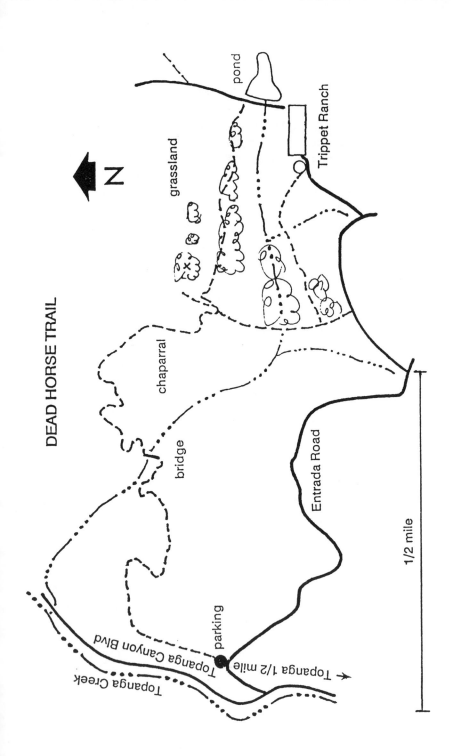

DEAD HORSE TRAIL

N

grassland

chaparral

bridge

pond

Trippet Ranch

Entrada Road

1/2 mile

parking

Topanga 1/2 mile →

Topanga Canyon Blvd

Topanga Creek

HIKE 51

DEAD HORSE TRAIL

in Topanga State Park

Maps:	SMMTS, East
Distance:	2½ miles roundtrip
Elevation:	400 feet gain and loss
Terrain:	Trail
Time:	1 hour
Trailhead:	Dead Horse parking lot on Entrada Road

A short hike — but an interesting hike — the Dead Horse Trail takes us on a tour of the western approach to Trippet Ranch in the west end of Topanga State Park. We will be introduced to dense streamside shade, grasslands, chaparral and oak groves. This particular area was burned in 1925 and 1948. The major fires of recent years have bypassed the area.

The hike begins at the Dead Horse parking lot, 200 yards from Topanga Canyon Boulevard, 1/2 mile north of the Post Office in the town of Topanga. We must take care driving to the parking lot — the turn onto Entrada is sharp and steeply uphill. The turn into the parking lot is on a blind curve. The gate is locked at night. The trail heads north through chaparral. Except for the imported gravel on the path up from the parking lot, the initial stretch of trail is on solid basalt, a fine grain volcanic rock. Later we will be on sandstone. After 10 minutes on the trail we cross Trippet Creek on a beautiful, rustic, wooden bridge. It was installed in 1986 without so much as disturbing a blade of grass — a highly responsible care for the environment. The streambed is interesting for those who would climb around on rocks and risk some Poison Oak. Sweet Cicely, Geranium, Grape, and 4 species of fern grow along the banks.

Cross the bridge and soon enter a Chamise chaparral forest. The trail contours along the south and west facing slope of a broad ridge. As the trail heads east we enter an oak woodland on the right and a meadow on the left. Upon reaching a road near the pond, turn right and walk across the earth and rock dam that impounds the water. California Roses have become established on the dam. Trippet Ranch is the Park headquarters. A ranger lives in the house south of the parking lot. Restrooms, drinking water, pay phone, picnic area, parking, and park Personnel are available.

We can return the way we came or locate a trail west of the parking lot that crosses a meadow and continues down the south side of the stream. In about 1/4 mile the trail intersects an east-west trail, which if followed north will join the Dead Horse Trail where we turn left and return to our cars.

HIKE 52

Maps: SMMTS, East
Distance: 4 miles round trip
Elevation: 600' gain and loss
Terrain: Trail and fireroad
Time: 1¾ hours
Trailhead: Trippet Ranch

We can make a loop hike using a fireroad for half the trip and trail for the other half. Most of the area of the hike was burned during the Topanga Canyon Fire of 1977, then again by a prescribed burn in June, 1984. This hike will duplicate a part of the Eagle Spring Loop trip but will go in reverse order and with more detail.

Reach the trailhead by turning east onto Entrada Road from Topanga Canyon Boulevard just north of the town of Topanga. Once on Entrada Road turn left at every street intersection and drive 1.1 miles to the entrance of Topanga State Park. Park in the lot; a fee is required.

From the east end of the parking lot go north on the macadam road near the left side of the pond. In about 100 yards, as the road goes over a little rise, turn right onto the trail. After crossing the east end of the meadow the trail quickly enters an enchanting riparian woodland of Oak, Laurel and Sycamore trees. The trail winds through the densely wooded area then comes out for a short glimpse of chaparral before dipping into the next streamside area of Fern and Scarlet Monkeyflower. The trail turns north and heads into chaparral before coming to the Musch Ranch area — which can be distinguished by a stand of Eucalyptus trees. An overnight campground, drinking water, restrooms, picnic tables, and horse corrals are available. Fires are not authorized. Check with a State Park ranger before planning to stay overnight.

Several branching trails may cause some confusion but keep in mind that the trail leads uphill to the east. Shortly after leaving

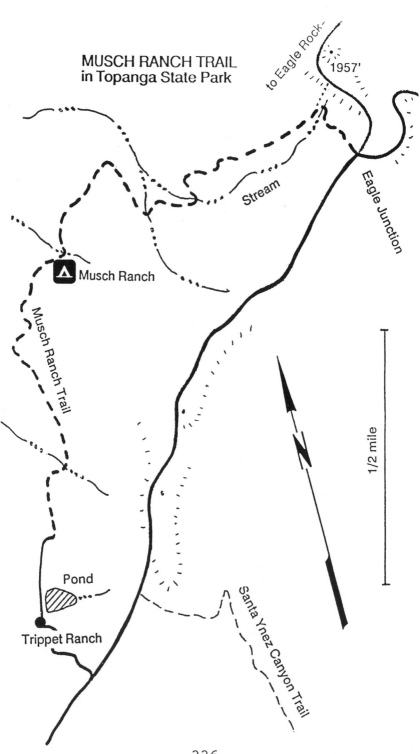

MUSCH RANCH TRAIL
in Topanga State Park

to Eagle Rock

1957'

Eagle Junction

Stream

Musch Ranch

Musch Ranch Trail

1/2 mile

Pond

Trippet Ranch

Santa Ynez Canyon Trail

the Musch Ranch area a side trail goes downhill from a low ridge at a point where we angle right and go uphill. The trail from this point on is generally to the east and after two more stream crossings begins a serious climb.

The Topanga Canyon fire of November 1977 swept down this slope and thoroughly burned the chaparral, then again when a prescribed burn was set. The chaparral is recovering nicely because many plants sprout on the root-crowns of burned plants and many seeds that have lain dormant in the topsoil sprout after a fire. The composition of the plant community is temporarily disrupted by fire — maybe for a 7-10 year period. Many flowers that normally do not thrive in chaparral have a few years of glory until they are again crowded out. We look for Bush Poppies as we climb up after the last stream crossing. These 8-10 foot high shrubs are scarce in chaparral but plentiful along this trail. The yellow blossoms appear in February and bloom for three months. Before smelling a blossom, I think "Watermelon," and with a little imagination it smells like watermelon. A stand of Bush Lupines dominates the area farther up the trail. A trip along this trail in February, March, or April will be remembered for the beautiful blue blossoms and the delightful scent.

After a vigorous climb we crest out on a fireroad at Eagle Junction and turn right. The walk on the fireroad stays high on the ridge. Topanga Canyon watershed is on our right and Santa Ynez Canyon on our left. We soon are able to look down on Trippet Ranch to the right and identify the pond, the buildings, and the parking lot. The goat pens can be seen north of the beginning of the Musch Ranch Trail. Goats were used in Topanga State Park as a means of reducing vegetation on the firebreaks. The program was discontinued several years ago. About 1/2 mile from Trippet Ranch the Santa Ynez Trail branches left. The hill southwest of this junction is of volcanic basalt that intruded into the sandstone about 14 million years ago. We keep to the right at road junctions in order to reach Trippet Ranch parking lot.

Trippet Ranch facilities include: picnic area, restrooms, drinking water, and bulletin board information center.

EAST TOPANGA FIREROAD

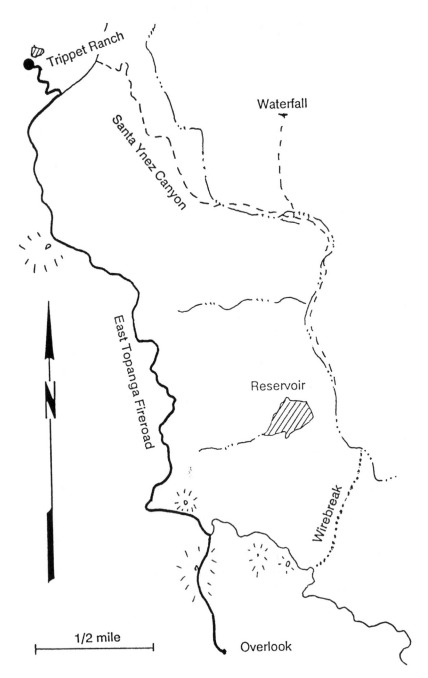

Trippet Ranch

Santa Ynez Canyon

Waterfall

East Topanga Fireroad

N

Reservoir

Wirebreak

1/2 mile

Overlook

HIKE 53   EAST TOPANGA FIREROAD

(Santa Ynez Fireroad)
from Trippet Ranch

Maps:	SMMTS, East
Distance:	6 miles roundtrip
Elevation:	1500' gain and loss
Terrain:	Fireroad
Time:	2-¾ hours
Trailhead:	Trippet Ranch

This trip is high on a ridge and gives an opportunity to look down into the deepest parts of both Topanga Canyon and Santa Ynez Canyon.

Reach the trailhead by turning east onto Entrada Road from State Hwy 27 just north of the town of Topanga. Once on Entrada Road turn left at every street intersection. Drive 1.1 miles to the entrance to Topanga State Park.

Leave the east end of the parking lot and go uphill on a fireroad. This road intersects a road that runs along the ridge at "the Latitude." Turn right and start a gentle climb along an oak shaded road that quickly crests out on the ridge between Topanga Canyon on the west and Santa Ynez Canyon on the east.

Notice the rock underfoot. Since leaving Trippet Ranch the base rock has been sandstone. Now we are on volcanic rock and have just crossed the east-west trending Topanga Fault. Volcanics intruded into the existing sandstone about 15 million years ago during a period of volcanic activity in the Santa Monica Mountains. For the next two miles most of the rock along the route is volcanic with a few areas of sandstone.

This east Topanga ridge gives breathtaking views of the lower part of Topanga Canyon and one can sense the power of the stream that has cut this gorge through the mountains to a depth of more than 1000 feet. Periodically Topanga Creek demonstrates this force by cleaning out some of the man-made structures such as roads. bridges, and buildings that impinge upon the creek bed.

The hillside housing on the west side of the canyon is the Fernwood tract of Topanga.

The Santa Ynez Canyon view is equally spectacular with its network of ravines, and massive sandstone slabs of tilted rock. Two trails drop down from the fireroad to Santa Ynez Creek. One, about a mile and a half from the start of the hike, leaves the road near Peak 1629. (This is a sandstone knoll west of the road.) The trail is east of the road and is difficult to pick up because of bulldozer activity destroying the first couple hundred feet about 1978, and the trail has not been used since. The trail is steep, going through a beautiful chaparral forest, and bottoming out through a lot of Poison Oak just before reaching the stream. The other trail begins about 450 yards farther south on the road and is really overgrown. These trails are not part of this hike and are mentioned only for those with a strong urge for adventure. When the land for Topanga State Park was being purchased for what is now the second largest urban park in the United States and the largest wildland within any city in the world, lower Santa Ynez Canyon was not included. This effectively blocked what could have been the main entryway for the people of greater Los Angeles. The housing development in Santa Ynez Canyon is Palisades Highlands.

Continue south along the ridge until coming to a road on the right about 2½ miles from the trailhead. This road turns to a firebreak as it follows a sandstone ridge out to "the Overlook," a high point with an exceptional view of the Pacific Ocean. Return the way we came.

HIKE 54

Musch Ranch Trail
from Trippet Ranch

Maps:	SMMTS, East
Distance:	7 miles roundtrip
Elevation:	900' gain and loss
Terrain:	Combination fireroad and trail
Time:	2-¾ hours
Trailhead:	Trippet Ranch

On Highway 27 just north of the town of Topanga, turn east on Entrada Road. Once on Entrada Rd, turn left at every street intersection, 1.1 miles to the entrance of Topanga State Park.

Take the trail up the hill from the parking lot. This intersects with a fireroad. A sign reads: "Eagle Spring 1.6 mi., Mulholland 4.6, Will Rogers State Historical Park 9.2." Turn left at this intersection and walk up a gentle grade, initially in the shade of Coast Live Oak trees — later along an open ridge. (We will pass the trail on the right leading to Santa Ynez Canyon.) Continue on the road for about 1 mile to a fork, Eagle Junction, go left and continue uphill, noting the view of Eagle Rock ahead. Later, from the backside of Eagle Rock, it is possible to take a short side trip, climbing to the top.

Continue east on the road, passing Penny Road entering from the left, until reaching an intersection with three roads, called "The Hub." Just before reaching this junction we could climb to a high point on the left. From there we would be at the apex of three watersheds. To the south is Santa Ynez Canyon with its intermittent stream draining into the ocean near Sunset Blvd. To the east is Rustic Canyon with its drainage outlet near Chautauqua Blvd. To the north is Garapito Canyon which joins with Topanga Canyon and the drainage is then south to the ocean, just west of where Hwy 27 meets the Coast Highway.

At "The Hub" are three other roads. First is Fireroad 30 on the

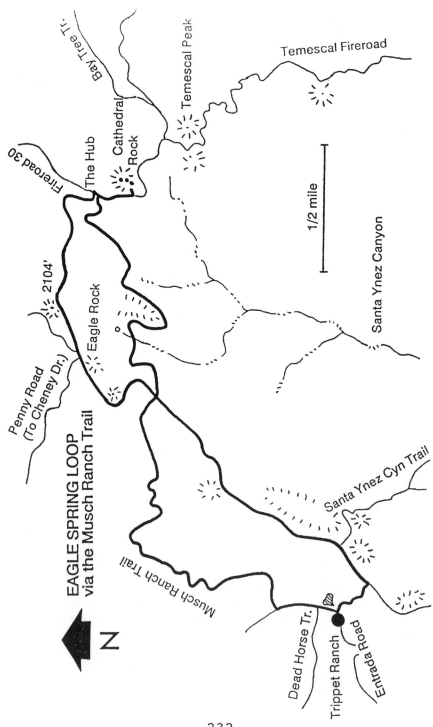

EAGLE SPRING LOOP
via the Musch Ranch Trail

N

Bay Tree Tr.

Fireroad 30

The Hub

Cathedral Rock

Temescal Peak

Temescal Fireroad

2104'

Eagle Rock

Penny Road
(To Cheney Dr.)

1/2 mile

Santa Ynez Canyon

Musch Ranch Trail

Santa Ynez Cyn Trail

Dead Horse Tr.

Trippet Ranch

Entrada Road

232

left which goes 2 miles north to Mulholland Dr. The next road which appears to be a continuation of Fireroad 30, is named Temescal Fireroad at this point and goes south along the north-south ridge, separating Santa Ynez and Upper Rustic Canyons. The third road which goes to Eagle Spring, we'll take later,

This hike goes south on Temescal Fireroad abut 1/2 mile to the intersection with Rogers Road on the left. Continue a short distance south of this intersection, leave the road and climb Temescal Peak, the highest point in the Park, 2126'.

Return to "The Hub" the same way we came. A nice lunch stop is at Cathedral Rock to the east of the road a few hundred yards before getting back to the junction and the road to Eagle Spring. Climb into Cathedral rock — there is room for 25 people — or maybe 50 good friends. At "The hub" turn left to go to Eagle Spring. At one time three large wooden tanks stored water from the year-round spring. They are now gone.

Eagle Spring Water Tanks

A short walk up the stream locates the spring, protected by abundant stands of Poison Oak.

Continue west on the road until coming to Eagle Junction. Cross the road to the west side where we will find the trail that goes down the slope through an area that burned in the November 1977 fire. This is the Musch Ranch Trail, so named because of the ranch at the base of the hill. Continue south on the trail heading down through the chaparral. The chaparral quickly gives way to quiet oak glens, moss covered rocks, and a stream that flows after each rain. Signs indicate the trail location in places. Cross a little meadow, pass the pond, and we have arrived at the parking lot.

The Old Footbridge on Musch Ranch Trail

HIKE 55

SANTA YNEZ CANYON
EAST TOPANGA FIREROAD
(on some maps shown as Santa Ynez Fireroad)
via the "Wirebreak"
from Trippet Ranch

Maps:	SMMTS, East
Distance:	8 miles roundtrip
Elevation:	1700' gain and loss
Terrain:	Trail, firebreak and fireroad
Time:	3¼ hours
Trailhead:	Trippet Ranch

On Highway 27 just north of the town of Topanga turn east on Entrada Road. Once on Entrada Rd turn left at every street intersection. It is 1.1 miles to the entrance of Topanga State Park. This is where we will park our car.

The hiking trail goes uphill from the east end of the parking lot. Turn left upon reaching the "Latitude," a point on the fireroad along the saddle. This road leads gently uphill through a grove of Coast Live Oaks. About 300-400 yards after leaving the Latitude there is another saddle that allows a good view of Santa Ynez Canyon on the right. Take this trail that crosses over to a little ridge, then after a left turn drops down into Santa Ynez Canyon. The upper part goes through part of the area burned in the fire of November 1977 and for a few years will be covered with wild flowers every spring until the chaparral returns. Starting down the trail presents a continuing change in the panorama of the lower canyon. Dense stands of Chamise, Ceanothus, Sumac and Toyon can be seen on the slopes to the west; massive sandstone can be seen on ridges below; and on a clear day the ocean is framed by the mouth of the canyon.

After dropping 700' rather steeply, the trail enters a cool riparian woodland shaded with Oaks and Sycamores. The trail makes a sharp turn left and becomes almost level as it gently follows the stream. Blackberry vines, Humboldt Lilies, and a myriad other plants carpet the banks of the stream. Farther on

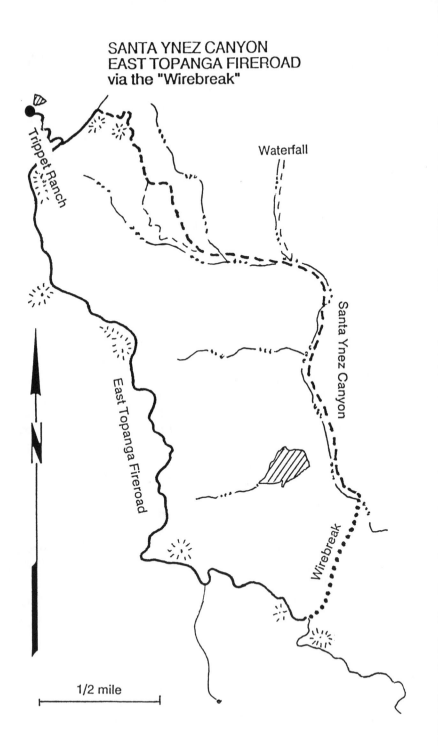

SANTA YNEZ CANYON
EAST TOPANGA FIREROAD
via the "Wirebreak"

Trippet Ranch

Waterfall

Santa Ynez Canyon

East Topanga Fireroad

Wirebreak

N

1/2 mile

down, just before the stream we are following joins with the Santa Ynez north fork, an old cabin site is off to the left in amongst some Poison Oak. About all that is visible now are two rock chimneys, one with a fireplace.

Continue downstream for a good 3/4 mile more and come to a large culvert which we once walked through. This is in the area of a housing development but if we stay down along the stream, none of the sense of the primitive is lost. If water running through the culvert prevents us from using it, we climb the steps on the left, cross the street and find a trail down to the stream below the culvert. Expect some problems in getting on the trail along the stream. We may elect to walk the sidewalk then down (south) on Palisades Drive, about one-half a mile to an entrance to Santa Ynez Canyon Park. Turn west into the Park. Follow the trail along the stream to the obscure crossing and the beginning of the "Wirebreak". Better yet go with someone who has recent experience with the trail conditions. Come out of the culvert on the left side of the stream and continue for about 450 yards, at which time look very closely for the trail on the other side of the stream that leads up to the firebreak. A help in locating this is a power line that goes up the middle of the firebreak.

The "wirebreak," so called because of the power line nearby, is 800 feet of elevation gain in less than 1/2 mile — just continuous uphill misery. Once on top, however, the road that we find is level by comparison. Turn right and follow this East Topanga Fireroad for about 3 miles to a junction where the road drops down to Trippet Ranch.

This section affords a view overlooking both Topanga Canyon on the west and Santa Ynez Canyon on the east as well as an ocean view to the south.

The variety on this hike is emphatic: oak grassland, chaparral, and riparian woodland; pristine wilderness bordered by a housing development; canyon depths and lofty ridge viewpoints; strenuous exertion and relaxed enjoyment — a full range of experience.

SANTA YNEZ CANYON WATERFALL

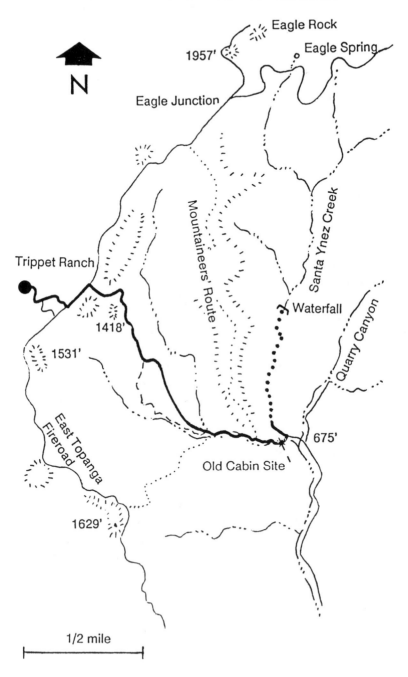

Eagle Rock

1957'

Eagle Spring

Eagle Junction

N

Mountaineers' Route

Santa Ynez Creek

Trippet Ranch

Waterfall

1418'

1531'

Quarry Canyon

675'

East Topanga Fireroad

Old Cabin Site

1629'

1/2 mile

HIKE 56   UPPER SANTA YNEZ CANYON

to the waterfalls
from Trippet Ranch

Maps:	SMMTS. East
Distance:	6 miles roundtrip
Elevation:	1100' gain and loss
Terrain:	Combination fireroad, trail, and steep ridge
Time:	3 hours
Trailhead:	Trippet Ranch

On Highway 27 just north of the town of Topanga, turn east on Entrada Road. Once on Entrada Road turn left at every street intersection, 1.1 miles to the entrance of Topanga State Park. Park your car.

From the east end of the parking lot take the trail past the right of the white brick building. Turn right on the Nature Trail and wind uphill through the woods. This trail goes across a grassy area that has a succession of attractive flowering plants every spring: Blue-eyed Grass, Owl Clover, Brodiaea, and Violet.

At the top of the hill turn left on the fireroad and continue uphill until the basalt knoll on the right is passed, then turn right and start down into Santa Ynez Canyon. This section of the trail is in the area burned over in November 1977. The chaparral was temporarily replaced by other vegetation: Mustard, Morning Glory, Filaree, Horehound, Wild Cucumber, Bush Lupine, Tree Tobacco, and many other flowering plants. Chaparral is reclaiming its territory and will dominate the hillsides. About half mile down the trail start looking for a side trail on the left, just after coming down a steep grade on a reddish-tinged sandstone. (It isn't well-marked and can be missed.) Take this side trail and descend along a rocky ridge.

Soap Plant (Amole) is everywhere along the ridge. Six foot tall plants bloom in May and June, the flowers opening in late afternoon. Farther down the trail, the ridge is covered by deerweed, which grows very thick after a fire. As the chaparral returns, the deerweed disappears to a great extent. The sandstone ridge dips steeply to the west, about 45°. The south end of the sandstone ridge has a number of round sandstone inclusions.

A couple of trails leave the ridge and drop down to the trail in the canyon to the west, or we may continue south on the ridge.

Upon rejoining the original trail down in the canyon, turn left. We are instantly in a new environment of Oak, Sycamore, and Walnut trees; Blackberries and Currants line the trail. About 500 yards down the trail are some caves in the cliff on the right. The wall of the canyon is very steep in this part of the Santa Ynez. If we look to the right we will see beautiful examples of conglomerate rock. To the left in about 200 yards and obscured by chaparral are two rock chimneys, all that remain of an old cabin site. The trail forks farther downstream. Take the left fork and go upstream.

Follow a trail upstream for about 3/4 mile. We will cross the stream several times — and may even run out of trail on occasion, because every storm brings down new sand and gravel and makes a few changes. By staying close to the stream we will come to some waterfalls. That is the objective of this segment of the hike. Eventually, rock-climbing ability and equipment are needed to proceed. This is a good place to turn around, retracing our steps to return to the roadhead.

A couple of variations in the route are available: (1) Instead of taking the ridge trail above the sandstone cliff, we can stay on the main trail and follow it all the way to the fireroad that leads to Trippet Ranch. (2) A bushwhack trail goes steeply up the ridge to the north, starting just a few yards west of the two chimneys. (3) An indistinct trail branches from the main trail about 400 yards west of the two chimneys and goes uphill on the left, heading southwest. This overgrown trail starts through a thick stand of Poison Oak, gains 900 feet, and tops-out on the East Topanga Fireroad. The trail is almost impossible to find because of the overgrown vegetation. Variations (2) and (3) are seldom explored. We would need to wear gloves, goggles, long sleeves and other protection.

Santa Ynez Waterfall

EAGLE SPRING, TEMESCAL FIREROAD, SANTA YNEZ CANYON LOOP

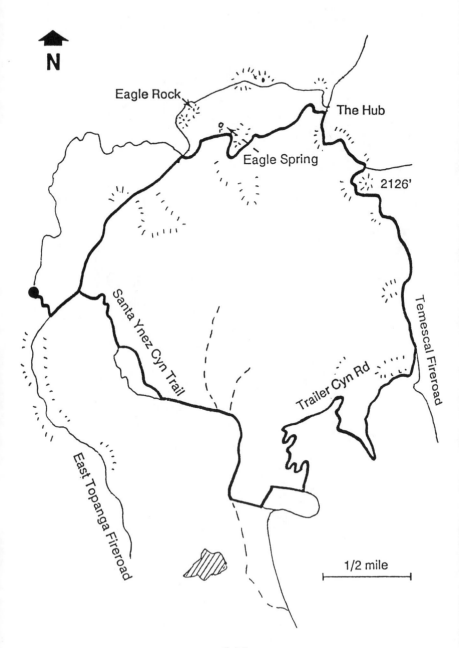

N

Eagle Rock

The Hub

Eagle Spring

2126'

Santa Ynez Cyn Trail

Temescal Fireroad

Trailer Cyn Rd

East Topanga Fireroad

1/2 mile

HIKE 57

Temescal Fireroad
Trailer Canyon
Santa Ynez Canyon Loop
from Trippet Ranch

Maps: SMMTS, East
Distance: 10 miles roundtrip
Elevation: 1800' gain and loss
Terrain: Fireroad and trail
Time: 4 hours 20 minutes
Trailhead: Trippet Ranch

On Highway 27 just north of the town of Topanga turn east on Entrada Road. Once on Entrada Road, turn left at every street intersection. It is 1.1 miles to the entrance of Topanga State Park. Park your car.

From the east end of the parking lot follow a trail up the hill on the right. Go a quarter mile to an intersection called the "Latitude" to a sign labelled "Backbone Trail." Turn left onto the Eagle Spring Road, go 1½ miles to another road junction (Eagle Junction), take either road. The road to the left gains some elevation right away and gets up on a ridge overlooking Garapito Canyon on the north and Santa Ynez Canyon on the south. The road to the right drops down to Eagle Spring. Either the upper road or the lower road is the same distance between Eagle Junction and "The Hub" — 1.4 miles. Four roads join at The Hub — Fireroad 30 coming south from Mulholland Drive, north loop Eagle Road, south loop Eagle Road, and Temescal Fireroad. If this loop trip is to take 4 hours and 20 minutes we should reach The Hub in 1 hour from the start of the hike, and are due for a ten minute rest. An interesting resting spot is in the "Cathedral Rock" area two minutes south on Temescal Fireroad.

Cathedral Rock may be reached by going past it on the road, then by cutting to the left and back, going up a steep slope to a gap in the rocks. The atmosphere within Cathedral Rock is one of feeling snug, serenely comfortable, secure. You can quickly change this aura by going to the edge of the cliff and looking onto Rustic Canyon. The view of Rustic is an unusual display of steep chaparral covered slopes in a near primitive state, wild and beautiful country that will be seen closer on other hikes.

The junction with Rogers Road is 10 minutes south on Temescal Fireroad. 100 yards farther is a firebreak on the left that goes up to Peak 2126, the highest point in Topanga State Park. Continuing on, we see a short spur road on the right that goes to Peak 2036. a sign nearby states "T.S.P. 4 miles." Continue south on Temescal Fireroad another half mile, to a road junction on the right.

Trailer Canyon Road leads us down into Santa Ynez Canyon. Trailer Canyon Road winds around a lot on the way down to Santa Ynez Canyon and drops 1300'. The road bottoms out in a housing area.

Overlooking Rustic Canyon from Cathedral Rock

244

Turn right on Michael Lane, following it several hundred yards until reaching a cross street, Vereda De La Montura. Turn right and follow it to the streambed.

A well-used trail goes upstream, gently for awhile, about a mile. There are several caves in the sandstone cliffs on both sides of the stream. A trail forks to the right going up quarry canyon. Stay to the left at this fork and the next one also. The trail follows the west fork of the stream through a dense riparian woodland until it makes an abrupt right turn and goes uphill steeply. Within 100 feet the trail is out of the canyon environment and in chaparral. The trail is steep uphill for an 800' gain in about a mile.

Upon reaching the Eagle Spring Road, turn left and return to the parking lot.

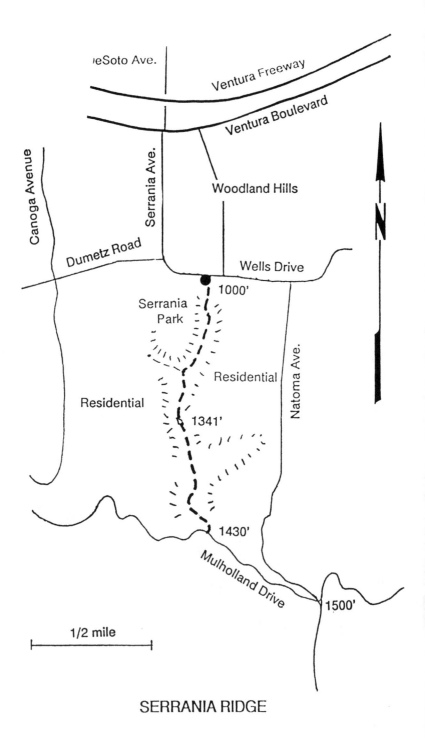

SERRANIA RIDGE

HIKE 58

to Mulholland Drive
from Serrania Park (loop)

Maps:	SMMTS, East
Distance:	2½ miles roundtrip
Elevation:	500' gain and loss
Terrain:	Road and trail
Time:	1 hour
Trailhead:	Serrania Park

This short hike is suitable for all degrees of hiking ability. It doesn't take us completely away from the city but does give us an opportunity to absorb some of the feeling of open space.

In Woodland Hills drive south of Ventura Blvd. on Serrania to the end to wells drive; park on the right.

The hike starts by going south along the ridge at the east side of Serrania Park.

Follow the fence along the east side of the Park until we come to a break. Leave the Park through the hole in the fence and continue south. The initial climb is rather steep, then the trail follows the ridge with some ups and downs. About ten minutes out puts us on a knoll that has a trail coming up from the left. Continue on, until reaching another cross-trail coming up from the left. At this point go left, staying on the ridge as it changes direction occasionally, until reaching Mulholland Drive — the turnaround point. The trail splits two times on this section of the ridge, but in both cases rejoins.

After turning around, return the way we came. It is possible to get on the wrong trail coming back so pay close attention going out.

EAGLE SPRING LOOP
by way of Fireroad 30

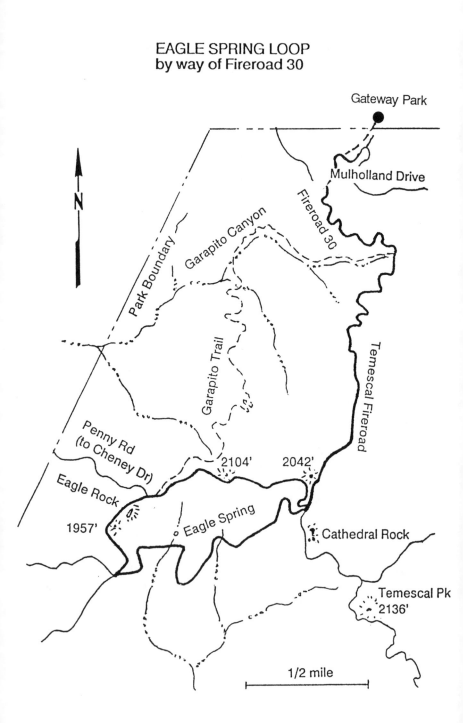

Gateway Park

Mulholland Drive

Fireroad 30

N

Park Boundary

Garapito Canyon

Garapito Trail

Temescal Fireroad

Penny Rd
(to Cheney Dr)

Eagle Rock

1957'

2104'

2042'

Eagle Spring

Cathedral Rock

Temescal Pk
2136'

1/2 mile

HIKE 59

EAGLE SPRING LOOP

by way of Fireroad 30
from Gateway Park

Maps:	SMMTS, East
Distance:	8 miles roundtrip
Elevation:	1100' gain and loss
Terrain:	Fireroad
Time:	3¼ hours
Trailhead:	Mulholland Drive

This is a trip in Topanga State Park that is on a fireroad and trail all the way, and although steep in a few places is a good introductory hike.

Drive to Marvin Braude Mulholland Gateway Park.. This is at the south end of Reseda Boulevard.

Go uphill from the Park on a dirt road. In about two hundred feet we will turn right onto a narrow trail contouring up to Mulholland Drive — a dirt road. Turn right and hike to fireroad 30 entrance to Topanga State Park. Walk around the fireroad gate south onto Fireroad 30 and go two miles until coming to The "Hub," an intersection of four roads. Of the three choices available take the one on the immediate right and go uphill. We will soon be on an east-west ridge that separates Garapito Canyon on the north from Santa Ynez Canyon on the south. On a reasonably clear day look south to see Santa Monica Bay and the coast line all the way to Palos Verdes Peninsula. If using a compass, Santa Catalina Island is 180° true (166° magnetic) from the ridge. On the clearest day of the year we might see the rather small Santa Barbara Island and San Nicolas Island farther out.

Continue west along the ridge. Penny Road comes in on the right and is another way of entering Topanga State Park. Just beyond this road but on the left is Eagle Rock, overlooking upper Santa Ynez Canyon. A short side trip will take us to the top of the rock, its sculptured caves, and the impressive view of the valley below.

Continue on the fireroad going downhill until reaching Eagle Spring Junction. Turn left and continue downhill toward Eagle Spring. Eagle Rock looms high overhead, dominating upper Santa Ynez Canyon with its imposing mass and exposed cliffs. Eagle Spring is announced by a sign on the left. The spring itself is upstream a short distance by trail. Beautiful patches of Poison Oak thrive in the area. A portable "Andy Gump" restroom is currently alongside the road.

Continue on the fireroad as it contours through the chaparral toward Hub Junction. The elevation gain is moderate, 400 feet in a little more than a mile. As we near The "Hub" we can see a lofty crag on the ridge to the right. "Cathedral Rock" holds a sheltered recess within its protective walls that makes an excellent lunch stop. This is south on the Temescal Fireroad and not on the loop of this hike, but does make an interesting short side trip.

At The Hub go north on Fireroad 30, retracing our steps for the two miles back to Mulholland. The walk is pleasant along this ridge road with the isolation of Rustic Canyon to the east and Garapito Canyon to the west. From here we walk the half mile to our cars.

Eagle Rock

HIKE 60

GARAPITO CANYON LOOP
by way of Fireroad 30
from Gateway Park

Maps:	SMMTS, East
Distance:	7½ miles roundtrip
Elevation:	1300' loss and gain
Time:	3½ hours
Trailhead:	Mulholland Drive

Garapito Canyon is steep, rugged and beautiful. Sierra Club volunteers began building a trail from Fireroad 30 in 1985 and completed it late in 1987.

Go to the Marvin Braude Mulholland Gateway Park at the south end of Reseda Boulevard. Hike uphill from the Park on a dirt road to turn right onto a narrow trail that contours up to Mulholland Drive. Turn right and hike to Fireroad 30. Walk around the fireroad. gate and go 1/2 mile to a point where some power lines cross. The trail into upper Garapito Canyon is on the right and begins here. Cross a small meadow then abruptly enter dense chaparral. The entire canyon last burned in 1961 and the chaparral has had time to fully recover. Trail building in l985 opened sunlit corridors so that dormant seeds that have lain in the duff since the l961 fire recovery period, could sprout. The spring of 1986 ushered in a riot of Giant Phacelia, Mustard Evening Primrose, Contorted Evening Primrose, White Pincushion, Yellow Monkey Flower, and other fire-following plants along the trail.

In the more than 500 feet of elevation loss, the trail takes us through a lot of Chaparral and occasional patches of Coastal Sage Scrub. Whenever we are near the streambed we will see Sycamores, and at one place several Cottonwoods. Geologically, the streambed and ravines are the Coal Canyon Formation, a marine sequence of sandstone, siltstone, and pebbly conglomerate that was laid down during late Paleocene and Eocene times, 60-50 million years ago. The trail crosses the main streambed, goes up and around a shoulder, and back down to a stretch along the

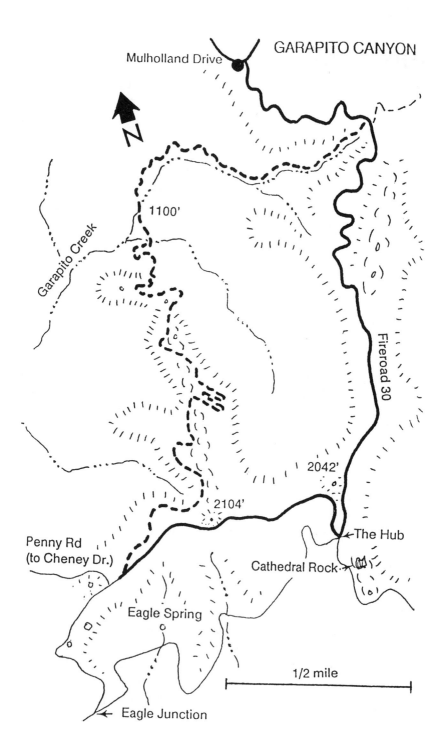

GARAPITO CANYON

Mulholland Drive

N

1100'

Garapito Creek

Fireroad 30

2042'

2104'

Penny Rd
(to Cheney Dr.)

The Hub

Cathedral Rock

Eagle Spring

1/2 mile

← Eagle Junction

stream to an oak grove. At this point we have walked about 2-3/4 miles from the trailhead — take a rest — we are about to start uphill, gaining 700 feet in the next mile and a half. A massive buttress, or ridge, drops down from Peak 2104 to our present location in the canyon. The trail works its way up the ridge at a comfortable walking grade, making switchbacks as it goes. Along one section of the lower trail we look across an arroyo at a spectacular conglomerate cliff. Later on after a couple of switchbacks, we find ourselves above and near the edge of the cliff. This hike offers lots of excuses to stop and rest. The panorama below unrolls continuously as we climb through the most dense mature Chaparral in the area. (I was going to say "in the world" but that may not be true.) We continue upward and get an idea that the crest is near when we go through some open spaces of California Buckwheat.

Upon reaching Eagle Spring Loop road, turn left. We might elect to go on a short side trip to the top of Eagle Rock from this point. If so we turn right, walk slightly uphill 650 feet, then walk over a rise on the east and climb the backside of Eagle Rock. The view of Santa Ynez Canyon, to the south, and the ocean is dramatic. The fireroad toward Trippet Ranch and East Topanga Fireroad are visible and so is more of the southern half of the Park. Look for Silver Lotus plants in bloom from March through June, growing in cracks in the sandstone of Eagle Rock.

The route out is east to the "Hub," about 1 mile from where Penny Road intersects Eagle Spring Loop road. Enroute we pass the highest point on today's hike near Peak 2104. Look at the road near the peak; the pattern of the rock is caused by the slow cooling of molten lava as it intruded through cracks into the sandstone about 15 million years ago. This lava is called diabase — we've given it the common name "Onion Rock" because it exfoliates concentrically somewhat like an onion would. At the "Hub," turn left and walk 2-1/2 miles to our cars at the Gateway Park.

UPPER RUSTIC CANYON
and BAY TREE TRAIL

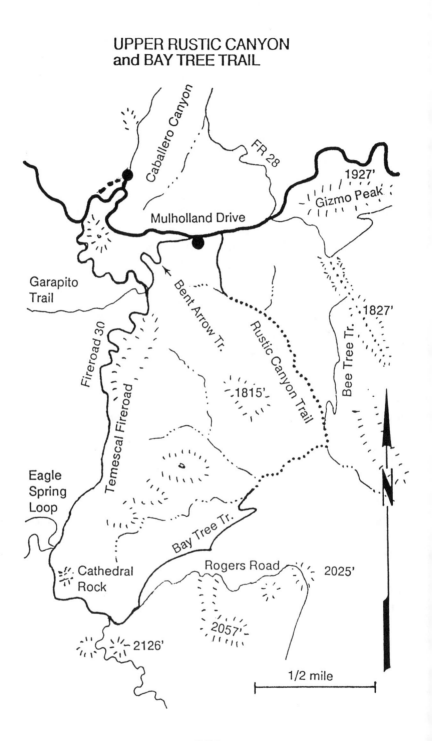

Caballero Canyon

FR 28

1927'
Gizmo Peak

Mulholland Drive

Garapito
Trail

Bent Arrow Tr.

Rustic Canyon Trail

Bee Tree Tr.

1827'

Fireroad 30

Temescal Fireroad

1815'

Eagle
Spring
Loop

Bay Tree Tr.

Cathedral
Rock

Rogers Road

2025'

2057'

2126'

N

1/2 mile

HIKE 61

UPPER RUSTIC CANYON

via Rustic Canyon Trail,
Bay Tree Trail, Rogers
Road & Fireroad 30
from Gateway Park

Maps:	SMMTS, East
Distance:	7¼ miles roundtrip
Elevation:	1300' loss and gain
Terrain:	Trail, streambed, and fireroad
Time:	3¾ hours
Trailhead:	Mulholland Drive

This "Rustic Ramble" presents a challenge to our trail finding ability in getting out of the canyon. We should expect to spend some extra time looking for the trail, so it's best to do this hike on a day when we are not on a precise schedule.

Drive to Marvin Braude Mulholland Gateway Park. This is at the south end of Reseda Boulevard. Go uphill from the Park on a dirt road until reaching Mulholland. Turn left and hike east on Mulholland past the Bent Arrow Trail on our right. Turn right on a very steep trail down into Rustic Canyon. If we have doubts as to the trail, look at a telephone pole across the road. It is number 112509M. Upper Rustic Canyon, being rugged and isolated, is seldom visited so we will be walking along a trail overgrown with brush, and rough spots underfoot.

After about 500 yards of very steep, "brushy" trail we will reach a streambed where we will turn left. Get ready for some boulder hopping. Rustic Canyon is full of rocks that resemble small "blackboard slates," "giant speckled eggs, " some "concrete" rocks, but no "spaghetti" rocks. Also look for tracks made by raccoon, coyote, and deer. Common with most streambed travel in these mountains is the fact that every storm changes the terrain so that last year's sandy trail can be this year's mosaic of boulders. The elevation drop along this intermittent stream is gentle and presents few hazards to travel. Twenty-five minutes after first reaching the stream we will come to another streambed entering from the right. This West Fork is the first major stream joining from the west, and although it is a significant stream it is possible to pass it by because of the trees and brush growing in the canyon.

Turn right and go upstream in the bed of the West Fork for nine minutes. At this point on the left (south) a trail goes up the steep hillside and heads southwest. As the beginning of this trail may be difficult to spot, I'll give my clues. It is about 750 yards from the fork in the stream where we turned right (but seems much farther). We will have passed an overgrown arroyo that enters from the north. The trail shows up soon after we make a right turn coming up the streambed. Two rows of rocks on the left give a hint of the trail and it seems enough. Overshooting is no problem — just come back. A crew of volunteers on maintenance work renamed it the "Bay Tree Trail," and it is justly named.

Follow the trail up through Sycamore, Oak, and Bay. Oh, that Bay!! If you have never experienced the clean pungent smell of fresh Bay leaves, you are due for a treat. Some call it Laurel. In Oregon it is Myrtlewood, but by any name you will long remember the scent of Bay. Take a deep breath because this trail will gain over 800 feet in not much more than a mile, mostly under a verdant canopy of leaves. Soon we will pass a spring — not gushing, but more of a seepage. Once a cup hung on the tree and the water was drinkable, but the cup is gone and leaves have settled into the small basin. We leave the water for coyotes. Later we will discover a sheltered recess that is sanctuary for a trickling stream. The vegetation changes as elevation is gained, and the charm of sylvan enchantment gradually shifts to views of rugged terrain. In fall and winter, dotting the slopes across the canyon are orange-red splashes of Toyon berries on a palette of green chaparral. On the skyline to the west the craggy outline of Cathedral Rock comes into view. Embracing the trail on either side, and adding to its enchantment, are the Holly-leaf Cherries, commonly called Islay. This big-seeded sweet cherry ripens late in the summer along this trail and is a favorite food of the coyotes. It is rare but there is also some Chaparral Currant along this trail. During the summer the Chaparral Currant drops its leaves in order to conserve moisture; but watch what happens a couple of weeks after the first fall rain — look for bare twigs with rose-colored flowers. Thanksgiving is an interesting time of year to be on this trail. The Chaparral Currant is pushing spring — and fall is hardly over. Now, continue climbing the trail until reaching Rogers Road, then turn right.

As we head west on Rogers Road, notice the beginning of Temescal Canyon on the left. Only a small part of Temescal Canyon is in view, but I mention it because on this hike we will be at the headwaters of five different watersheds: Temescal, Santa Ynez, Garapito — which drains into Topanga — Caballero, and Rustic. After a short uphill walk on Rogers Road the route joins Temescal Fireroad at the crest of the ridge. We should then turn right and walk north. A third of a mile northwest on this relatively level fireroad, look to your right for an imposing rock formation. "Cathedral Rock" dominates this part of the ridge and is an ideal lunch stop. The easiest way is to walk up the steep southwest slope through a gap in the rocks into a sheltered amphitheater that can comfortably hold a group of 25-50 people (if you're very good friends). The view to the east from this massive hard coarse conglomerate rocky crag is spectacular. The entire panorama of the first part of the hike is spread out below and the ruggedness of upper Rustic Canyon is impressive.

Now that our hunger has been satisfied, and our pack lightened a bit, continue north on the fireroad and upon reaching Hub Junction go straight ahead toward Mulholland Drive. The road stays on the ridge separating Garapito Canyon on the west from Rustic Canyon on the east. We hike the 2 miles to Mulholland, turn right and keep our eyes peeled for a trail on the left taking us to our cars.

GEOLOGICAL COMMENT

On this trip we see a variety of geological features that could be of interest to the casual observer as well as to the serious geologist.

With the exception of the first part of the hike coming down to the streambed, all of Upper Rustic Canyon and the trail to the Temescal Fireroad is on Santa Monica slate, a dark-gray to black rock that was formed 150 million years ago during the jurassic epoch. Subsequent granitic intrusions into the Santa Monica Slate are not in evidence in the canyon but some granite boulders could have eroded from the granitic outcropping just east of Gizmo Peak (Pk 1960).

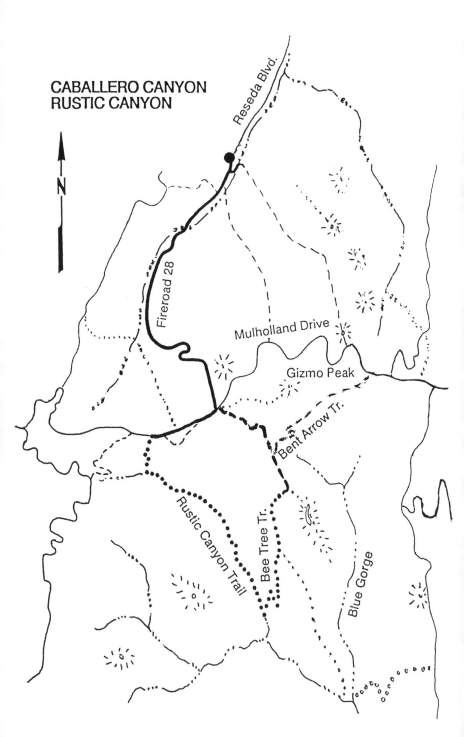

CABALLERO CANYON
RUSTIC CANYON

N

Reseda Blvd.

Fireroad 28

Mulholland Drive

Gizmo Peak

Bent Arrow Tr.

Rustic Canyon Trail

Bee Tree Tr.

Blue Gorge

HIKE 62

CABALLERO CANYON
RUSTIC CANYON
from Tarzana (loop)

Maps:	SMMTS, East
Distance:	6 miles roundtrip
Elevation:	1200' gain and loss
Terrain:	Trail, streambed, and fireroad
Time:	3 hours
Trailhead:	Reseda Blvd. at Caballero Trail

In Tarzana drive south on Reseda Boulevard. After passing Paseo Nuevo Drive on the right and El Caballero Country Club on the left, park along Reseda.

Our trail is on the east side of Reseda and heads south at an angle toward the creek. We join a trail that once was Fireroad 28 and follow it about one and a half miles to Mulholland Drive. In at least one place the old road has been washed out so the trail dips down to the streambed and then back up. At this same area the Pipeline Trail goes up a ridge on the right to Mulholland. The Pipeline Trail has been modified, making it easier to hike and is part of a loop trail with the one we are on.

Upon reaching Mulholland turn left momentarily and take the eastern section of the Bent Arrow Trail, starting on the other side of the road. This trail takes us uphill on the south side of Gizmo Peak on a ten to fifteen minute walk to a north and south ridge. Turn right and follow the ridge for about 400 yards hiking up and down about three small knolls. Up ahead we spot a larger knoll. We do not go there but look to our right for a sloping open area. Bee Tree Trail starts at the west end of the open area. Don't expect a sign at the trail. Because this trail is hard to find without a map, it is not used often. It is steep and not maintained but this isn't all bad, we have lots of branches to hang onto on the steep slope. We will descend more than six-hundred feet in three quarters of a mile.

When we reach the streambed the chaparral, mostly ceanothus, gives way to Oak and Sycamore. In the spring we will look for Bush Monkey Flower, Blue Larkspur, Clarkias, and several species of ferns and a lot more native plants. We pick our way carefully upstream, avoiding Poison Oak and other brush. Each winter a few trees fall and add to the navigational interest. Even the Bee Tree fell several years ago and has deteriorated — the bees have gone but the name lives on. We could sit in shade and have a snack or lunch. Before leaving we might call for a "split break".

The upstream segment is slow going; some of our speed may depend upon how dry the streambed is and if winter rains have rearranged the canyon bottom. To me rustic Canyon is a great place to be. I am in no hurry to leave. Someone else must have had the same feeling many years ago. On a level spot about fifteen feet up from the east bank we can find the remains of an old cabin. I would like to know the history. As we may have noticed the rock formations on the canyon walls are of a black-grey slate, the bed-rock of the Santa Monica Mountains. 'Blue Gorge" downstream of today's hike and difficult to beat our way into is of Santa Monica Slate. It is not really blue but when wet it might have a blue tint. But would you go to a place called "Gray Gorge"? Santa Monica Slate is the first sedimentary deposit made on the ocean floor 190 to 135 million years ago, during the Jurassic Period. Nowhere in the Santa Monica Mountains is the original ocean floor exposed.

To continue uptrail we keep in mind that even though it seems longer (thank goodness) we have but one mile before reaching Mulholland from the bottom of the Bee Tree Trail. Someone could keep track of time and near twenty-five minutes of upstream travel should alert us to watching for a chance to turn right into a narrow sidestream. The trail we are looking for is well-defined about one hundred feet into the side canyon. It is possible to miss the canyon, and if we find ourselves heading west with a steep light-colored rock slide up ahead, we've gone too far.

Once on the trail out of the streambed we come to the steepest trail of the hike. One of the best aerobic exercises around. In ten minutes we are on Mulholland. Turn right, walk five minutes to Caballero Trail (Fireroad 28), turn left and head for the parked cars.

HIKE 63

BAY TREE/
BEE TREE TRAIL Loop
from Gateway Park

Maps:	SMMTS, East
Distance:	8 miles
Elevation:	1600' loss and gain
Terrain:	trail, streambed, and fireroad
Time:	2¼ hours
Trailhead:	Gateway Park

We have hiked upper Rustic Canyon by coming downstream and by going upstream. Now we will cross the canyon when we enter it from the west by dropping down the Bay Tree Trail and exiting east climbing out on the Bee Tree Trail. Almost half a century ago, with a great deal of foresight, Los Angeles County Sanitation District bought both Rustic and Sullivan Canyons. The purpose, of course, was to provide convenient garbage disposal facilities. The good news is that we now have some of the most remote backcountry hiking in the Santa Monica Mountains, all within reasonable range of millions of people eager for the outdoor experience. Credit goes to our Sanitation District. They have planned well and in a sense have prevented a development of this great recreation area. Who would build in or near a future garbage dump? The bad news is the possibility of a garbage dump in these two canyons exists. So today we will get some exercise and visit a spectacular, remote area seldom visited.

Quite often "Dirt Mulholland" is often closed to automobile traffic so we start our hike on Reseda Boulevard. This adds a half mile each way — but it is a pleasant half mile. Go to the Marvin Braude Mulholland Gateway Park at the south end of Reseda Boulevard. Hike uphill from the Park on a dirt road and turn right on a narrow trail that contours up to Mulholland Drive. Turn right and hike to Fireroad 30. Walk around the gate and go south to the "Hub", a distance of two and a half miles from Gateway Park.

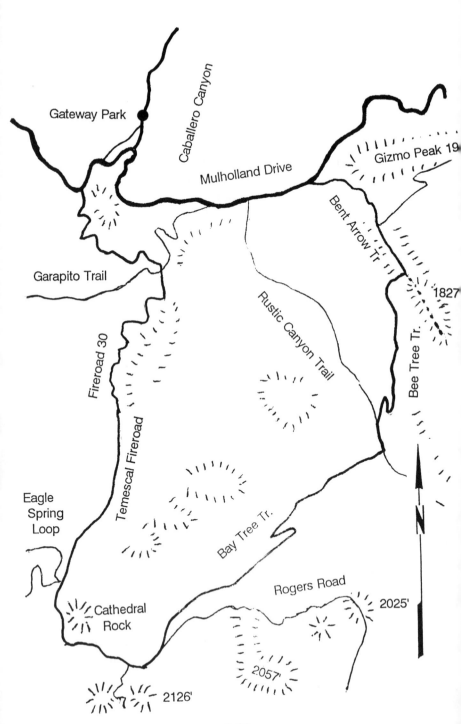

Gateway Park

Caballero Canyon

Mulholland Drive

Gizmo Peak 19

Bent Arrow Tr.

Garapito Trail

Rustic Canyon Trail

1827

Bee Tree Tr.

Fireroad 30

Temescal Fireroad

N

Eagle
Spring
Loop

Bay Tree Tr.

Rogers Road

2025'

Cathedral
Rock

2057'

2126'

We look east for a great view of the canyon of today's hike. A bulletin board and a portable "outhouse" are the only signs of the "Hub's" civilization. We will not see any of either until the hike is over.

Continuing south we pass Cathedral Rock on the left. We look for a low perennial shrub growing on the rocks. Silver lotus is worthy of note because it is rare in our mountains. From March to June we can look for the 3/8 inch long pea-like yellow floweers. This entire hike is through a chaparral plant community, with the exception of streamside environments. Chaparral (ceanothus, chamise, manzanita, mountain mahogany, scrub oak, and laurel sumac as well as many small shrubs) will normally use all the water and sunshine available so that many other plants cannot gain a foothold. Alongside roads and trails where a strip of bare space occurs, some flowering plants can take hold. We are likely to see Bush Poppies and Lupine along Temescal Motorway and in a few minutes upon turning left onto Rogers Road will see Bush Monkey flowers. Two or three hundred yards easterly on Rogers Road down in a saddle look for the head of Temescal Canyon on the right and the beginning of Bay Tree Trail on our left. Walking down Bay Tree is a delight. Much of it is in shade on a north facing slope. We will see a wide variety of flowers in the spring. Larkspur, Clarkia, Lupine, Fiesta flower; all worth coming to look for. In late summer we find Holly-leaf cherries. They are mostly seed but the flavor is good. Down in the canyon I know of a place where I can pick a cup of blackberries. In late November Chaparral Currant begins to bloom about the time the leaves come out. Currant, as many chaparral plants, have a winter growing season and a summer dormant season.

We will see a spring near the bottom of the trail. More of a seepage than a spring, but enough water for a deer or coyote. Upon reaching the West Fork stream we follow it for about three - eighths of a mile where it reaches Rustic Creek. We turn left and in eight minutes will see the Bee Tree Trail on the right. It is a trail not seeing much use at present and only occasional volunteer maintenance, so we aren't going to expect too much from it. The bee tree that once gave us a guide to the trail, has fallen down and deteriorated. Bee Tree Trail is steep. We will gain 650' in three quarters of a mile, which does include some level walking.

At the top of the trail turn left onto the ridge and follow it over a few knolls, but as we approach Gizmo Peak notice a section of the Bent Arrow Trail and turn left to follow it to Mulholland. We follow Mulholland to the west for about one mile and turn right to go down the road to our parked cars. We will be careful to go a full mile, and not turn too soon. Fireroad 28 would take us down Caballero Canyon and not to Gateway Park.

HIKE 64

"LEMMING" HIKE

San Fernando Valley to the
ocean via Caballero Canyon,
Bent Arrow Trail, Eagle Rock,
East Topanga Fireroad, and
a chaparral ridge (shuttle)

Maps:	SMMTS, East
Distance:	15 miles one way
Elevation:	2000' gain
	2900' loss
Terrain:	Trail, fireroad, streambed, chaparral bushwhacking.
Time:	7 hours
Trailhead:	Reseda Blvd.

The concept of a "Lemming Hike" is rather lightly based on the lemmings' mad dash to the sea where they swim out and drown. There are no lemmings in the Santa Monicas, but the hike simulates the senseless rush to the sea that lemmings might take, were there any.

Several challenges are presented: finding the way requires close attention to the directions; 15 miles on a variety of terrain requires physical stamina; and dropping down through a dense, virtually impenetrable chaparral while losing 1600 feet of altitude is no picnic. A difficult hike.

This is a one way trip so a car shuttle is necessary. We should leave some transportation at Topanga Beach, where the hike ends. Proceed to the beginning of the hike by crossing the mountains on Highway 27. Upon reaching Ventura Blvd, turn right and drive east into Tarzana; turn right on Reseda Blvd. and travel south to the end where we will park our cars.

From this point we take a trail south onto what was once Fireroad 28 but is now a trail — the Caballero Canyon Trail. About fifteen minutes into the hike a part of the group is likely to stay on Fireroad 28 while another part breaks away and will hike a modified version of the Pipeline Trail. All to meet on Mulholland to continue

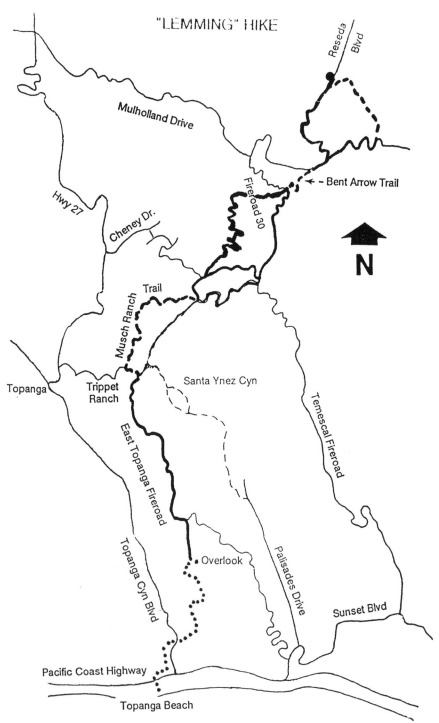

"LEMMING" HIKE

Reseda Blvd

Mulholland Drive

Hwy 27

Cheney Dr.

Fireroad 30

← Bent Arrow Trail

N

Musch Ranch Trail

Topanga

Trippet Ranch

Santa Ynez Cyn

Temescal Fireroad

East Topanga Fireroad

• Overlook

Palisades Drive

Sunset Blvd

Topanga Cyn Blvd

Pacific Coast Highway

Topanga Beach

west, turning left onto the Bent Arrow Trail. The Bent Arrow contours along the steep south-facing slope of a peak until reaching Fireroad 30. At this juncture the more adventuresoms part of the group crosses the road onto the Garapito Canyon Trail while the remainder turns left to follow on Fireroad 30 for one and a half miles to the "Hub" while gaining 400 feet. That group will split again, some taking the low road past Eagle Spring, the others hiking the high road past Eagle rock. Both meeting (in theory) at the Eagle Spring Junction. Two routes to Trippet Ranch are available at this point: one, stay on the fireroad; the other, turn right and hike the two miles to Trippet Ranch and lunch. Meanwhile the Garapito Canyon group exits on the high road and travels to Eagle Spring Junction where they may split; one group staying on the fireroad, the other hiking down Musch Ranch Trail.

In order for this to function well we have some constraints: two qualified leaders must be in each group. That means we must have four leaders in each group for it to divide. Nearly always we come into Trippet in four different groups. We have eight leaders scheduled for our annual "Lemming Hike".

I have some comments about the different views on the various trails. Garapito Canyon Trail was built by the Sierra Club Volunteers, some of whom are avid leaders in the Santa Monicas. One is likely to hear tales told on this segment by people who helped build the trail. Some of the tales might be true. Design and construction of this trail is absolutely astounding. Spectacular views and exceptional trail building seem to be the average for this volunteer team.

The high road is about one and a third miles long and at one spot is the highest point of this hike. Look at the road under our feet to note a geometric pattern of volcanic rock. This diabase is a 15 to 12 million year intrusion into the land when it was under the sea. Slow cooling of lava allowed large crystal-like formations. Now exposed and with the release of intensive pressure it exfoliates like an onion so we call it "Onion Rock". The sandstone "Eagle Rock" is also along this section of trail. We can take fifteen minutes out for a side trip and climb the back side if we choose. Each trail segment has its merits, and each group has incidents to relay when we meet for lunch.

After lunch the entire group stays together as a unit until we reach Topanga Beach. Upon leaving Trippet Ranch our route is

East Topanga Fireroad. The road follows along the crest of the ridge east of Topanga Canyon. We are presented a precipitous view of the angular rock canyon 1000 feet below. Santa Ynez Canyon is on the east side of the ridge and offers a few of massive sandstone slabs tilted on edge down in the canyon next to the stream. We continue south until reaching a branch road or firebreak on the right. We take this road to a prominence called "The Overlook", aptly described as it overlooks the ocean and canyons and sprawling Los Angeles.

It is worthwhile in terms of future comfort and peace of mind to carefully scan the terrain to the south and plan the route, because later when deep in chaparral, your attitude may lack the serenity and composure that is possible now. The route down from this point is on a deer trail that begins at a high point about 100 yards northwest of the Overlook. The route heads 200° magnetic for about 1/4 mile, at which point there is a choice of dropping down to one of the two ridges. Nearly always we turn too soon and find ourselves on an extremely steep slope that drops down to Parker Canyon — a place we want to avoid. Force yourself to continue on the 200° heading and when reaching a somewhat level area look for a trail on the left. By heading 120° magnetic you will drop to the left ridge. Between these two ridges is a canyon that is going to be the exit route to Highway 27 and the sea. There is a semblance of a trail on the left ridge, so head for it and expect to find it at the base of the steepest part of the slope just as the ridge becomes gently sloping. Follow the trail south along the top of the ridge watching very closely for a trail on the right that cuts back sharply and heads down to the creekbed. The trail disappears so we bushwhack. This area has been completely overgrown in the last year or two making it impossible to follow a trail. Getting to the creekbed is a matter of staying on the high part of the small ridge leading to the stream but the chaparral is severe and you are tired.

If it becomes impossible to get through, go back to the north-south ridge and a local trail does exist. Go south toward the community of Parker Mesa and a steep down-climb puts us on Shoreheights Drive if the hole in the cyclone fence hasn't been repaired. Avoid private property; dogs are nervous and people are sensitive.

If we've come this far the rest is easy. Cross PCH at the light and walk to our cars.

If you don't use the escape route, once in the creekbed continue downstream until reaching Highway 27, then cross the road and head for the beach. The only rule left for all true "lemmings" is that you must enter the water to some degree. It is not necessary that you go all out and try to swim someplace; you may just take off your boots and wade a little.

Complete the car shuttle
don't leave any stragglers on the beach — and we have completed another great, long day!

HIKE 65

CABALLERO CANYON

Maps:	SMMTS, East
Terrain:	Steep trail
Trailhead:	Reseda Blvd

Because of urban expansion on both sides of Caballero Canyon, the hiking community must make some adjustments. Fireroad 29 has disappeared, the old East Ridge Trail has been bulldozed and so has the East Canyon Trail. Caballero Canyon is centrally located on the southern edge of the San Fernando Valley. It is the gateway to the northern entry to Topanga State Park and in time will become an exceptional corridor to the largest urban park in the United States. The loss of three important trails needs alleviation and until such time as a new trail system can be designed and built we must do the best we can to make use of the canyon.

Some trail remnants remain. I'll briefly describe some possible hikes, in addition to those already described. Hike to Mulholland by either the East Ridge Trail or Fireroad 28. Turn left and walk east on Mulholland Drive. Distances to trails, along the road, are shown in the chart. West to East:

Fireroad 28	to	East Ridge Trail [on north]	1 mile
	to	Fireroad 27 [on north]	1.2 miles
	to	Fireroad 26 [on south]	1.5 miles
	to	San Vicente Park [on south]	2 miles
	to	Encino Reservoir Overlook [on north]	2.6 miles

Eighty-five feet east of the East Ridge Trail a trail heads north on a ridge. This spur goes about 1/4 mile then nears the future housing area. The trail ends here.

Fireroad 27 begins at a locked pipe gate and heads north losing altitude all the way. Encino reservoir is in view to the east. A steep trail drops down into the canyon to the left of the road and now ends at the building area. A colony of rabbit-brush (*chrysothamnus nauseosus*) once grew in the canyon bottom but has been eliminated by construction. This was the only known habitat of this plant in the Santa Monica Mountains. The fireroad ends at a locked gate so turn around before then.

The Encino Reservoir Overlook is reached by a trail heading north beyond a locked pipe gate. We can get a good view of the reservoir without leaving Mulholland but a short walk down the trail leads to a level spot. The ridge beyond has been bulldozed, it is steep and seriously eroded. We may not want to proceed. Mulholland along this segment is gated so that motor vehicles do not have access at night. Sometimes the gate is also not open during the day.

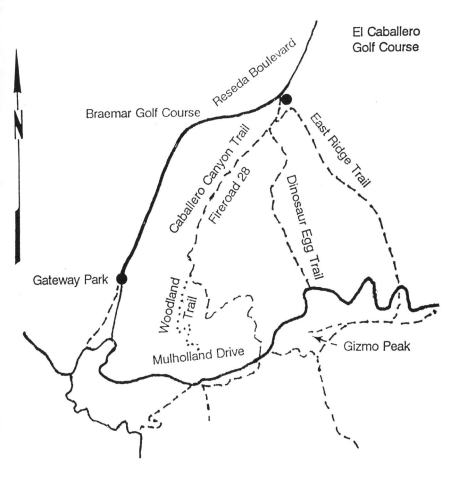

HIKE 66

GIZMO PEAK
from Reseda Blvd.

Maps:	SMMTS, East
Distance:	3 miles roundtrip
Elevation:	1100' gain and loss
Terrain:	Steep trail
Time:	1 hour and 45 minutes
Trailhead:	Reseda Boulevard

Drive south on Reseda Boulevard past Paseo Nuevo Drive on the right and El Caballero Country Club on the left, park along Reseda. The East Ridge Trail is in view across the Caballero creekbed. Take the trail down to the stream, turn left and get on the trail up the ridge. It is steep, eroded and not maintained. A 950-foot gain in slightly over 1 mile puts us on Mulholland. A steep trail on the opposite side of the road will take us to the top of Gizmo Peak with an added one-hundred-fifty foot gain. Or we can go left on Mulholland to take a trail up from the east end of the ridge.

The view from Peak 1927 and Peak 1960 at the far end of the ridge is worthwhile. The San Fernando Valley stretches out to the north and on a clear day or night is really spectacular. Caballero Canyon is below, and on the other side of the ridge to the northeast is Encino Reservoir, a part of the municipal water system. The immediate view south is of Rustic Canyon. Beyond is the ocean, the beach cities, Palos Verdes, and Santa Catalina Island. The view west shows some of Mulholland Drive and part of the Bent Arrow Trail. Some exceptional sunsets can be seen from here.

We have several options for the return trip. Number one, we can go back the way we came, making a 3-mile roundtrip. Number two, we can return to Mulholland, walk one mile west to Fireroad 28 and take it to the trailhead for a roundtrip total of four and a quarter miles. Number three, we can leave Gizmo Peak by trail on the south side, turn right on the Bent Arrow Trail to Mulholland, near Fireroad 28. Go to the trailhead for a total of about 4 miles roundtrip.

GIZMO PEAK

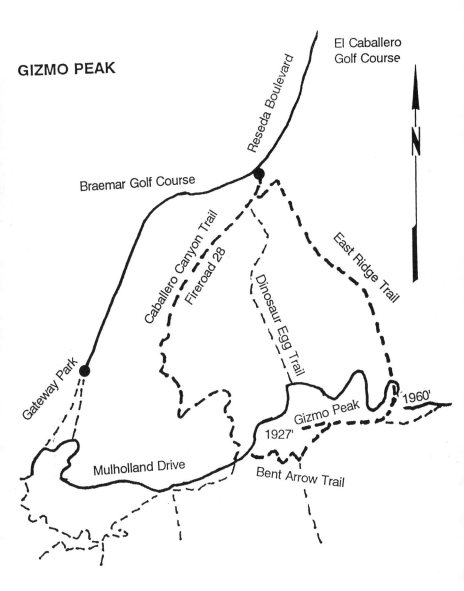

El Caballero Golf Course

Reseda Boulevard

Braemar Golf Course

Caballero Canyon Trail

Fireroad 28

Dinosaur Egg Trail

East Ridge Trail

Gateway Park

Gizmo Peak

1960'

1927'

Mulholland Drive

Bent Arrow Trail

N

HIKE 67

BLUE GORGE

from down in Rustic Canyon

Maps:	SMMTS., East
Terrain:	Class 2 rock climbing, streambed, some trail
Trailhead	Rustic Canyon stream and West Fork Junction.

I've had complaints about my write-up on Blue Gorge. One man lost his wallet, another caught poison oak, I've seen a couple of rattlesnakes, the trail isn't maintained, (as a matter of fact there is no trail in Blue Gorge). Nonetheless, Blue Gorge is worth seeing, but getting there isn't for everybody. One might not want to use this hike as an introduction to the mountains.

Using Hikes #61, #62, or #63 to get us down in to Rustic Canyon, I'll describe the route from the confluence of rustic Creek and its West Fork. From that point we hike downstream about one half mile during which time a mountain is on our left. When we see a streambed on the left we turn and follow upstream. We don't expect a trail so we will follow the streambed, boulder hopping along for about ten minutes when we begin to feel the gorge closing in. The stream becomes steeper with small rapids swirling around the rocks. The canyon narrows to about fifteen feet. We easily climb over a three-foot waterfall, continuing another one hundred feet when almost suddenly, a dark blue-gray, thirty-foot-high rock wall appears ahead. Our feet may get wet, but the lower five foot waterfall that blocks the narrow entry to the gorge can be climbed. We are then in a narrow flat area about fifteen feet long with another five-foot waterfall ahead. Above us the gorge narrows to four feet in one place but is generally six to eight feet wide.

Moss and ferns grow from the walls. A part of the rock on the east side is covered with a layer of limestone that has percolated down and changed the dark shiny stone to a light textured pattern. The blue-gray base rock is the oldest geological formation in the mountains. Santa Monica Slate was formed 150 million years ago

274

when this area was under water. The dark rocks are water-worn and smooth; many small grotto like caves have been carved in the walls giving a never ending change to the pattern. A particular quality of cool serenity surrounds this place. In a way I am glad that there is some difficulty reaching it.

Overhead, with roots in solid rock, grow a half dozen Maple trees — one with a diameter of more than twenty-four inches. The leaves are 5-lobed, and some are nearly a foot wide; the winged seeds start development early in spring and drop in the fall with Maples in a verdant microcosm, surrounded by chaparral — it's unbelievable.

Climb the next waterfall and the gorge widens. Three waterfalls, each about one and a half feet high, with pools at their base are in immediate view. Bay trees shade the stream and Humboldt Lilies are plentiful and bloom in June. This is indeed a beautiful place. Leave the area by going back downstream until reaching the center fork — about 10 minutes of walking — then turn right and go upstream. Fifteen minutes after starting up the Center Fork we were back at the West Fork injunction. We may have been gone forty-five minutes and can now continue our hike.

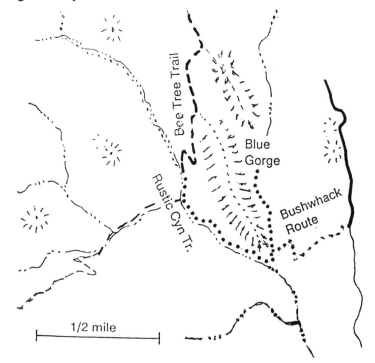

LOS LIONES TRAIL

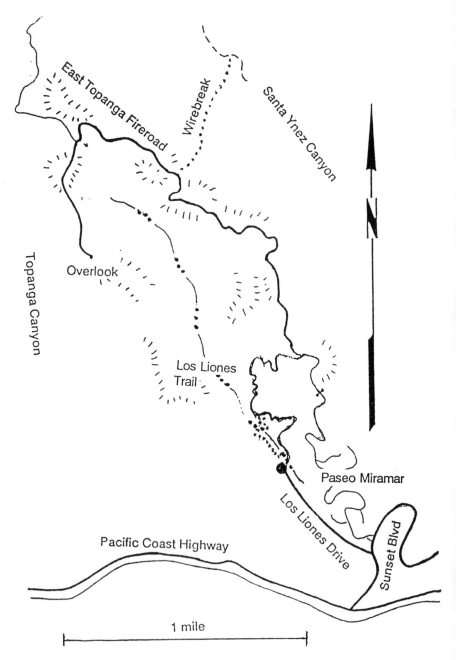

HIKE 68

Map:	SMMTS, East
Distance:	6 miles roundtrip
Elevation:	1500' gain and loss
Terrain:	Trail and fireroad
Time:	3 hours
Trailhead:	Los Liones Drive

Los Liones Canyon is a rugged steep-sloped, secluded area near civilization yet apart from the urban scene. A hiking trail in this part of Topanga State Park is welcome.

Drive east .3 mile on sunset Blvd. from the Pacific Coast Highway to Los Liones Drive and turn left. Park at the end of the street in a small parking area, avoiding the Church parking lot. Enter on the right side of the stream and start to climb east on a north facing steep slope. In five or six hundred yards we make a switchback left to continue our climb, now on a south facing slope. German Ivy grows every place. When we are 15 minutes out, notice a trail on the left that cuts back downhill. This is the old trail and can be used, but it is steep! This trail has many switchbacks and makes a lot of turns, losing elevation gained on occasion. In a little over a mile we gain 750 feet. Abruptly, the East Topanga Fireroad nears and we turn left and follow it uphill. The road continues uphill until easing up in about two-thirds of a mile and a 500 foot gain. About 20 minutes later we look for a trail that follows the top of a ridge heading south. One half mile along the ridge brings us to the "Overlook", an area with a great view of the ocean and the seacoast. Palos Verde Peninsula and Catalina Island are visible on clear days.

The 1973 Trippet fire burned the slope south of the Overlook and for a few years a passable route went down the south ridge, but the chaparral has recovered so that the route is not in use.

Return the way we came but take the time to look west into Topanga Canyon and the 1300 foot drop to the stream. One-half mile along East Topanga Fireroad we can look left down the "Wirebreak" and see Santa Ynez Canyon.

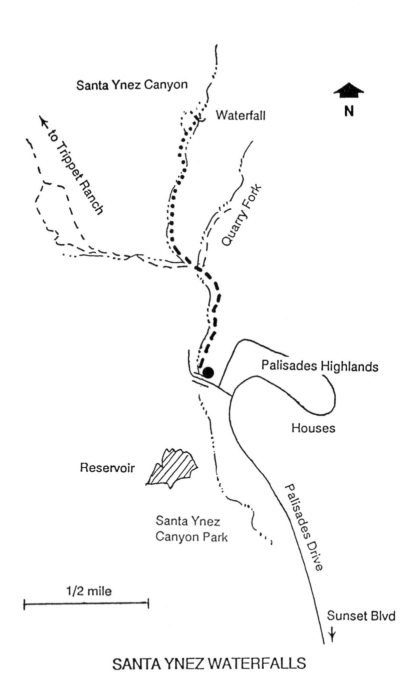

Santa Ynez Canyon

Waterfall

N

to Trippet Ranch

Quarry Fork

Palisades Highlands

Houses

Reservoir

Palisades Drive

Santa Ynez
Canyon Park

1/2 mile

Sunset Blvd

SANTA YNEZ WATERFALLS

HIKE 69

SANTA YNEZ WATERFALLS
from Palisades Highlands

Maps:	SMMTS, East
Distance:	4 miles roundtrip
Elevation:	300' gain and loss
Terrain:	Trail and Boulder hopping
Time:	2½ hours
Trailhead:	Palisades Drive

This is not a strenuous trip at all unless we elect to climb up the waterfalls in the canyon. The footing can be difficult because the winter rains wipe out trails and bring down small trees and brush.

The trailhead is reached from Sunset Boulevard. Turn north on Palisades Drive (three-tenths of a mile from Pacific Coast Highway), and drive north to Vereda de la Montura. Turn left, drive two blocks and park on either side of the street. An entrance to the trail is upstream.

In previous editions of the book we started this hike at Santa Ynez Park, but because of vegetation growth, the immediate trail downstream of the culvert is not recommended.

The canyon narrows, and some cliff-forming sandstone rock becomes prominent on both sides of the stream. Caves, or rockshelters, can be seen near stream level as well as higher on the cliffs. An intermittent stream comes down steeply from the right. At that point, and for 100 feet, look for a limestone outcropping along the trail and showing in the stream.

Continue upstream and we soon come to a gate. Immediately beyond the gate is a fork in the stream and the trail. Take the left fork as the right fork goes to Quarry Canyon. Before crossing the stream notice a large sandstone rock that has a mortar hole on the top side. The size and shape indicate that this was used by the Indians for grinding acorns. Cross the stream and continue 100 yards, reaching another fork in the trail. This time, turn right, cross the stream, and follow the north fork upstream. An old Cabin Site is on the point of land between the streams above their junction. Two stone chimneys about 30 feet apart are all that remain of the buildings. Trees have grown up into what was once the building and have all but completely hidden the chimneys. The vegetation is so thick that we have some difficulty getting to the area. Part of the vegetation is Poison Oak; and to further dissuade careless exploration, a resident rattler (as of May 1980) owns the indistinct trail leading to the site.

Twenty minutes on the north fork of boulder hopping and some trail, takes us through a lot of Poison Oak, Ferns, Humboldt Lilies and water-loving plants. Look for Pacific tree-frogs on overcast, cool days, or in sheltered places; tadpoles can be found in April and May. When hearing the "kreck-eck" of the Pacific tree-frog we might expect to see a large animal, if measured by the sound volume; but look for a 1½ inch long frog that blends with the surroundings and is not likely to be close to a tree. Also notice the characteristic black stripe that runs from the nostril to behind the eye.

Rock Shelter in Lower Santa Ynez Canyon

The canyon walls become steep and rugged, the stream narrows, and we feel that the waterfalls are close. Several small falls come first, and we are challenged in climbing up some rock; then around to the right of a turn in the canyon is a beautiful, twelve-foot waterfall. Occasionally climbers with ropes will continue farther and even go to the source of the stream at Eagle Spring; but this is the turnaround point of this hike because of the difficult rock climbing.

We return the way we came, and remind ourselves to come back again at the tail end of a good rainstorm for a real spectacle.

HIKE 70   SANTA YNEZ CANYON PARK

In Palisades Highlands

Santa Ynez Canyon Park is a small park alongside Palisades Drive. Part of the entrance road is surfaced and suitable for wheelchairs and walkers. I go there because of the great variety of wildflowers. Some places are suitable for picnics in the shade and in time to come I would expect improvements to develop greater use by families.

The Trailhead is reached from Sunset Boulevard, three-tenths of a mile from Pacific Coast Highway. Turn north to drive one and three quarters of a mile on Palisades Drive to Santa Ynez Park. Parking is along the curb, entrance is around a locked gate on the west side of the street. A one-half-mile trail leaves the gate entering the Park, and stays on level ground on the way to the upper end. A riparian woodland characterizes the plant community although many introduced plants result from homes near the Park. Open spaces allow for a mix of spring wildflowers.

Features include a stream running through the Park, a fenced-in reservoir, and access to the "Wirebreak" trail beginning two to three hundred yards along the trail, then going west across the stream and uphill into Topanga State Park.

HIKE 71

Maps:	SMMTS, East
Distance:	17.5 mi. roundtrip
Elevation:	3300 ft. gain and loss
Terrain:	Fireroad
Time:	8 hours including lunch
Trailhead:	Temescal Canyon

This hike starts at the north end of Temescal Road in Pacific Palisades, goes to Mulholland Drive, and back by way of Fireroad 30. Because we go and return by the same route, we have the option of turning around short of the destination or of arranging a car shuttle at the north end at Gateway Park. The hike crosses Topanga State Park in a south to north direction by use of a dominant ridge. Excellent views are presented of Santa Ynez, Temescal, Rustic, and Garapito Canyons. The San Fernando Valley can be seen from the north end of the hike and the Los Angeles Basin from the south. This route clearly shows the expanse of wildland that exists within the city.

Walk north along the road about 100 feet beyond the gate, and take a trail on the left to go uphill. The route parallels the stream far enough away so as to avoid the housing area. Once beyond the last house the trail drops down to follow the creekbed upstream along a washed-out road then climbs through the narrow gorge of the canyon. An uncommon plant, French Broom, is seen in at least one area along the trail. This 10-foot bush produces yellow blooms in March through May. The gorge offers some interesting features: a thin waterfall called "The Drip", on the east side of the trail could become serious after a rainstorm; cliff forming conglomerate rock adds a rugged accent to the steep canyon walls; and Temescal Creek cascades down a narrow gorge.

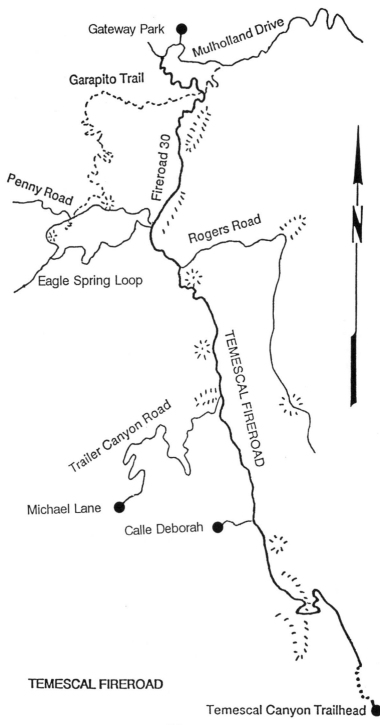

Gateway Park

Mulholland Drive

Garapito Trail

Fireroad 30

Penny Road

Rogers Road

Eagle Spring Loop

N

Trailer Canyon Road

TEMESCAL FIREROAD

Michael Lane

Calle Deborah

TEMESCAL FIREROAD

Temescal Canyon Trailhead

The trail crosses the stream on a new bridge where a wooden bridge once spanned the 15 to 20 foot distance from bank to bank. The Mandeville fire of 1978 came through Temescal Canyon and burned the old bridge. A waterfall is in our view from the bridge. The trail crosses the stream, makes a switchback to the left as it goes steeply up the wall of the canyon, then tops out on a ridge going northwest. The fireroad stays near the crest of the ridge, gaining altitude moderately. Upper Temescal Canyon to the east is totally undeveloped, whereas both Pulga Canyon and Santa Ynez Canyon to the west show building activity. This part of the hike was in the path of the 1978 Mandeville fire and was completely blackened. The recovery by resprouting chaparral and flowering plants is striking, and few signs of the fire are evident.

Calle Deborah Road comes in on the left, and about 1 mile farther north, Trailer Canyon Road comes up from Santa Ynez Canyon. A microwave facility, locally called "Radio Peak," is about half way between the two points. The route continues north on a reasonably level grade, intersecting with Rogers Road about 1½ miles beyond the Trailer Canyon intersection. The highest point in Topanga State Park, Temescal Peak (2126'), is near the intersection and may be climbed by a short but steep firebreak for a good view of the head of Temescal Canyon and of Rustic and Santa Ynez Canyons.

Continue north on the fireroad, which is a segment of the Backbone Trail at this point, passing Cathedral Rock in 1/2 mile, then on to the "Hub" — a four-way intersection. The left road goes to Trippet Ranch by way of Eagle Spring; the next left road goes to Trippet Ranch by way of Eagle Rock; and the road straight ahead is a continuation of Fireroad 30, the route of this hike. One-and-a-half miles from the Hub, the Bent Arrow Trail has its beginning by clinging to the wall of Upper Rustic Canyon and working its way east, eventually to parallel Mulholland Drive. On the west, opposite the Bent Arrow Trail, look for the beginning of Garapito Trail. We turn back at Mulholland.
You have:---

—   just walked through a wilderness area—all within the city limits —
and probably have met other hikers and some animals
but not many distractions.
—   You should be tired. Unless a car shuttle has been set up,
turn around and walk the 8-3/4 miles back.

HIKE 72

PHIL LEACOCK
MEMORIAL TRAIL

Maps:	SMMTS, East
Distance:	2+ miles [includes loop to
Elevation:	600' [Temescal Ridge Tr.)
Terrain:	Trail
Time:	1 hour and 15 minutes
Trailhead:	Bienveneda

This trail connects the western part of Pacific Palisades with the north-south Temescal Ridge Trail and the Temescal Canyon Trail. Although a short trail, it is an important trail. Important for several reasons; it perpetuates the memory of Phil Leacock who volunteered himself for the Santa Monica Mountains; the trail is beautiful in its own right, and it performs an important function by connecting with the Temescal trails.

Find the trailhead by driving on Sunset Boulevard in Pacific Palisades, turn north on Bienveneda and go about one mile. We can park along the curb of Via Floresta or Bienveneda. Leacock Trail begins on the east side in a narrow passageway that starts uphill. At the first turn a smooth trail turns rocky, and uphill turns to wooden steps anchored to the ground. Just short of ten minutes later we notice an intersecting trail on the left. This is Bienveneda Trail and after making a loop we will return on it. For now we go southeast and hike around to the south-facing slope of the ridge, as we continue to gain altitude but at a gentle rate.

We come to a trail junction. Actually the Leacock Trail intersects Temescal Ridge Trail. If we see anyone coming up the trail from below on our right they will be breathing hard because of the near 700 foot gain from Temescal Gateway Park. We can turn around at this point and go back the way we came and we will have walked the Leacock Trail both ways. Or we could turn left to walk north about two-thirds of a mile on Temescal Ridge Trail. In about fifteen minutes we arrive at an overlook point. A memorial is placed for a young lady. The government has placed a marker giving the geographic location. Five minutes after leaving the overlook point the Bienveneda Trail joins the Ridge Trail on the left. To complete a loop hike we will turn left and follow the Bienveneda Trail to the Leacock Trail, turn right and return to the trailhead.

This hike has great views of the city, the ocean and canyons. Only hikers (runners, and walkers) use this area. People out of respect (and the law) walk their dogs elsewhere. Bicyclists ride on the fireroad north of this area but avoid this trail complex.

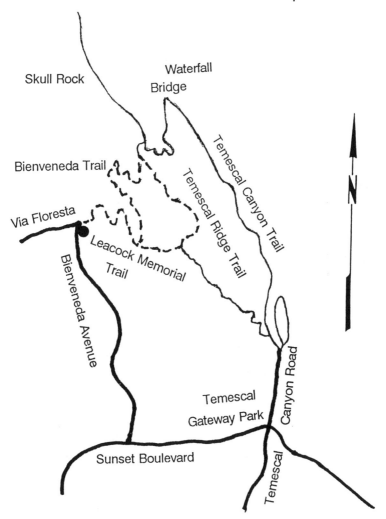

HIKE 73

ROGERS RIDGE

from Will Rogers State
Historic Park

Maps:	SMMTS, East
Distance:	5½ miles
Elevation:	1300' gain and loss
Terrain:	Trail, very steep with poor footing at times
Time:	2½ hours
Trailhead:	Will Rogers S.H.P.

This hike combines exercise with a bit of nostalgia. Will Rogers bought the ranch in 1922 and it became a state park in 1944. The house and grounds are preserved as they were. Although Will was astride a horse when he travelled these trails I believe no one had a closer feel for this land.

Go 4.6 miles from the Pacific Coast Highway on Sunset Boulevard. Drive north into Will Rogers State Historic Park. If we come by RTD bus, get off at the Evans Rd stop on Sunset Blvd. A trail leads into the Park.

Hike north along the trail near the tennis courts west of Park Headquarters. The trail goes uphill onto the ridge overlooking Rivas Canyon and passes close to Inspiration Point, then forks left beginning a steady uphill climb.

The trail is steep in places, and rocky. Shade is rare so wind and sun play an important part in our comfort. The ridge we are on separates Rustic Canyon on the east from Rivas Canyon on the west, as we go higher, the canyon views and the ocean scene are spectacular. The trail levels out comfortably on top with some slight up and down as we go from one little peak to another. A trail breaks right and goes to the floor of Rustic Canyon. Farther on, as we start up a slight rise, a trail angles off to the left into Rivas Canyon. Take this trail and follow along the east slope of the canyon. Staying on this road takes us to the head of Rivas Canyon and the saddle overlooking Rustic Canyon. This is the turnaround point of the hike. A 4-trunked Oak tree provides a sheltered spot

to rest and relax. Rogers Road continues into Topanga State Park.
  We can return the way we came or come back on the **Ridge Trail**. To do this we go east and uphill to the ridge.

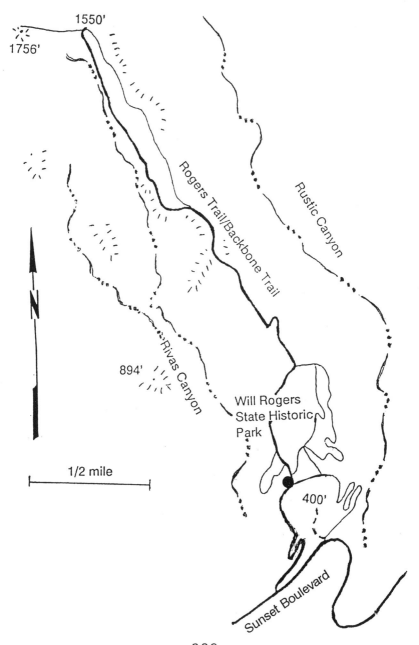

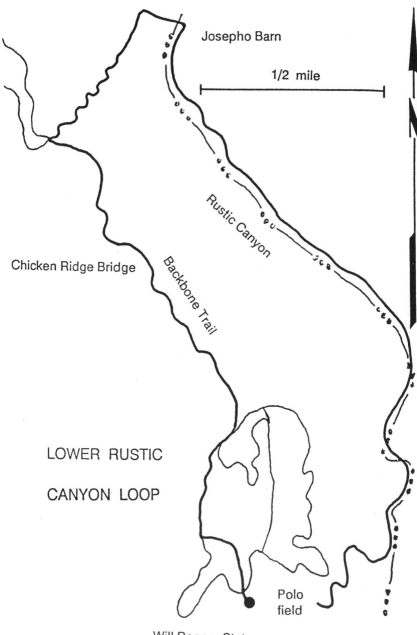

Josepho Barn

1/2 mile

N

Rustic Canyon

Chicken Ridge Bridge

Backbone Trail

LOWER RUSTIC

CANYON LOOP

Polo
field

Will Rogers State
Historic Park

HIKE 74   LOWER RUSTIC CANYON LOOP
from Will Rogers State Historic Park

Maps:	SMMTS, East
Distance:	5 miles
Elevation:	1050' gain and loss
Terrain:	Steep trails, fireroad, boulder hopping
Time:	2 hours, 45 minutes
Trailhead:	Will Rogers State Historic Park

This hike quickly takes us to Rogers Ridge then down to the bottom of Rustic Canyon. The steep trails and some boulder hopping in the canyon will challenge our stamina. We will find class 2 rock climbing in the lower canyon and some wet stream crossing when the water is running. If heights bother you, Rogers Ridge will make you nervous.

Begin our hike at Will Rogers State Historic Park. If coming by RTD bus, get off at the Evans Road stop on Sunset Boulevard and walk up the trail to the polo field. This will add about 1/2 mile each way. If we drive, park in the lot. Start near the tennis courts west of Park Headquarters and head uphill on a trail bordered with a white wooden fence. Upon reaching the fireroad, we are given a choice of turning left and walking on a gentle route, or crossing the road onto a steep rough trail. Take the steeper route — we need the mental preparation for some steeper trails ahead. The trail heads north by west, short-cutting the fireroad. Turn right when we next reach the fireroad higher on the ridge. At the next fork in the road go straight ahead (left of the two options). In a few minutes another fork to the left gives a glimpse of a Kiosk with information on the Backbone Trail. Go to the Kiosk and start uphill to the north. If at anytime we take a wrong turn up to this point, we are likely to end up on Inspiration Point. Look north and see the Kiosk and the trail.

The trail up Rogers Ridge is gravelly, steep and rutted. Views south become spectacular and only get better as we gain altitude.

After one and a half miles we cross Chicken Ridge bridge. Much of the excitement of this ridge is gone now that the bridge increases the safety. Will Rogers and Anatol Josepho are reported to have designed this route, but had also scouted out a lower trail to the east to avoid the knife-edge of Chicken Ridge. The Chicken Ridge route became the riding trail between the two ranches — the trail we are on today. Beyond the bridge the trail hangs on a steep rock slope. Severe trail erosion makes the footing difficult so we take care. In less than one-half mile we walk along a scrub oak ridge and come to a trail junction. The Backbone Trail splits going north with one route on the ridge; the other contouring on the slope facing Rivas Canyon. We turn right and walk down to Rustic Canyon. Some great views of Rustic Canyon develop as we descend. Sycamore, cottonwood and walnut trees show a ribbon of green along Rustic Creek every spring. The trail crosses the stream and heads toward a large wooden barn enclosed by a cyclone fence. A large, attractive, multi-trunked sycamore shades the upstream side of the barn. Look for some coast redwoods planted here years ago. The other buildings of the Josepho ranch burned in a fire.

The trail downstream drops into the streambed at times, but for the most part stays on the left bank. Ruins of burned-out homes and old foundations are spaced along the bank. The large two-story metal framed structure was part of the Murphy complex. It appears to have been a workshop on the ground floor, and dormitory above. The concrete building to the south housed a power station with two large generators. A large steel diesel fuel tank still stands hidden in the trees of a side canyon. A series of concrete steps will take us up the slope, all the way to Sullivan Ridge west if we can find the route.

Farther south a burned cabin is all that remains of Will Rogers' hideaway. The double fireplace remains among the rubble. No one lives in this part of the canyon now. Look for some large bay trees. We'll pass by some large jointed cactus, and be somewhat careful as we pass a beehive in a bay tree.

The trail forks right and crosses the stream. The left fork goes to the top of the dam built by the Santa Monica Land and Water Company about 1900. The dam is now silted to the top so no water is impounded. Go around the dam by trail. We can go back up the stream to the base of the dam for a look.

The route downstream more or less follows the creek but can no longer be called a trail. We will get our feet wet when the canyon narrows, and will resort to class 2 rock climbing on occasion. Will Rogers built a road up the creek among these rocks. A narrow and steep detour around the dam allowed him to drive through rustic Canyon in his Ford touring car. He built a small log cabin in the canyon. Floods have removed the road and fire has taken the log cabin. We wonder how anyone would have the optimism to put a road through this narrow, rocky gorge. About the time we have had enough of wet boots and slipping on rocks, a trail takes us uphill about 1/3 mile to the east end of the polo field. Many people walk to the stream and back on this, the Rustic Canyon Trail, to Rustic Canyon. Secluded ravines, wood bridges, cliffs, rocks, and the canyon with a stream makes this a special place.

HIKE 75

RUSTIC RAMBLE #4

via Sullivan Canyon from
Queensferry Road (loop)

Maps:	SMMTS, East
Distance:	10½ miles roundtrip
Elevation:	2100' gain and loss
Terrain:	Gravel streambed, road, trail, chaparral, bush-whack, and class 2 rock climbing
Time:	8 hours incl. lunch and side trips
Trailhead:	Queensferry Road

This trip is difficult, requiring hiking experience and some rock climbing ability. The route finding is involved — it is best done in a group led by someone that knows the terrain. The route crosses Boy Scout property at Camp Josepho. Prior permission is required.

Arrive at the start of the hike by driving 2.3 miles west of the San Diego Freeway on Sunset Blvd. Turn north onto Mandeville Canyon Road for 0.3 mile to Westridge Road, turn left and follow the twists and turns for 1.1 miles turning left at Bayliss Road, then 0.3 mile to Queensferry Road, turn left and park.

Walk north along the floor of Sullivan Canyon for about 3 miles, passing a Eucalyptus tree. Depending on storm damage, there should be a road at this point that goes north, becoming steeper as the head of the canyon is reached. The road makes a climbing U-turn to the left then swings right and intersects the Sullivan Ridge Road west (Fireroad 26). Turn right and continue to Mulholland Drive. If on schedule you are now 2¼ hours out from the trailhead.

Turn left on Mulholland and walk 1/4 mile, coming to Fireroad 27A, on the left. Go around the gate and follow the fireroad 1/3 mile west along the Gizmo Peak ridge until coming to the Bent

Arrow Trail on the left. The trail makes a couple of switchbacks coming out on the firebreak south of the peak. Travel the firebreak on the ridge about 1/2 mile until coming to a trail on the right. This trail is difficult to spot. Look for a cleared area that extends west of the firebreak. This precedes the low place before the last knob on the ridge. Go to the edge of the clearing and drop straight down a trail to the west. After losing 250 feet of altitude we make a turn left and head south. Stay with the trail until it turns right and drops down to the center fork. Get off the trail and continue following the ridge. At least two rattlers reside in the area and might be obscured by the heavy low buckwheat brush, so exercise more than usual care.

Drop down the south point of the ridge through light chaparral, losing 500 feet. We will reach the stream in an Oak shaded lunch spot about 3½ hours after leaving the trailhead.

After lunch we take an optional side trip. The ridge that we came down separates the main fork of Rustic Creek and the east fork. Take a 35 minute roundtrip up the east fork to "Blue Gorge." This broad canyon soon begins to narrow and after ten minutes of walking we will enter the gorge.

Water, running through the east fork for centuries, has carved a narrow canyon through the blue-black rock. Blue Gorge is a rare little world set aside to be witnessed by only the hardy and daring. We sense the adventure that lies ahead while walking upstream. Suddenly a massive smooth rock grotto 30 feet high confronts us. A five foot waterfall spills into a pool at our feet. Upon closer approach we see that the appearance of a cave is deceptive because the narrow passage turns as it comes through the rock. Climb to the top of the waterfall and we are in a cool microscene of smooth rocks, waterfalls, Humboldt Lilies, Moss, Ferns, Bay and Maple Trees overhead. It is difficult to believe that 100 feet up the mountain is a stand of tough chaparral.

Upon leaving the lunch area, head downstream. Ideally the route follows the stream to Camp Josepho, then up the road to Sullivan Ridge; but unless permission has been obtained to cross the Boy Scout property, an alternate route must be used. (a) The point of a ridge comes down to the stream below the east fork entry. This slope is steep at the bottom but becomes gentler after about 200' gain. It is the best route to Sullivan Ridge Road. (b) A more difficult route goes up the steep baranca just 200 yards south of the ridge. The baranca received the name "Falls Gorge" because of the many 8 to 12 foot waterfalls we climbed up. This route takes close to an hour and a half to gain 600 feet to Sullivan Ridge Road. From that point go south on the road, coming to a small clump of Oak trees with a board wedged in for a seat. Continue south on the ridge to the side road that drops down to Camp Josepho on the west.

My recommendation is to follow the streambed to Camp Josepho rather than fight chaparral climbing uphill. Upon reaching Camp Josepho walk up the road to Sullivan Ridge on the east. Turn right and walk one-third mile and look for the trail down to Sullivan Canyon. While still on the road we will cross under some telephone wires and go around a bend in the road to the right. A few hundred feet beyond a pole with the number 43975 we will find the trail on the left. The trail is overgrown and steep, but is solid footing compared with some of the day's travel. Upon reaching the streambed, turn right for the easy one-half-mile-walk to the trailhead and our car.

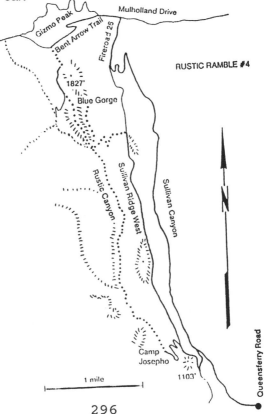

RUSTIC RAMBLE #4

HIKE 76

Maps:	SMMTS, East
Distance:	9½ miles roundtrip
Elevation:	1250' gain and loss
Terrain:	Road and gravel streambed
Time:	4 hours 15 minutes
Trailhead:	Queensferry Road

In Brentwood go 2.3 miles west of the San Diego Freeway on Sunset Blvd. Turn north onto Mandeville Canyon Road for 0.3 mile to Westridge Road, turn left and follow the twists and turns for 1.1 miles turning left at Bayliss Road, then 0.3 mile to Queensferry Road, turn left and park. The trail is on a private road.

This hike is along the floor of a narrow steep-walled canyon. During the heavy flood stage, water covers the entire floor and distributes a large amount of 150 million year old gravel (called Santa Monica Slate) rather indiscriminately along the entire area. The floods of early 1980 eliminated most of the road and trails in the canyon, restoring it to a near pristine state.

We pick our way along the bottom of the canyon as it very gently ascends to the north. We will cross the stream many times. This will be of concern only early in the year when the water is high. As soon as summer arrives, the surface water disappears but the stream continues to flow down in the gravel several feet below.

The floor of the canyon is shaded with Sycamore trees, Coast Live Oaks, Walnuts, and other moisture-loving trees. A wide variety of native wild flowers, some grasses, and small shrubs including Poison Oak are found here. Both sides, up from the canyon floor, are covered with chaparral. A fire early in 1978 burned the slopes and ridges except at the head of the canyon, but the chaparral recovered immediately by rootsprouting and new lush plant growth.

Two pipelines run down the valley floor, usually covered from view but sometimes exposed by flood waters. Remnants of a dirt

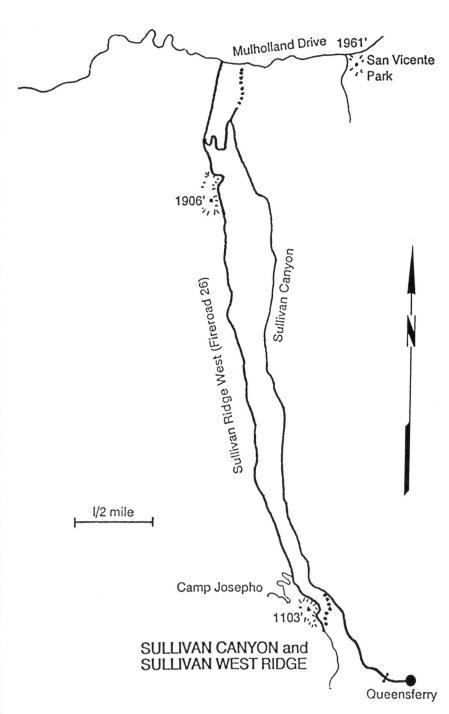

Mulholland Drive 1961'

San Vicente Park

1906'

Sullivan Ridge West (Fireroad 26)

Sullivan Canyon

N

1/2 mile

Camp Josepho

1103'

SULLIVAN CANYON and
SULLIVAN WEST RIDGE

Queensferry

service road exist for a short distance on the east slope a hundred feet or so up. Trails go to both ridges but are presently overgrown and difficult to locate from below. Only one is in good condition, going to the west ridge.

The canyon floor continuously presents shady rest spots without many significant landmarks. About 1½ miles from the trailhead we see a 6' waterfall on the east side. This dries up early, but is clear cool water in the spring. Occasional outcroppings of the Santa Monica Slate bedrock can be seen on both sides of the canyon. The blue-gray color is sometimes covered by a layer of limonite that was deposited by percolating waters along joints and bedding planes. This brown color is deceptive because it makes the slate difficult to recognize. Farther up the canyon a tall Eucalyptus tree on the left makes a good landmark. It has reseeded and now some smaller ones are growing. This point is about 3 miles from the trailhead and is often used as a turnaround point for a shorter hike, as the trail becomes steeper from here on.

Continuing up the stream, we will be on an old road that is high enough above the stream to avoid being washed out. In about a half mile, a road forks to the right and dead-ends into a steep trail going up through the chaparral to Mulholland Drive. I prefer the left fork, staying on the road until reaching the fireroad on the ridge. Turn right and follow this to Mulholland.

The return trip presents two options: we may go back the same way we came or go back by way of the Sullivan Ridge Road West (Fireroad 26). The fireroad stays high on the ridge and goes south without many turns. It's best to pick a cool day for this trip as little shade exists except for a small clump of Oaks about half way.

A little over 3 miles from Mulholland a road goes downhill on the right to Camp Josepho. Stay on the ridge and one third mile farther a trail on the left leads down to the floor of Sullivan Canyon. Watch closely for the start of this trail as it is not marked. While still on the road, we pass under some telephone wires and go around a bend to the right; look to our left. A pole with the number 43975 is a good indicator. Go a few hundred feet farther to find the trail, overgrown and steep. In 15 minutes we reach the streambed and turn right. It is one-half mile to the end of the hike.

HIKE 77

EAST SULLIVAN RIDGE ROAD
(Fireroad 25)
from Westridge Road

Maps: SMMTS, East
Distance: 7¼ miles roundtrip
Elevation: 1050' gain and loss
Terrain: Fireroad
Time: 3 hours
Trailhead: Westridge Road

In Brentwood from the corner of Sunset Blvd. and Mandeville Canyon Road go north on Mandeville 3/10 mile to Westridge Road. Turn left and follow Westridge to the end of the road at the locked gate. In this residential area, only street parking is available.

Walk around the gate onto the dirt road that heads north along the ridge. This is Fireroad 25 and stays close to the ridge between Mandeville Canyon on the east and Sullivan Canyon on the west.

The altitude gain is moderate and the footing good. Most of the gain is during the first two miles with an almost level ridge road to Mulholland. The view to the west into Sullivan Canyon is rugged and impressive. The floor of the canyon is 750' below the trail, making the trail down in the canyon look narrow. Sullivan Ridge is a favorite evening hike. Some spectacular sunsets are seen over the ridge to the west. In the summer, late afternoon is a lot cooler on this shadeless ridge.

Farther along the ridge the road follows the eastern edge of the crest giving a good view of Mandeville Canyon on the east. The floor of the canyon here is also 700-800 feet below the trail. A number of homes have been built in this narrow canyon. About one half mile before reaching Mulholland Drive a trail on the east drops down to Mandeville Canyon Road.

The fireroad comes to an inactive military installation near San Vicente Mountain, now a city park. By taking the road turning left at the gate and climbing a short distance to the top of the knoll, a magnificent view of the San Fernando Valley and the Los Angeles Basin spreads before you. Return the same way you came.

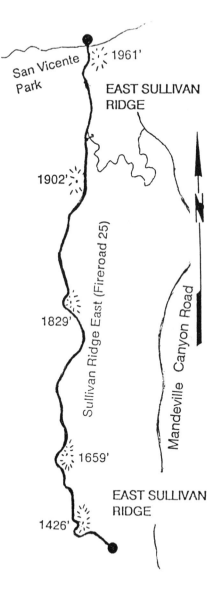

San Vicente
Park

1961'

EAST SULLIVAN RIDGE

1902'

Sullivan Ridge East (Fireroad 25)

Mandeville Canyon Road

1829'

1659'

EAST SULLIVAN RIDGE

1426'

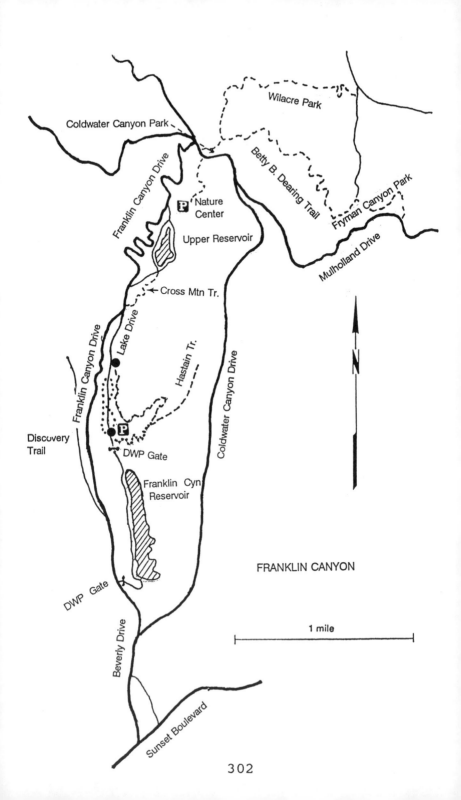

Coldwater Canyon Park

Wilacre Park

Franklin Canyon Drive

Betty B. Dearing Trail

Fryman Canyon Park

Nature Center

Upper Reservoir

Mulholland Drive

Cross Mtn Tr.

Franklin Canyon Drive

Lake Drive

Hastain Tr.

N

Coldwater Canyon Drive

Discovery Trail

DWP Gate

Franklin Cyn Reservoir

FRANKLIN CANYON

DWP Gate

1 mile

Beverly Drive

Sunset Boulevard

302

HIKE 78

Maps:	Thomas Bros. Street Maps
Distance:	2 miles
Elevation:	400 ft.
Terrain:	Steep trail, Fireroad
Time:	45 min.
Trailhead:	Franklin Cyn Ranch

Franklin Canyon Ranch is part of the multi-agency and multi-organizational recreational complex of the Cross Mountain Park. National Park Service rangers and docents from William O. Douglas Outdoor Classroom (WODOC) provide outdoor educational programs on a reservation basis and the general public can use the area without charge. Facilities include a parking lot, restrooms, drinking water, pay telephone, picnic area, trails, National Park Service Ranger Station Nature Center.

Both above and below the ranch, the L.A. City Department of Water and Power maintains reservoirs. These are part of the scenery for the hikes, but are closed to the general public. WODOC provides environmental educational programs on a reservation basis at the upper reservoir. The special facilities include trails for senior citizens, a handicapped and Braille trail, and a series of student educational trails. Open seven days a week throughout the year, WODOC provides an exceptional schedule of opportunities for many who would not have a chance for outdoor experiences.

Reach Franklin Canyon from Beverly Hills by driving north on Beverly Drive from Sunset Blvd. 1.2 miles from the Coldwater Canyon Drive intersection, turn onto Franklin Canyon Drive. The road is narrow and winding with a 15 mph speed limit. After 1.7 miles more, turn right onto Lake Drive. Go to the parking lot.

From the San Fernando Valley drive south on Coldwater Canyon Avenue until reaching Mulholland Drive. Cross Mulholland onto Franklin Canyon Drive and go 1.7 miles to Lake Drive, turn left and go to the parking lot. Part of Franklin Canyon Drive is not paved and should not be used in wet weather.

To hike the Hastain Trail counterclockwise we leave the lower parking lot and walk south across the lawn toward a lath house. Look behind an avocado tree to find the trailhead. A steep trail leads us up the east flank of the ridge. Immediately we are surrounded by a mixed plant community of Coastal Sage Scrub and Chaparral. In bloom seasonally are Popcorn Flower, Bush Sunflower, Everlasting, Peony, Golden Yarrow and many others. The trail switches back as it climbs, and the narrow trail is steep. In 15 minutes we will intersect a fireroad and are entitled to a rest to view the canyon and reservoir below. We have climbed 400 feet. A right turn onto the fireroad will take us higher on the ridge and give views of the canyons below, Los angeles, and on a clear day, the ocean. A left turn at the fireroad will take us downhill at a comfortable slope for about 1 mile before intersecting Lake Drive. Turn left and return to the parking lot.

Discovery Trail is an almost level self-guided walk over a trail on one side of Lake Drive and back down on the other side. Begin at the southeast corner of the parking lot and walk north on the trail. On occasion we use the road because of the steep hillside. "Discovery" is a good title because this trail allows us to notice the plants and animals about us. We will see Walnut Trees, Elderberry Bushes, Poison Oak, and many different flowers. A colony of Poison Hemlock (an introduced plant that gained fame in 399 B.C. when Socrates died in Athens) grows along the road. Don't even touch it. Cross the road and come back along the trail.

The Canyon Trail, and others are available for exploration.

Fryman Canyon Park, Wilacre Park and Coldwater Canyon Park, in conjunction with Franklin Canyon Ranch and two Franklin Canyon reservoir areas, are referred to as the Cross Mountain Park.

WILACRE PARK

Wilacre Park is 129 acres of rugged ridges and canyons in Studio City. Surrounded by residential areas, this park is a greenbelt of wild land set aside for recreational use. Access is gained by three trailheads: one from Coldwater Canyon Park on Mulholland Drive, one from Laurel Canyon Boulevard, and the other from the upper end of Iredell Street. I'll describe a hike from Laurel Canyon on the Betty B. Dearing Trail.

Reach the trailhead by driving 1.6 miles south of the Ventura Freeway on Laurel Canyon Boulevard to Fryman Canyon Road, and park. This is about the 3500 block on Laurel Canyon Blvd. Limited curb-side space is available; there is no parking lot.

We walk west on a paved road that is restricted to non-motorized vehicles and those on foot. Dogs are allowed on leash. We immediately begin an uphill climb that will total a 500 foot elevation gain when we reach Coldwater Canyon Park. Plan for a 30 minute brisk walk through the shade of Walnut trees, some introduced pines, but mostly chaparral. We will notice several levelled places that may in time become overnight campgrounds. Upon reaching Coldwater Canyon Park, a right fork at station #14 will put us on the "Magic Forest" nature trail and we can make a loop into the Park.

A left turn at station #14 takes us on a near level trail heading south. In ten minutes we become hemmed-in on the left by a cyclone fence and almost immediately find ourselves on Iredell Street. We are now out of the Park but continuing ahead, another trail starts up from the right. You may elect to turn around at this time or proceed southeast on the trail as it contours around to Fryman Canyon, and then up to Fryman Canyon Overlook. Part of this trail is on private property over which the owners have granted trail access.

FRYMAN CANYON PARK

Fryman Canyon is a steep chaparral-covered 59 acres of north facing hillside near Mulholland Drive. The Trailhead for the Betty B. Dearing Trail is on Mulholland Drive 2 miles east of Coldwater Canyon Park and .8 of a mile west of Laurel Canyon Boulevard. Ample parking for cars and a few buses is provided at a scenic overlook.

The trail goes downhill, initially, and later contours west through a chaparral forest. We cross an intermittent stream in the shade of riparian woodlands and, incidentally, walk by an automobile graveyard — I counted 10. The trail intersects an old road and continues west. We return the way we came, or continue on to Coldwater Canyon Park or to Wilacre Park. A car shuttle could be set up if we don't want to climb back up the hill.

COLDWATER CANYON PARK

Coldwater Canyon Park is a 12 acre Los Angeles City, Department of Recreation and Parks property managed under lease by the Tree People. The focus of activities is on a variety of educational and community services, using a number of buildings left when fire station 108 vacated the premises in 1977. A forestry nursery, landscaping display, and nature trail are some of the features. Trails connect with the Wilacre Park trail system.

Coldwater Canyon Park is located on the north side of Mulholland Drive, east of Coldwater Canyon Avenue. A parking lot, drinking water, restrooms, and an information center are available.

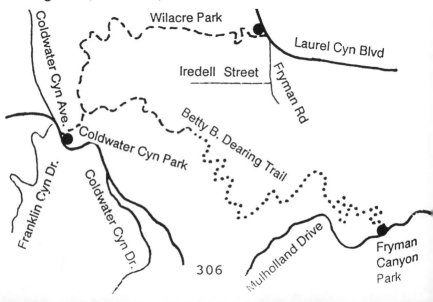

306

HIKE 80   MOCO-CAHUENGA CANYON

Maps: Hollywood Street Map
Distance: 1/2 mile roundtrip
              (at most)
Terrain: path
Time: 15 minutes
Trailhead: Fern Dell Drive

This isn't a hiking trail in the same sense as most of the trips to be found in this book; it is a secluded spot within a city where one may escape the busy streets, relax for awhile, or take a romantic stroll.

In Hollywood near the intersection of Los Feliz Blvd. and Western Avenue go north on Fern Dell Drive to Red Oak Drive. The entry gate is on the east side of Fern Dell.

Moco-Cahuenga Canyon is a verdant haven in a populated area. A stream courses through the canyon, dappling over waterfalls into pools surrounded by ferns and moss covered rocks. Overhead a dense canopy of large Sycamore trees shades this narrow strip of a Park.

Moco-Cahuenga is an Indian Language name with "Moco" meaning the post and council grounds and "Cahuenga" identifying the chief of that tribe.

Surprise yourself some day when in Hollywood — take a few minutes and relax in this truly delightful spot.

307

HIKE 81

Maps:	Griffith Park map
Distance:	2 miles roundtrip
Elevation:	500' gain and loss
Terrain:	Trail and bridle path
Time:	1 hour
Trailhead:	Griffith Observatory

In Hollywood, drive north on Vermont Avenue past Los Feliz Blvd. where the name changes to Vermont Canyon road. The road passes several picnic grounds, a golf course, the Greek Theatre, and a bird sanctuary. After climbing a short distance, the road ends at the Griffith Observatory parking lot.

We walk toward the Observatory and before reaching the building we go left toward the shrubs and trees. The trail starts down the hill, gently at first but with some loose rocks and a perceptibly steeper grade farther on. As we leave the activity at the observatory the remoteness of the area is apparent. Vegetation, mostly chaparral, lines the trail but is not so dense that good views of the valley and city below are blocked out. After about 350 yards down the trail we have a choice of several routes; take the second trail on the right and continue downhill.

In a few hundred yards more another fork in the trail gives us a choice. This time take either one — they both lead to the picnic grounds. I like the left trail because the source of the Ferndell stream starts near the trail. The stream stays within sight and sound all the way to the picnic grounds, which are complete with restrooms, tables, charcoal grills, trees, a running stream, and grass.

The Moco-Cahuenga Canyon is just downstream of the picnic grounds. This little park is a delightful retreat of waterfalls, moss and ferns. Moco-Cahuenga is a mini-hike of its own, but if you have extra time on this hike, it is certainly worth a few minutes' visit.

Return to the Observatory by going upstream through the picnic grounds. Stay on the west side of the stream until picking up the bridle path that starts at the bend of Western Canyon Road as it makes a big left turn upon leaving the picnic area. Stay on the path as it climbs through the broad canyon. Do not be concerned that the Observatory is not visible; a ridge separates this path from the one on which we descended and obscures the view. The path stays on the left of the streambed and is a gradual climb making a big wide sweep to the right. Western Canyon Road parallels the path and is uphill on the left. As the path nears the ridge, it crosses Western Canyon Road, at which time we turn right and follow the paved road to the parking lot. We can avoid walking along the road by crossing it and continuing up the path until it reaches the ridge and intersects the trail between Mt. Hollywood and the Observatory. Turn right and follow the trail to the parking lot.

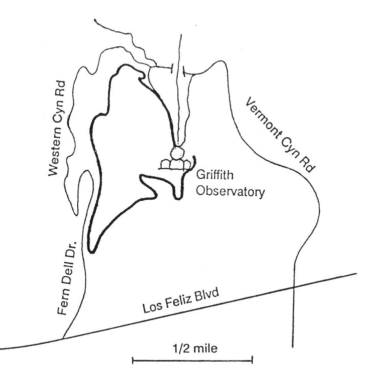

HIKE 82

MT. HOLLYWOOD
from Griffith Observatory

Maps:	Griffith Park
Distance:	2½ miles roundtrip
Elevation:	500' gain and loss
Terrain:	Bridle path and foot trail
Time:	1 hour 15 minutes
Trailhead:	Griffith Observatory

The path leaves the north end of the Griffith Observatory parking lot climbing gently along a tree-lined ridge. In about 350 yards the path crosses along a ridge that is above the Mt. Hollywood Drive Tunnel. At this point the bridle path coming up from the Ferndell picnic area joins from the left. Continuing uphill we notice a steep side trail on the right. This also leads up to Mt. Hollywood, but is steeper and rougher going. The path climbs gently, but steadily, making a big switchback to the west. In less than 1/3 mile after the switchback a path branches in from the left.

Take this path, heading north at first as it circles around the west then the north side of Mt. Hollywood. A grove of trees and benches and cool drinking water shortly appears to the left of the path. This is known as Captain's Roost and is a fine place for lunch or a rest. Continue up the trail as it circles the peak and we notice several bridle paths coming up from the left. One of these leads to a water tank, another comes up from Mt. Hollywood Drive, another from Vista Del Valle. Mt. Hollywood can be climbed from a number of different points so it is worth noting that there are a lot of trails leading back down the mountain, most of which don't lead to the parking lot, so it pays to be observant. We continue on the path, and at the first opportunity turn right to go to the top of Mt. Hollywood. We find a bench, a sign, and an exceptional view of the city.

For variety, return by a slightly different route. Leaving the peak, retrace our steps for about 250 yards to the road, turn right, then at the next junction turn right again — the plan being to circle the peak meeting up with the path that brought us up. Notice Dante's View, a cool grove of trees with benches and water — another beautiful lunch stop. Continue along the path to the junction then head downhill back to the parking lot.

Several well defined trails lead down the ridge to the observatory. If you become adventurous and explore, keep an eye out for a steep trail leading down the east slope. This goes to the bird sanctuary rather than the parking lot, but is not a serious problem; a 1/2 mile walk up Vermont Canyon Road would put us back in the parking lot.

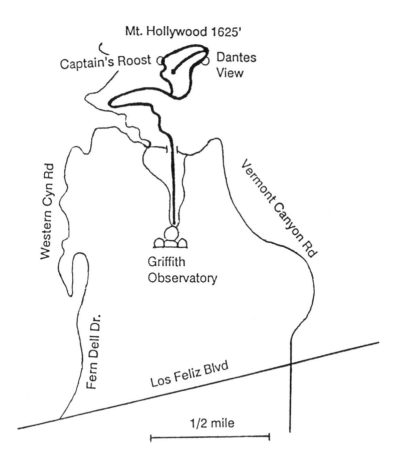

HIKE 83

from Griffith Park
Headquarters

Maps:	Griffith Park Map
Distance:	2 miles roundtrip
Elevation:	250' gain and loss
Terrain:	Bridle path and foot trail
Time:	1 hour
Trailhead:	Griffith Park Hdqtrs

From the parking lot at the Griffith Park Ranger Station go west on Griffith Park Drive about 100 yards, crossing the road at the intersection. At the end of the fence a trail goes up the hill; take this trail about 100 ft. until it meets a bridle path, then turn left. After about 300 yards the bridle path forks; take the left fork. Almost immediately we will see a sign pointing out "Bee Rock Trail" to the right.

The trail up to Bee Rock initially follows a stream that has debris control dams constructed across it. Most of the season will find the stream dry, but a heavy rain brings down sand and gravel. Along the streambed, Sycamore, Walnut, and Oak are the dominant trees. As the trail gains altitude and leaves the stream, Toyon and Laurel Sumac become plentiful. Some Poison Oak is near the trail.

Thirty minutes after leaving the parking lot should find us at a ridge. Turn left and walk out onto Bee Rock. A fenced-in corridor has been placed to prevent falling. A good view of the eastern end of the Park is possible from the top of the rock. The Park Ranger Headquarters, Park Center and merry-go-round area can be seen through the trees.

This is a short, easy hike; return the way we came.

HIKE 84　GRIFFITH PARK FERN CANYON
NATURE TRAIL

Maps:	Griffith Park Map
Distance:	1/2 mile roundtrip
Elevation:	100' gain and loss
Terrain:	Trail
Time:	1/2 hour
Trailhead:	Griffith Park

This trail begins southwest of the Griffith Park merry-go-round on the other side of the road.

Built near an intermittent stream in chaparral, this self-guided nature trail identifies a number of plants. The plant selection includes chaparral, as well as streamside vegetation. Markers are set up along the trail and a guide pamphlet may be available. I have made comments for each station, but keep in mind that plants grow up and die, markers get changed, and other factors enter into the chance that this trail could change.

1. This tall tree is a Deodar Cedar and is not native to this area. It has been planted extensively in southern California and lines both sides of Los Feliz Blvd.
2. The berries of the Sugar Bush have a tart waxy covering. Soaking them in water makes a drink used by Indians.
3. Coffeeberry, also called Pigeon Berry and Yerba del oso, is not eaten; but when roasted and ground, the seeds make a palatable coffee substitute. Coffeeberry bark is known to be a laxative.
4. The Blue Elderberry Bush produces an edible berry late in the summer. It is edible only when fully ripe. The leaves and stems of the plant are mildly poisonous, but are used as a diuretic and purgative.

5. Oak tree.

6. The light gray-green tree near the stream is a white alder. This tree is native to the area and may grow to 100 feet in height.

7. The mottled light green and gray barked tree across the stream is a California Sycamore. This tree will grow only near a perpetual or intermittent stream or in moist gulches. It prefers poor, rocky soil.

8. Poison Oak. As a skin irritant the juice of the plant is very poisonous. Direct contact anytime of the year will cause a severe skin rash. If you view this in the fall or winter the red leaves may have fallen to the ground. They are still poisonous.

9. The tree on the opposite side of the dam is an Arroyo Willow, or Creek Willow. This is an important flood and erosion control plant, the sturdy but flexible branches can catch debris and slow running water.

(Don't bump your head on that California Walnut.)

10. The Holly-leaf Cherry across the stream is an evergreen bush that produces a tasty cherry that is mostly seed. Islay is its common name. It is an important plant of the chaparral.

11. This Southern California black walnut is usually found on margins of streams in gravelly or sandy soils but sometimes on dry hillsides. The nuts are edible — small and hard to crack, but of excellent Flavor.

12. This tall bush is Toyon, or "California Holly." It thrives in the deep soil of canyon bottoms, or competes well in the chaparral.

13. The Lemonade-berry Bush is similar to the Sugar Bush (Station 2).The berry can be soaked in water to make an acid drink. The Wild Blackberries, also seen here, grow near streams.

Cross the stream on a footbridge then turn right. From this point on, most of the numbered posts are missing. Recross the stream and go up the trail to the ridge. Cross the ridge and follow down the stream on the other side.

14. Laurel Sumac is related to Lemonade-berry and Sugar Bush. This aromatic bush grows well throughout the Santa Monicas.

15. This is a Coast Live Oak. The leaf curls some — to the degree that if it were to fall in the water upside down it would float like a boat. The bark of the tree is rough and corky looking.

16. This fern-like plant is Poison Hemlock, and although not native to this hemisphere it is widely distributed in the moist

areas of the Santa Monicas. The plant dries up in the summer holding some of the seeds on the tall stalks. In early October the new plants start growing at the base of the old plant. All parts of this plant are poisonous.

17. This is another toyon. To the left is a Fuchsia Flowering Gooseberry. This plant dries up in late summer and drops its leaves, thereby reducing its need for water.

18. This is another gooseberry. You may notice the three very stout spines at the branch nodes. In general, gooseberries have spines; currants do not.

    The small single needle pine (*Pinus edulis*) is not a native of the Santa Monicas.

19. Burned over area across the arroyo. There are some everlasting plants on the uphill side of the trail. These flowers have an odor resembling brown sugar — even when dry.

20. Lemonade-berry, Gooseberry, and Walnut. A Scrub Oak is on the other side of the trail.

21 This is a clump of Giant Rye Grass. A native in the Santa Monicas and used by the Indians, it dries up in the fall.

22. The Yucca plants on the hillside across the arroyo are commonly called Our Lord's Candle. In the spring when in bloom, the plant has a tall spike covered with cream colored blossoms. By late summer a dry spike remains. The Indians used the fibers from the leaves to make baskets and as thread. The seeds were ground and made into mush.

23. Notice the small oak seedling near the base of the larger oak. Also, the seasonal California wall fern or licorice fern grows here. Don't expect to see it after a long dry spell.

24. This hillside has a number of Black Sage plants growing three or more feet high. The leaf and flower whorls on the stems give rise to other names of Ball Sage and Button Sage.

This description was in our First Edition of *Hiking Trails of the Santa Monica Mountains* published in 1980. Plants do die out and new plants come in but this area has remained fairly constant. Some of these same species may have been here for hundreds of years, and if we elect to let nature take its course most of the species will be here in the future.

HIKE 85

CHEESEBORO-
LOWER PALO COMADO LOOP

Maps: National Geographic SMMTS NRA
Distance: 6 miles
Elevation: 1000'
Terrain: Trail and dirt road
Time: 2 hours 30 minutes
Trailhead: Cheeseboro parking lot

Today's hike is a loop, going north in Cheeseboro Canyon then to cut across a ridge and down into Palo Comado Canyon. We continue our counterclockwise route by going to the south end of Palo Comado before we turn east to climb a ridge and come down the Modelo Trail. Our trip takes us through the valley oak savannah, over a sage scrub plant community, a riparian oak woodland and a grassland.

Cheeseboro Canyon Parking lot is reached by turning north on Chesebro Road from Ventura Freeway in Agoura Hills. Drive slowly about one half mile then turn right into the park and follow the road to a parking lot. A ranch road follows the stream about three miles through a wooded area gaining about 250 feet. We turn left on Ranch Center Trail and in the next 1.1 mile will gain and lose 400 feet. Most of the route is in the open with an opportunity to identify a variety of spring wildflowers. Good views of Cheeseboro Canyon to the east and Palo Comado Canyon to the west might give us cause to slow down and look at these two canyons that parallel each other one mile apart. As we descend west we enter where ranch buildings once stood. People lived in the old farm house, now gone, and a friendly dog barked, then came out to the road to be petted. Palo Comado has reverted to more of a pristine state and all but one structure is gone.

Our trail bends left and merges with the southbound Palo Comado Canyon Trail. The trail is almost level, losing slightly over 100 feet in the next mile and a third. A side trail on the right would take us uphill and into a residential area. We won't go on it today. When we reach a fence turn left to go east gaining about 350 feet in a mile. This is the Palo Comado Connector Trail which soon joins the Modelo Trail. Modelo is named for a light-colored laminated, cleavable, rock structure that formed on the bottom of the ocean somewhere around 10 million years ago when the Santa Monica Mountains were ocean floor. The trail heads south at this point and drops three hundred feet in one and a third miles to hike's end.

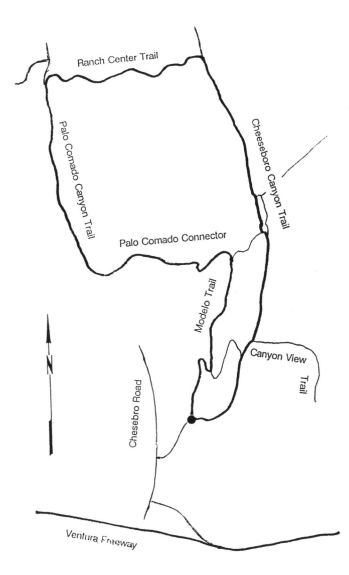

HIKE 86

PALO COMADO TR.
CHEESEBORO LOOP
Shuttle

Maps:	National Geographic, SMMTS NRA
Distance:	8½ miles
Elevation:	800' gain, 1,000' loss
Terrain:	Trail and dirt road
Time:	3½ hours
Trailhead:	Sunny Crest Drive -- beginning Cheeseboro parking lot -- end.

Today's hike will take us up a fireroad in Palo Comado Canyon, then across to Shepherds' Flat and down Cheeseboro Canyon. We will see canyons, cliffs, streams, chaparral, and oak woodlands. A great adventure.

Shuttle means to leave half the transportation at the end of the hike, so everyone drives to the Cheeseboro Parking Lot. Get there from the Ventura Freeway in Agoura Hills by taking the Cheeseboro off-ramp and go north on Chesebro Road turning right into the parking lot. This is where the hike will end. All hikers carpool to the hike's beginning at Sunny Crest Drive. Get there by going west on the freeway, turn north on Kanan Road and drive 1.9 miles to Sunny Crest Drive. Turn right, go .8 mile, and park at the curb.

We go east on a dirt trail up a little rise, then down to Palo Comado Canyon. Cross the stream and turn left onto Palo Comado Canyon Trail. Our trail is almost level at first but becomes steeper as we hike toward the head of the canyon and pull away from the stream. We will pass a steep trail on the right in about 20 to 25 minutes, then 15 minutes later we take a trail on our right that makes a sharp right turn and climbs 2 or 3 minutes to a saddle overlooking Cheeseboro Canyon. This trail takes us east to Shepherds' Flat in about 20 minutes. Steady hiking should put us at Shepherds' Flat about 1 hour and 15 minutes after starting the hike. Many places along the route are great lunch stops. A couple of large Oaks west of the Flat give lots of shade, and most of the remaining trail down Cheeseboro Canyon is shaded.

We turn right and head south on Sulphur Springs Trail which becomes Cheeseboro Canyon Trail. We start downhill through a Chaparral forest, mostly Hairy-leaved Ceanothus and Hoary-leaved Ceanothus. These two species of wild lilac can start blooming late in January and last through April. When we near the stream we enter a riparian woodland of Oak and Sycamore and later Valley Oak Savannah, lasting for the rest of the hike. About one and a third miles from Shepherds' Flat we will pass Sulphur Springs. Another three and a third miles takes us to the end of the hike.

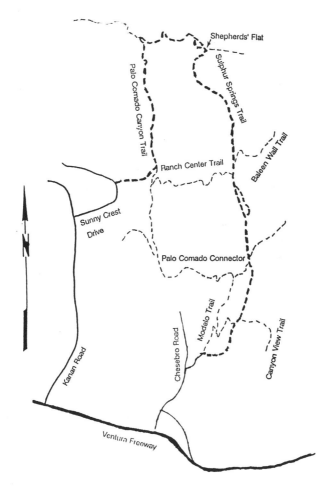

HIKE 87

**CHINA FLAT and
SIMI PEAK - Loop**

Maps:	National Geographic SMMTS NRA
Distance:	8 miles
Elevation:	1700'
Terrain:	Rocky trail and dirt trail
Time:	3¼ hours
Trailhead:	King James Court, Ventura County

China Flat is a grassland and oak woodland. The trail to it is steep and rocky, gaining one thousand feet on a sun exposed slope before reaching the Flat. Simi Peak is a 400' elevation gain from China Flat but on a reasonable grade on a respectable trail. China Flat itself is near a state of original purity. Mother Nature's changes to man's occupation are gradually restoring the land to its natural splendor. This is a treasure to be preserved.

In Westlake Village go north of the Ventura Freeway on Lindero Canyon Road and enter the community of Oak Park. After Lindero makes a sweeping right turn and heads east, look for King James Court on the left. Park on Lindero; walk north one block on King James to the trailhead.

A sign posted at the China Flat Trail asks that we use the "Primary access" trailhead just east of King James Court. I have done this alternate several times and I do not recommend it. Parts of it are at a 30° grade on unstable rock with an unnecessary exposure to injury. The improved trail at the end of King James Court is steep enough and much safer so use it. Yesterday (9/10/1998) thinking I could be prejudiced, I walked the trail east of King James. When halfway up the 30° grade on this miserable section I looked up to see a more or less friendly Southern Pacific Rattlesnake watching my struggles. He was in the middle of the trail and must have concluded that I was having enough trouble so he moved to the side and let me pass. Needless to say I was alert on my entire hike yesterday and at the end exited at King James Court.

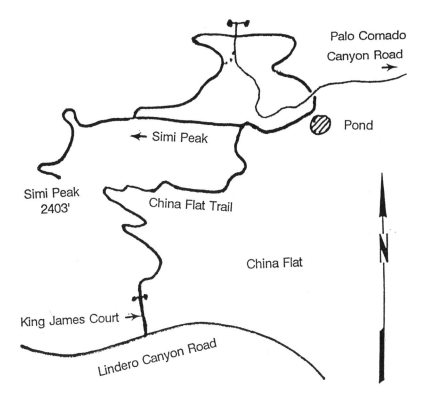

We start uphill, and most of us should deliberately conserve energy because a one-thousand-foot gain on a rocky trail deserves respect.

Fifteen minutes into our hike we notice a short trail headed toward a moss covered wall of rock. Water drips from a seven foot cliff into a clearwater pool. Scarlet Monkey Flower and Fuchsia survive where moisture is present. A nearby cave — just big enough for one person — might have been a shelter for a native family hundreds of years ago.

Although Yerba Santa and Santa Susana Tarweed are found elsewhere in the local mountains, they are usually growing in places that require individual energy to find. I cherish their presence here. Santa Susana Tarweed is on the endangered species list but is prolific here. Hundreds of plants border the trail and are among the rocks and cliffs. Run your hand along the leaves, it smells like raspberries to me. When we get to China Flat we will see Slender Tarweed that has a similar appearance, but not the raspberry smell.

We reach the crest of our trail in fifty minutes. A row of huge boulders and a substantial, locked gate prevent trucks and other motor vehicles from making the mistake of trying to use the trail we just came up. We go around the gate and start a big turn left as we descend into China Flat. We soon leave a chaparral forest to enter an oak woodland. Fifteen minutes and a 200-foot elevation loss later, look for and take a trail on our left.

This trail heads west and contours around the northeast slope of Simi Peak as it climbs 400 feet in about one mile to reach the summit. We may already be winded but the view from atop Simi Peak will leave us gasping. At 2403 feet it is the highest point in the area. We look south and see the streets and houses of Oak Park. To the north Simi Valley comes into view. On the southern horizon, both east and west, the Santa Monica Mountain range dominates the view. We deserve the view — we climbed up here.

On our return from the peak we can take a left fork in the trail when we have walked about ten minutes. Steep in a few places and not as well used as the main trail, it takes us to the north border of the Park. This may change in time, but for the last few years this trail takes us from meadow to meadow of Turkey Mullein, an annual, spreading, gray plant. Flowers bloom all summer until October but it doesn't matter, we need a magnifying glass to see them. We then turn right to go east two thirds of a mile — passing a cave on our left and crossing a north/south road. As the trail makes a sweeping right turn, it loses altitude. A pond and other signs of ranch use is in view. A trail leaves the north end of the pond and for awhile parallels the road (Palo Comado Canyon Road) going west. In less than one half mile we intercept the trail we came in on and follow it to the trailhead.

HIKE 88

UPPER PALO COMADO LOOP
from Sunny Crest Drive

Maps:	National Geographic, SMMTS NRA
Distance:	7½ miles
Elevation:	1050 feet
Terrain:	Trail and road
Time:	3 hours
Trailhead:	Sunny Crest Drive

Palo Comado Canyon is a north-south canyon with its upper origin at China Flat in the Simi Hills. Today's hike takes us on a counter-clockwise loop into Cheeseboro Canyon and across the head of that canyon back into Palo Comado. Of Course this loop may be done clockwise for variety.

We locate the Sunny Crest Drive trailhead by turning north on Kanan Road from the Ventura Freeway and drive 1.9 miles. Turn right on to Sunny Crest Drive, go .8 mile, and park at the curb.

A dirt trail goes east uphill over a one-hundred-foot rise, then down the other side to Palo Comado Road (all roads in the Park are dirt). This is a ten minute walk unless the stream is running high, then we always figure out the best way to cross. Turn right on Palo Comado and walk 200 yards where we find a road on our left going uphill and signed "Cheeseboro Canyon", shown as Ranch Center Trail on the map. We are tempted but do not take the first left road — the one going past a building area. That road takes us to a very steep climb. In the event we do this anyway, we can follow a trail south along the ridge and in 4 minutes reach Ranch Center Trail. Ranch Center Trail gains 400 feet then loses it going down to Cheeseboro Canyon.

We turn left on Cheeseboro Canyon Trail/Sulphur Springs Trail to begin a gentle upstream walk shaded by Oaks and Sycamores. After 350 yards we see the Baleen Wall Trail start up the slope on our right.

Eight to ten minutes later we will see a sign indicating that we stay left to be on the Sulphur Springs Trail. Up until now the stream runs clear but the Sulphur Springs input gives a milky color.

This color dilutes out downstream. We don't need to be told when we pass the spring.

Dense riparian woodland transitions to chaparral as the trail climbs out of the canyon. For a while we are on a rocky trail with short steep sections. This levels out soon and when we reach Shepherds' Flat, about one hour after leaving Ranch Center Trail, we are indeed on flat land. Turn left and quickly come to a fork in the trail. Both routes meet again. I prefer the left route because we pass several large Oaks that furnish a great place for lunch.

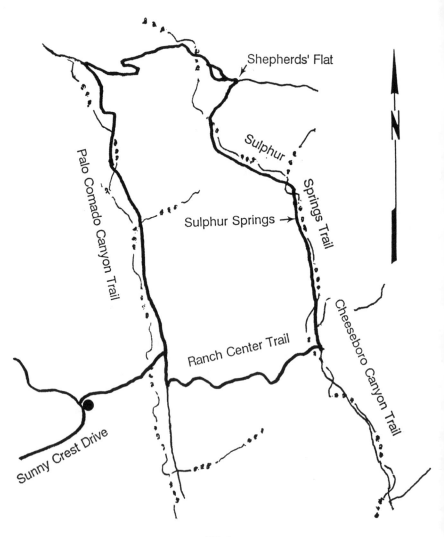

Continuing west the route goes through mild climbs and descents for about twenty minutes then climbs up the ridge to overlook Palo Comado Canyon. Enroute we pass several trails on our left. We avoid these because of the overgrowth, but one that goes south along a ridge is unusual in that several piles of bleahed cow bones can be seen. Our trail angles right and descends to Palo Comado Canyon where we turn left for a gentle downhill mile before it levels out near the stream and in shade of Oaks. One half hour after starting down Palo Comado we look for the trail on the right that takes us to Sunny Crest Trailhead. Fifteen minutes puts us at our cars.

HIKE 89

An Equestrian Adventure in the mountains
of Lower Zuma Canyon
by
Patti Keenan

We began our ride at 2:20 p.m. on Monday, September 14,1998.

Our aim was to begin earlier — but at the last minute, decided to pony a pack horse. We chose Puzzleberry.

This turned out to be a grand idea for three reasons: 1) it would save our mounts the extra burden; 2) Puzzleberry wanted to go; 3) we learned how to use my pack equipment.

This trail loop is only advisable if your horse and you are in good condition. It reaches elevations of 1,700 ft. Gentle though it might be, it requires great stamina and endurance.

A few pinches of bicarbonate of soda before a strenuous ride will assure your horse's chances of not "tying up" out there on the trail. This can cause serious liver damage if left untreated. If your horse has ever trembled after a hard ride — this home remedy will likely resolve the problem.

Our journey kicks off at the Edison/Kanan Dume Road's trailhead staging area, recognized by large boulders lined up along the bottom of the hill. This is located just north of Cavalleri Rd and north of the white house surrounded by the white wrought iron fence, on Kanan Dume Road.

This "proposed" staging area will someday allow horse trailers to utilize this trailhead, but at this point in time, two plus axles are forbidden in either direction on Kanan Dume Rd. Except up to and not past Cavalleri Road.

Our maximum speed is walk/trot. The day is glorious — with views of mountain and ocean forever!

In eight minutes we reach the first junction. The signage points left for the Ocean View Trail. This takes you into Bonsall

Canyon, aka, Zuma Canyon — and gently drops you into the canyon below. Two more minutes and we are at the junction of the Canyon View Trail, to the left. We fork right, to the Zuma Canyon Connector, staying on the Edison Road. The fireroad is wide and newly graded. It is maintained by the National Park Service and they have done a superb job this summer on all the trails here.

Around the first bend the ascent begins and we will parallel Kanan as we wind slowly upwards to 1,700 feet. The mountain and ocean views only get better by the minute.

In about 25 minutes we reach another junction. The sign indicates Edison Road continues right. We turn left up onto the newly cut Zuma Canyon Connector Trail. We begin a switchback that will carry us right to the top of a mountain ridge. Now you will see a resplendent white water view of Zuma Beach that, besides this experience, only flying can provide.

Traveling along this mountain ridge we are headed due north and we're probably at our 1,700-foot level. With the ocean breeze at our backs we have the feeling we are on the top of the world! There is only chaparral at this height. At the end of this ridge the sign points left. It's 3:30. We have made several stops up 'til now — taking advantage of shady spots and photo ops. Now we are headed due West and the breath-taking sights of Point Dume and Zuma Beach lie below in all of their splendor.

Now we begin our descent, gently working our way into the canyon below. There are a few places of caution, where the trail may narrow, but not badly. Mostly, it remains a nice wide fireroad. Obstacles, such as soft shoulders, rocks, water seepage and erosion, can appear from one ride to the next — on any trail. Always be alert.

We noticed water coming from the rock face at one point and it travels along, leaving a thin slice down the trail. We stopped and offered the horses a chance to wet their lips but it didn't smell like home, so they passed. The little stream finally crossed our path and dropped over the edge into the canyon to join the creek below.

It's 4:00 now and we've stopped one last time before our rest stop at the creek. We stop at the red painted culvert, where we find a large boulder that has fallen from the rocky mountain side, a lovely sycamore, and three oak trees casting a welcome shadow of shade across the trail.

We jump down, tighten our saddle girths, adjust Puzzleberry's lopsided saddlebags and pack saddle and take a cool swig of water (we froze our water bottles) providing ice water all day.

We pushed off and moving at a great downhill pace, we arrive at the most lush and fragrant part of the trail ride as we enter a grove of bay laurel trees. It is now 4:15.

Two more minutes and we are at the creek. Lovely shade, running water, huge rocks and sand. Our horses gladly step into the stream, but still aren't interested in drinking. We tied to assorted branches and shrubs, loosened the girths and lightened Puzzleberry's burden of snacks and drinks, threw down the old lace tablecloth and found a comfortable rock to sit on.

There is a "proposed" hitching post — but it must first go through all proper channels of government before final decisions on priority, location, etc. can be established. We hope for sooner than later. The importance of hitching posts should be emphasized. The equestrian would much prefer a safe hitching post rather than damage a tree or trample the flora, or rub against poison oak!

At 5:25 all parties rested. We loaded Puzzleberry — a lighter burden now — and began our ascent.

Initially this trail is a bit rough — due to overgrowth and erosion— but nothing you can't step over. After a while it's a breeze! The horses are happy at a fast trot.

About a half mile before the top there is water for horses only, on your left. It's a big white barrel and sports a nose-press waterer. It bears a warning "Not fit for human consumption." It runs very slowly and the horses only lick at it, but don't have the patience to work at it.

It is now 6:10 and we've reached the west ridge above Zuma Canyon. We are now on the Zuma Ridge Fireroad and the sign ahead indicates a right turn takes you to Encinal Canyon Road, toward Buzzards Roost — left will take us down towards Bonsall and Zuma Canyon, to the Busch Trailhead. We head left, back to the ocean breezes and views forever.

It's 7:00 when we reach the Busch Trailhead. We make a sharp left, toward the step-over and the sign reads Zuma Canyon Connector Trail. This trail too has been cleared and repaired by NPS and the California Conservation Crew. It is a lovely switchback, that drops you right onto the canyon floor. From there we veer left, following the signage to the Ocean View Trail. We travel along the canyon floor, cross the creek and pass through lush and assorted shrubs and plants. Sycamore, walnut and sumac are the dominant trees. Wildflowers abound.

This trail now becomes a switchback that climbs back out of the canyon on the eastern-most side. At the top we find ourselves right back where our journey began, on the Edison Road trail. Turning right, we head downhill to the staging area on Kanan Dume Road. It is 7:45 and we pull out our trusty flashlights for the last few minutes.

Your other option of course, is to begin and end your loop in the parking lot at the end of Bonsall Drive.

When we arrived home we were so exhilarated by our day of fun and sun that everyone was ready to go out again! Except Puzzleberry !

THINGS TO PACK:

collapsible bucket	snacks
water/for horse and rider	flashlight
halter & lead rope	hat/visor
long rope (for a picket line)	sun block
long-sleeved shirt or jacket	chaps
bug repellent	camera

Participants of this ride are

Patti Keenan, riding Bart

Sandy Mitchell, riding Hailey

Jennifer Skophammer, riding Blackfoot

Patti Keenan is President of Malibu Trails Association

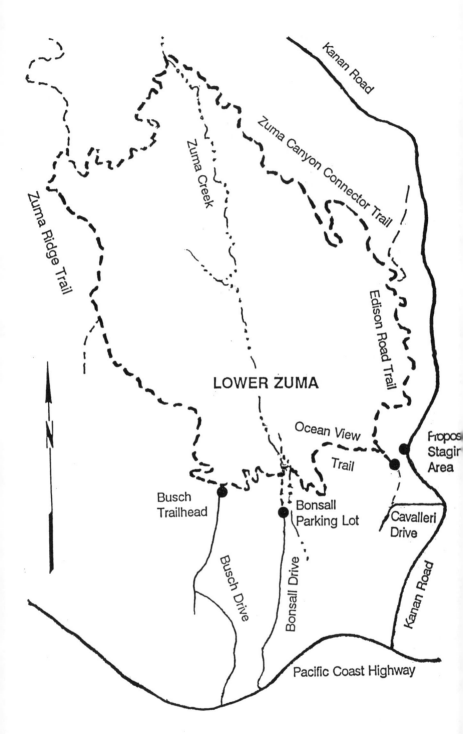

Kanan Road

Zuma Canyon Connector Trail

Zuma Creek

Zuma Ridge Trail

Edison Road Trail

LOWER ZUMA

Ocean View

Trail

N

Busch
Trailhead

Bonsall
Parking Lot

Propos
Stagir
Area

Cavalleri
Drive

Busch Drive

Bonsall Drive

Kanan Road

Pacific Coast Highway

BACKBONE TRAIL

The Backbone Trail is a 69 mile (more or less) equestrian, hiking, and quite often biking trail that runs west and east through the Santa Monica Mountains. The western terminus is at the Pacific Ocean at Point Mugu State Park, the eastern terminus, at Will Rogers State Historic Park. Parts of the trail have been in existence many years, other segments are still on the drawing board. Land for the eastern half has been procured; we have major gaps in land acquisition of the western half.

The concept of a Backbone Trail has been talked about for many years, not always by the name "Backbone," but the idea of an east-west ridge trail is certainly not recent. Work to procure land, design the trail, and build it has been going on for several years. Cooperative effort of the California State Park system, the Santa Monica National Recreation Area, the Santa Monica Mountains Conservancy, the Sierra Club, elected representatives, and a great number of volunteers has had a direct positive effect on keeping the project moving.

The following maps and brief descriptions are meant to give an overview of the trail, rather than a detailed description. Those segments of the trail that have been completed should not present a route finding problem but for the segments not yet built, the information here should be augmented with topo maps and personal contact with someone who has walked the route, before attempting it on your own.

The names of the trail segments listed here are temporary until either common usage dictates or someone with authority to name trails does so. A problem with naming a trail segment that hasn't been built is that the builders of the trail are the ones that will, for one reason or another, come up with an appropriate name. As an example, "The Dead Horse Trail" had no name during construction — but a lot of suggestions were being made — until one day as the trail neared completion, the crew arrived at the trailhead to find that overnight someone had buried a horse (pony) in the trail. "Dead Horse Trail" has been the accepted name since. So until such time as designated names are established, I would like to consider these as "working" names to be temporary for this edition of the book, and will plan to update later.

Locations listed are identifiable places on the maps, usually a trail junction, or road or stream crossing. Information as to the location of water or restrooms is included. In general, the niceties and conveniences of a well-established trail are missing. We don't expect trail signs or mileages to be posted in the immediate future and those of us who choose to walk this trail in the next few years should do so with an explorer's attitude. A group of us walked the trail as an annual pilgrimage, starting in 1983.

In 1990 we discontinued this and have since concentrated on November as "Backbone Trail" month. We celebrate the "Trail" in a number of ways, but for us hikers the Sierra Club leads several Backbone Trail hikes each Sunday. Other organized groups are honoring the recognition of the trail.

KEY:

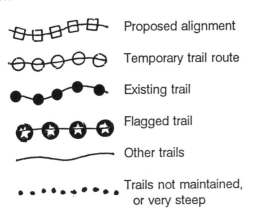

Proposed alignment

Temporary trail route

Existing trail

Flagged trail

Other trails

Trails not maintained,
or very steep

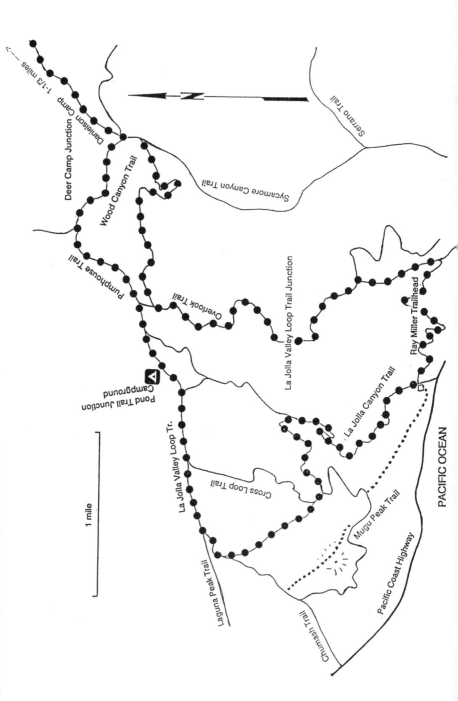

Deer Camp Junction

1-1/3 miles

Danielson Camp

Wood Canyon Trail

Pumphouse Trail

Sycamore Canyon Trail

N

Serrano Trail

Overlook Trail

La Jolla Valley Loop Trail Junction

Ray Miller Trailhead

Pond Trail Junction

Campground

La Jolla Valley Loop Tr.

Cross Loop Trail

La Jolla Canyon Trail

1 mile

Laguna Peak Trail

Mugu Peak Trail

Chumash Trail

Pacific Coast Highway

PACIFIC OCEAN

SEGMENT OF TRAIL	LOCATION
La Jolla Canyon Trail	Ray Miller Trailhead, La Jolla Cyn Jolla Valley Loop Trail Junction
La Jolla Valley Loop Tr	La Jolla Canyon Trail Junction Mugu Peak Trail Junction Cross Loop Trail Junction Oak Grove Mugu Peak Trail Junction Laguna Peak Trail Junction Cross Loop Trail Junction Pond Trail Junction Campground Trail Junction Overlook Trail Junction
	Pumphouse Trail Overlook Trail Junction Deer Camp Junction
Wood Canyon Trail	Deer Camp Junction Sycamore Canyon Trail Junction
Sycamore Canyon Trail	Danielson Camp

6 miles between Ray Miller Trailhead and Danielson Camp

The Ray Miller trailhead is an excellent staging area for the beginning or the end of your hike along the Backbone Trail. A large parking lot, locked at night, gives us a good assembly spot. Restroom facilities and drinking water are available. Overnight camping is available at nearby La Jolla Beach and at Sycamore Campground. A walk-in campground is located at mile 4 of the trail (two miles from the trailhead by short-cutting). Restrooms, drinking water, and picnic tables are available at the walk-in camp. Restrooms and picnic tables are also available at Deer Camp Junction. Total elevation gain for this segment is about 1000'.

The La Jolla Canyon trail is closed to all but foot traffic. Because the Backbone Trail is a multi-use trail, when possible, alternate routes have long been considered. The Chumash Trail could not be changed because to do so would constitute a gross irreverence to its heritage of being one of the oldest foot trails known in continuous use (possibly for the last 7000 years). The Ray Miller Trail, constructed in 1989, heads east and connects to the Scenic and Overlook Trails. Horses and bicycles can also use this trail.

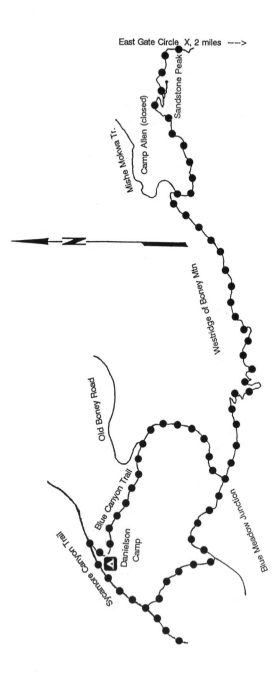

East Gate Circle X, 2 miles --->

Sandstone Peak

Camp Allen (closed)

Mishe Mokwa Tr.

Westridge of Boney Mtn

Old Boney Road

Blue Canyon Trail

Sycamore Canyon Trail

Danielson Camp

Blue Meadow Junction

SEGMENT OF TRAIL	LOCATION
Sycamore Canyon Trail	Danielson Camp
Blue Canyon Trail	Danielson Camp Blue Meadow Junction
Westridge of Boney Mtn Trail	Blue Meadow Junction
	Camp Allen (closed) Sandstone Peak East Gate Circle X

10 miles between Danielson Camp and East Gate of Circle X

The original plan for the Backbone Trail route was to use the segment of the Guadalasca Trail that goes uphill east of Sycamore Canyon.   This trail is more than 20° steep in many places and would require complete rebuilding.   A decision has been made to reroute the Backbone Trail along Sycamore Canyon as far as Danielson Camp.   This change allows a moderate grade and the benefit of having a campground with many facilities.

The Westridge Trail segment was built primarily by California Conservation Corps crews during 1990.   A reliable source of water does not exist between Danielson Camp and the Ranger Station at Circle X Ranch.   The Altitude change, the distance, and the remoteness of this section mandate careful planning for anyone attempting this hike.

Three   other trails connect Sycamore Canyon with the Westridge Trail.   Each one is unique and worth hiking.   The Serrano Canyon Trail is not suitable for horses.

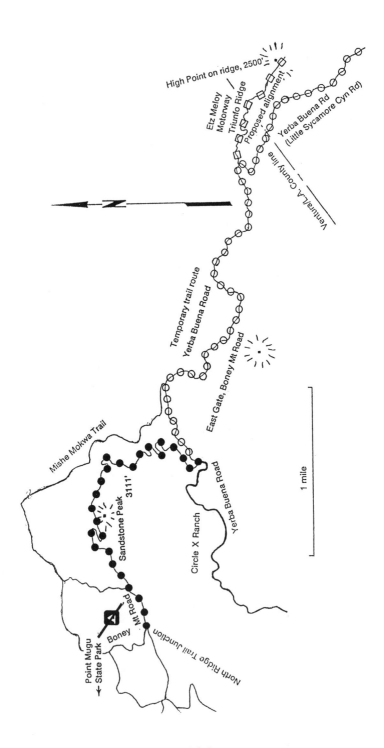

SEGMENT OF TRAIL	LOCATION
Boney Mt Road	Trail to Sandstone Peak
Yerba Buena Road Triunfo Pass segment (Property has not been procured and trail does not exist)	East Gate, Boney Mt Road Triunfo Ridge
Triunfo Ridge (Property has not been procured and trail does not exist)	Yerba Buena Road Junction Ventura/L.A. County line High Point on ridge, 2500'

5-1/4 miles between East Gate of Circle X and Clarke Ranch Road.

Access is available by trail from (1) Yerba Buena Road and (2) Point Mugu State Park.

This section of the Backbone Trail has not been constructed, with the exception of existing routes in Circle X Ranch. The status of land procurement is not known.

Boney Mountain Road climbs to 3000'. Reach Sandstone Peak by climbing a trail from the road to the top. At 3111' Sandstone Peak is the highest point in the Santa Monica Mountains. I can give no reliable explanation why this massive volcanic mountain is called "sandstone." Because of his many years of devoted work to develop Circle X Ranch as a Boy Scout camp, W. Herbert Allen was honored by having the peak named after him. The new name was not officially accepted so it remains "Sandstone Peak."

Upon reaching Yerba Buena Road, the trail no longer exists until arriving at Clarke Ranch Road. Until such time as a corridor is procured we can walk on Yerba Buena Road and then Mulholland Highway to the beginning of Clarke Ranch Road, a total of 5.2 miles. Pavement on a decent grade might even be welcome after the rock on Boney Mountain. The proposed route is on Triunfo Ridge along Etz Meloy Motorway.

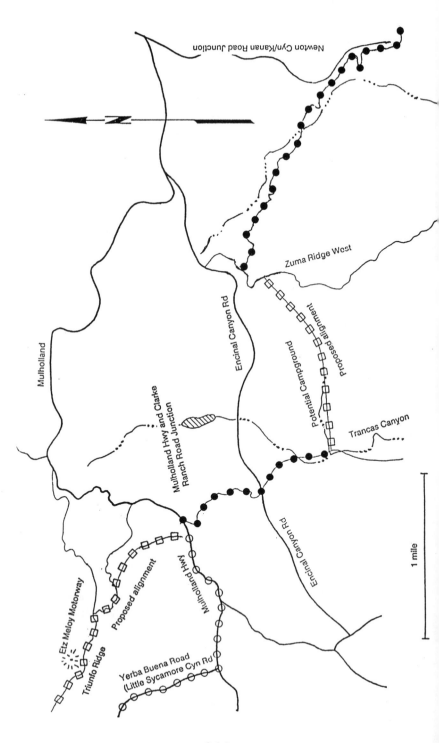

SEGMENT OF TRAIL	LOCATION
Clarke Ranch Road	Mulholland Hwy Junction
	Encinal Canyon Rd Junction
Trancas Canyon	Encinal Canyon Rd Junction
	Potential Campground
	Zuma Ridge West
Zuma Canyon	Zuma Ridge Trail
Kanan Road	Newton Cyn/Kanan Road Junction

Actual distance between upper Clarke Ranch Road and Kanan Road could be 7 - 9 miles.

The Actual proposed route is unknown. The distance is based upon the terrain and elevation change.

Access is available from (1) Little Sycamore Canyon Road, (2) Mulholland Highway, (3) Encinal Canyon Road, and (4) Kanan Road.

This section of the Backbone Trail promises to be of exceptional interest. Areas for potential campgrounds are found in both Trancas and Zuma Canyons. Trancas Canyon is a steep walled winding slit through massive rock and offers great chances for exploration. Zuma Canyon is known for spectacular waterfalls, rock pools and fern covered grottos. Lower Newton canyon between Zuma Canyon and Kanan Road supports three waterfalls, two of which are dramatic.

A large parking area along Kanan Road, at the north end of the tunnel nearest the ocean, can be used for a staging area for this trail section. Room for horse trailers is no problem.

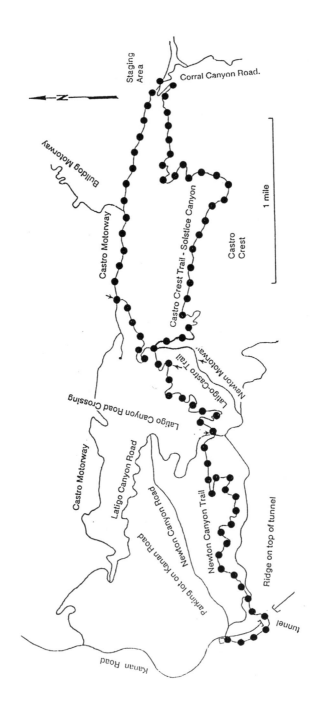

N

Staging Area

Corral Canyon Road.

1 mile

Bulldog Motorway

Castro Motorway

Castro Crest Trail - Solstice Canyon

Castro Crest

Latigo-Castro Trail

Newton Motorway

Latigo Canyon Road Crossing

Castro Motorway

Latigo Canyon Road

Newton Canyon Road

Parking lot on Kanan Road

Newton Canyon Trail

Ridge on top of tunnel

tunnel

Kanan Road

SEGMENT OF TRAIL	LOCATION
Newton Canyon Trail (Trail flagged but not built)	Parking lot on Kanan Road Ridge on top of tunnel Latigo Canyon Road Crossing
Latigo-Castro Trail	Latigo Canyon Road Crossing Newton Motorway Junction
Newton Motorway	Latigo-Castro Trail Junction Castro Motorway Junction
Castro Motorway	Newton Motorway Junction Bulldog Motorway Junction
Corral Canyon Road	Corral Cyn Rd Parking lot and Corral Crest Trail Junction

6-1/2 miles between Kanan and Corral Cyn Road via Castro M/W; 7 miles if by upper Solstice Trail.

Access is available from (1) Kanan Road (Southern-most Tunnel), (2) Latigo Canyon Road, and (3) Corral Canyon Road.

The trail follows the old road south to the ridge on top of the tunnel, then turns east. The property owner has granted a trail easement to the National Park Service from the tunnel to a driveway. Please respect the rights of the property owner and stay on the trail.

The trail from Latigo Canyon Road to Newton Motorway is complete and in use. Newton Motorway is a steep climb, 300' gain, to Castro Motorway. Six-tenths of a mile after getting on Castro Motorway, Bulldog Motorway comes up from the left. An alternate — and maybe favored — route starts on Bulldog, drops down to Malibu Creek, and follows it into the floor of the valley.

Otherwise, stay on Castro Motorway until you reach Corral Canyon Road staging area. There are no facilities.

Another alternate route takes us to Corral Canyon Road staging area via Solstice Canyon. This is preferred as a west-to-east route because it eliminates the steep climb up Newton Motorway to Castro Motorway. This may be 1/2 mile longer than the fireroad but on a beautiful trail.

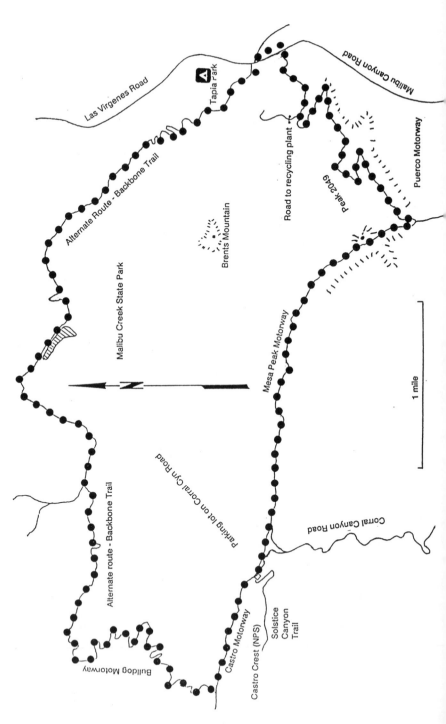

SEGMENT OF TRAIL	LOCATION
Mesa Trail	Parking lot on Corral Cyn Road Mesa Peak Motorway Junction
Mesa Peak Motorway *	Mesa Trail Junction Peak 2049 Puerco Motorway Junction Road to recycling plant Malibu Creek Road Junction
Malibu Canyon Road	Mesa Peak Motorway Junction Parking lot at Tapia Park

5-1/2 miles between Corral Canyon Road and Tapia Park.

* The 1/2 mile between Malibu Canyon Rd and the road to the recycling plant is "technically" not Mesa Peak Motorway.

This section of the Backbone Trail is on existing Fireroads.

Access is available from (1) Corral Canyon Road and (2) Malibu Canyon Road.

A ridge trail all the way has good views of Malibu Creek State Park on the left and Corral Canyon on the right. After passing Peak 2049 and starting down to the east we are treated to grand panoramas of Malibu Creek.
At Malibu Canyon Road we cross the road and turn left. Cross the bridge on the walkway, then recross Malibu Canyon Road and walk to Tapia parking lot.

Restrooms, drinking water, and picnic tables are available at Tapia.

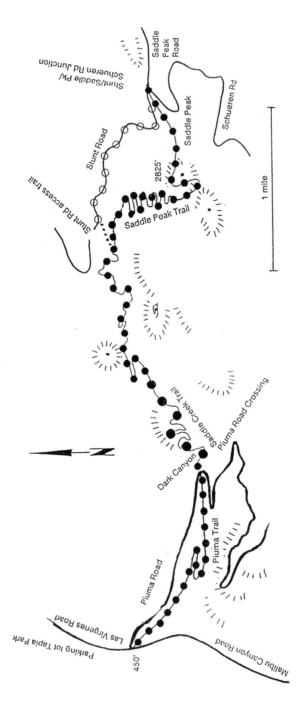

Saddle Peak Road

Stunt/Saddle Pk/
Schueren Rd Junction

Saddle Peak

Schueren Rd

Stunt Road

2825'

Stunt Rd access trail

Saddle Peak Trail

1 mile

N

Saddle Creek Trail

Piuma Road Crossing

Dark Canyon

Piuma Road

Piuma Trail

Parking lot Tapia Park

Las Virgenes Road

450'

Malibu Canyon Road

346

SEGMENT OF TRAIL	LOCATION
Piuma Trail	Parking lot: Tapia Park Piuma Road Crossing
Saddle Creek Trail	Piuma Road Crossing Dark Canyon Stunt Road access trail
Saddle Peak Trail	Stunt Road access trail Saddle Peak Stunt/Saddle Pk/Schueren Rd Junction

7 miles between Tapia and the top of Stunt Road east of Saddle Peak. 7-1/2 miles if we go to the top of the Peak.

Access is available from (1) Malibu Canyon Road, (2) Piuma Road, (3) Stunt Road, and (4) Stunt Road/Saddle Peak Road Junction.
It is characterized by elevation changes from 450' at Malibu Creek to 2825' on Saddle Peak. Most of the trail is in chaparral.

A great display of Chaparral Pea is found near Saddle Peak. May has the best blooms, and heat of summer ends the blooming season. On top of the peak we find a great display of Spanish Broom.

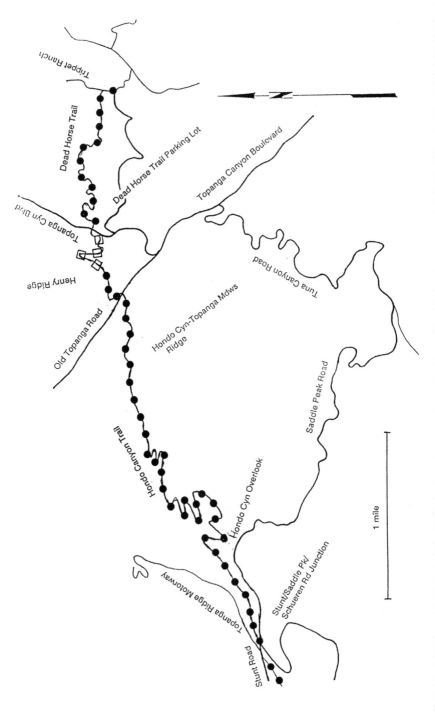

Tripper Ranch

Dead Horse Trail

Dead Horse Trail Parking Lot

Topanga Cyn Blvd

Topanga Canyon Boulevard

Henry Ridge

Old Topanga Road

Tuna Canyon Road

Hondo Cyn-Topanga Mdws Ridge

Saddle Peak Road

Hondo Canyon Trail

Hondo Cyn Overlook

Topanga Ridge Motorway

Stunt/Saddle Pk/ Schueren Rd Junction

Stunt Road

N

1 mile

SEGMENT OF TRAIL	LOCATION
Hondo Canyon Trail	Stunt/Saddle Peak Rd Junction
	Hondo Cyn Overlook
	Hondo Cyn-Topanga Mdws
	Ridge (1214')
	Old Topanga Road Crossing
	Henry Ridge
	Topanga Cyn Blvd Crossing
	Dead Horse Trail Parking lot
Dead Horse Trail	Dead Horse Trail Parking lot
	Trippet Ranch

7 miles between the top of Stunt Road and Trippet Ranch.

Access is available from (1) Stunt/Saddle Peak/Schueren Road Junction, (2) Old Topanga Road, and (3) Dead Horse Trail Parking lot, and Trippet Ranch.

The western half mile of this section (Fossil Trail) follows an obscured trail parallel to Saddle Peak Road. Upon dropping down into Hondo Canyon we will enter an area that has been isolated from use by steep slopes and dense brush. Rock formations and precipitous views dominate the high part of the area. The Grasslands and Oak Woodlands of Topanga Meadows make a radical change in scenery as the trail crosses the ridge south of Hondo Canyon. From the east side of Old Topanga Road the trail will cross Henry Ridge north of Topanga school. Even though the trail hasn't been flagged, the route is not difficult and drops down a ridge to Greenleaf Road and Topanga Canyon Boulevard crossing. The Dead Horse Trail segment is complete and in use. Restrooms are available at both Dead Horse Trailhead and Trippet Ranch.

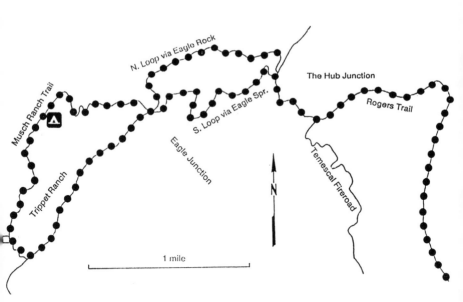

The section of the Backbone Trail between Trippet Ranch and Will Rogers State Historic Park has been in existence for a number of years.

Access is available from (1) Trippet Ranch and (2) Will Rogers State Historic Park.

Trippet Ranch is headquarters of Topanga State Park and offers a Ranger Station, pay telephone, picnic tables, restrooms, drinking water, and a bulletin board. Will Rogers State Historic Park, at the other end of this section of trail, offers all this plus tours of the home, a bookstore, and a museum. In between are 10 miles of good walking on fireroads and trails.

Immediately, at Trippet Ranch, two routes are offered: (1) the fireroad to Eagle Junction; and (2) Musch Ranch Trail (goes past an overnight camping area). Both trail segments are about 2 miles long and meet at Eagle Junction. At Eagle Junction two more options are available: (1) North Loop past Eagle Rock and, (2) South Loop past Eagle Spring. Both Segments are about 1.4 miles long and meet at the Hub. From the Hub the route is south on ridges, losing altitude as we approach Will Rogers State Historic Park.

350

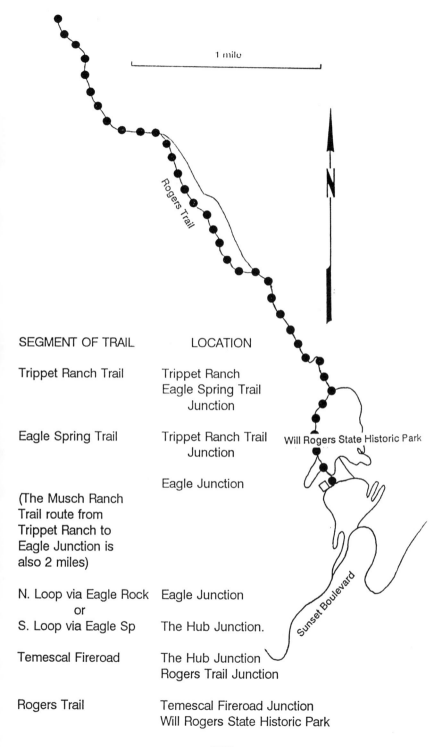

1 mile

N

Rogers Trail

SEGMENT OF TRAIL	LOCATION
Trippet Ranch Trail	Trippet Ranch
	Eagle Spring Trail
	Junction
Eagle Spring Trail	Trippet Ranch Trail
	Junction
	Eagle Junction
(The Musch Ranch Trail route from Trippet Ranch to Eagle Junction is also 2 miles)	
N. Loop via Eagle Rock or	Eagle Junction
S. Loop via Eagle Sp	The Hub Junction.
Temescal Fireroad	The Hub Junction
	Rogers Trail Junction
Rogers Trail	Temescal Fireroad Junction
	Will Rogers State Historic Park

Will Rogers State Historic Park

Sunset Boulevard

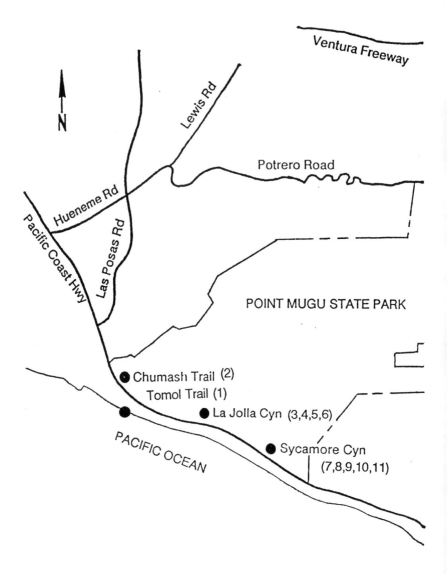

Ventura Freeway

Lewis Rd

Potrero Road

Hueneme Rd

Las Posas Rd

Pacific Coast Hwy

POINT MUGU STATE PARK

Chumash Trail (2)
Tomol Trail (1)

La Jolla Cyn (3,4,5,6)

Sycamore Cyn
(7,8,9,10,11)

PACIFIC OCEAN

TRAILHEAD MAP

These six map pages cover the
Santa Monica Mountains from
West to East.

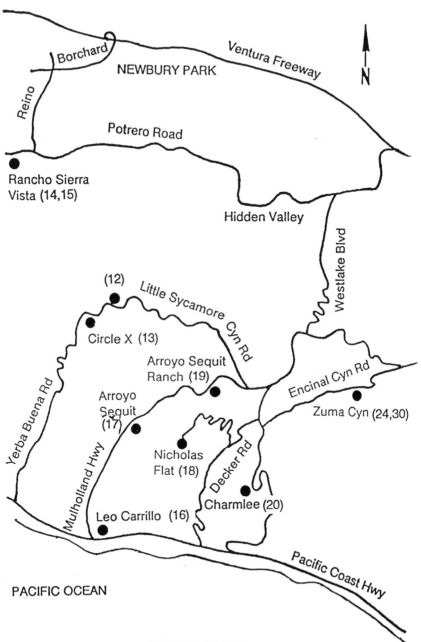

Borchard
Ventura Freeway
N
NEWBURY PARK
Reino
Potrero Road
Rancho Sierra
Vista (14,15)
Hidden Valley
Westlake Blvd
(12)
Little Sycamore Cyn Rd
Circle X (13)
Arroyo Sequit
Ranch (19)
Yerba Buena Rd
Encinal Cyn Rd
Arroyo
Sequit
(17)
Zuma Cyn (24,30)
Nicholas
Flat (18)
Decker Rd
Mulholland Hwy
Charmlee (20)
Leo Carrillo (16)
Pacific Coast Hwy
PACIFIC OCEAN

TRAILHEAD MAP

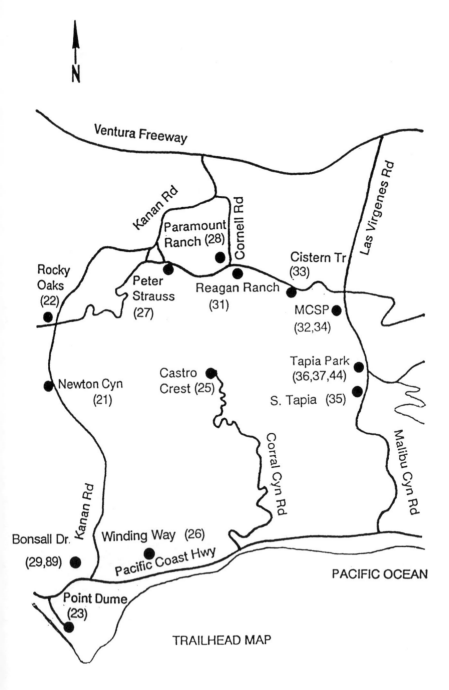

TRAILHEAD MAP

354

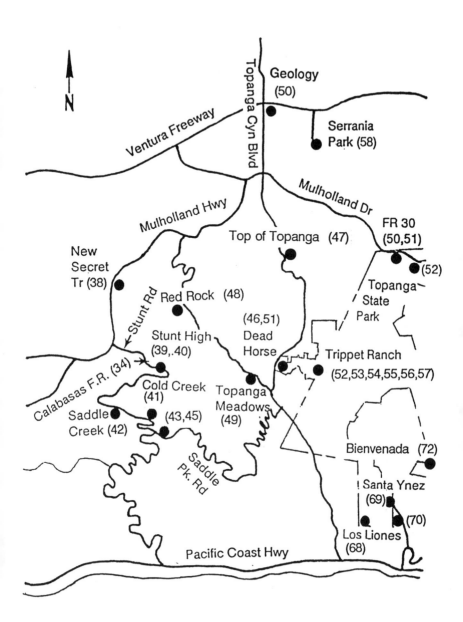

TRAILHEAD MAP

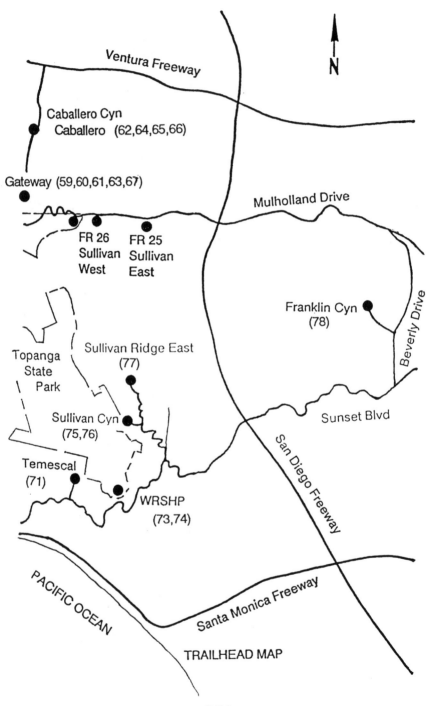

Ventura Freeway

N

Caballero Cyn
Caballero (62,64,65,66)

Gateway (59,60,61,63,67)

Mulholland Drive

FR 26
Sullivan
West

FR 25
Sullivan
East

Franklin Cyn
(78)

Beverly Drive

Topanga
State
Park

Sullivan Ridge East
(77)

Sullivan Cyn
(75,76)

Sunset Blvd

Temescal
(71)

WRSHP
(73,74)

San Diego Freeway

PACIFIC OCEAN

Santa Monica Freeway

TRAILHEAD MAP

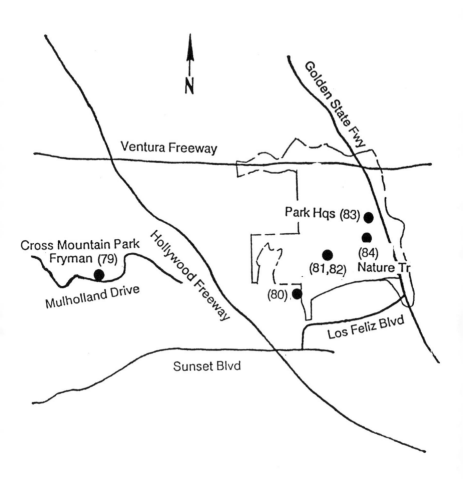

N

Golden State Fwy

Ventura Freeway

Park Hqs (83) ●

(84) ●

Cross Mountain Park
Fryman (79) ●

● (81,82)

Hollywood Freeway

Nature Tr

Mulholland Drive

(80) ●

Los Feliz Blvd

Sunset Blvd

Santa Monica Freeway

TRAILHEAD MAP

GENERAL INDEX
OF PLANTS

Flowering and Herbaceous

Baby Blue-eyes *(Nemophila menziesii)*	March-April
Bedstraw *(Galium spp. [3])*	March-June
Bleeding Heart *(Dicentra ochroleuca)*	May-June
Blow-wives *(Achyrachaena mollis)*	April
Blue Dicks *(Dicholostemma pulchellum)*	March-April
Blue-eyed Grass *(Sisyrinchium bellum)*	March-April
Boykinia *(Boykinia spp [2])*	May-July
Brodiaea *(Brodiaea jolonensis)*	April-May
Buttercup, Calif. *(Ranunculus californicus)*	Feb.-March
Calabazilla *(Cucurbita foetidissima)*	June-Aug.
California Fuchsia *(Zauschneria spp. [2])*	Aug.-Nov.
California Poppy *(Eschscholzia spp. [2])*	March-May
Canchalagua *(Centaurium venustum)*	June-July
Catchfly [Indian Pink] *(Silene laciniata)*	April-June
Checkerbloom *(Sidalcea malvaeflora)*	May-June
Chia *(Salvia columbariae)*	March-April
Chinese Houses *(Collinsia heterophylla)*	April-May
Chocolate Lily *(Fritillaria biflora)*	Feb.-March
Cinquefoil *(Potentilla glandulosa)*	May-July
Clarkia *(Clarkia spp. [5])*	April-June
Clematis [Virgin's Bower] *(Clematis spp. [2])*	March-May
Cliff Aster *(Malacothrix saxatilis)*	April-Nov.
Clover *(Trifolium spp.[11])*	
Coreopsis, Annual *(Coreopsis bigelovii)*	March-May
Corethrogyne *(Corethrogyne filaginifolia)*	June-Sept.
Cream-cups *(Platystemon californicus)*	April-May
Crimson Pitcher Sage *(Salvia spathacea)*	March-May
Curly Dock *(Rumex crispus)* *	March-June
Dock *(Rumex spp [3])*	
Dodder *(Cuscuta spp. [4])*	March-June
Dudleya [Live-forever] *(Dudleya spp. [3])*	April-June
Dudleya, Chalk-leaved *(Dudleya pulverulenta)*	August
Eucrypta *(Eucrypta chrysanthemifolia)*	March-April
Evening Primrose *(Camissonia spp. [5])*	April-May
Evening Primrose, Hooker's *(Oenothera hookeri)*	May-June
Everlasting [Cudweed] *(Gnaphalium spp. [7])*	Jan.-Oct.

Fennel *(Foeniculum vulgare)* *	May-July
Fiddleneck *(Amsinckia spp. [2])*	March-May
Fiesta Flower *(Pholistoma auritum)*	March-April
Figwort *(Scrophularia californica)*	March-June
Filaree [Storksbill] *(Erodium spp. [4])**	Feb.-May
Fire Poppy *(Papaver californicum)*	April
Fleabane *(Erigeron foliosus)*	May-June
Four O'clock *(Mirabilis laevis)*	March-June
Gilia *(Gilia spp. [2])*	April-May
Globe Lily *(Calochortus albus)*	April-May
Goldenbush *(Haplopappus spp [4])*	
Goldenrod *(Solidago spp [2])*	Aug.-Nov.
Golden Yarrow *(Eriophyllum confertiflorum)*	April-May
Golden Stars *(Bloomeria crocea)*	April-May
Goldfields *(Lasthenia spp. [2])*	April-May
Gourd *(Cucurbita foetidissima)*	June-July
Ground Pink *(Linanthus dianthiflorus)*	April
Groundsel, Bush *(Senecio douglasii)*	April-May
Groundsel, Common *(Senecio vulgaris)* *	Jan.-May
Gumweed *(Grindelia robusta)*	April-June
Hedge Nettle, Rigid *(Stachys rigida)*	March-Aug.
Hedge Nettle *(Stachys bullata)*	March-May
Hedge Nettle, White *(Stachys albens)*	June-Aug.
Heliotrope *(Heliotropium curassavicum)*	June-Aug.
Hemlock, Poison *(Conium maculatum)* *	May-July
Horehound *(Marrubium vulgare)* *	March-May
Humboldt Lily *(Lilium Humboldtii)*	June-July
Indian Paintbrush *(Castilleja spp. [4])*	March-May
Indian Warrior *(Pedicularis densiflora)*	Feb.-April
Jewel-flower *(Streptanthus heterophyllus)*	March-April
Jimson-weed *(Datura wrightii)*	May-July
Lacepod [Fringepod] *(Thysanocarpus curvipes)*	March-May
Larkspur, Blue *(Delphinium spp. [2])*	March-May
Larkspur, Scarlet *(Delphinium cardinale)*	June-July
Leather Root *(Psoralea macrostachya)*	June-Aug.
Lomatium *(Lomatium spp. [4])*	Jan.-May
Lotus *(Lotus spp. [7])*	March-Aug.
Lupine *(Lupinus spp. [8]*	March-May
Man-root [Wild Cucumber] *(Marah macrocarpus)*	Jan.-April
Mariposa Lily,, Butterfly *(Calachortus venustus)*	May-July
Mariposa Lily, Catalina *(Calochortus catalinae)*	March-April
Mariposa Lily, Lilac *(Calachortus splendens)*	May-June
Mariposa Lily, Plummers *(Calochortus plummerae)*	June-July

Mariposa Lily, Yellow *(Calochortus clavatus)*	May
Matilija Poppy *(Romneya coulteri)* *	April-May
Microseris *(Microseris spp [4])*	
Milkmaids *(Cardamine californica)*	Feb.-April
Milkweed, Calif. *(Asclepias californica)*	March-June
Milkweed, Narrowleaf *(Asclepias fascicularis)*	May-Sept.
Miners' Lettuce *(Claytonia perfoliata)*	March-April
Monkeyflower, Bush *(Diplacus longiflorus)*	April-June
Monkeyflower, Common *(Mimulus guttatus)*	March-May
Monkeyflower, Scarlet *(Mimulus cardinalis)*	June-Aug.
Monkeyflower, Slimy *(Mimulus floribundis)*	April-Aug.
Monkeyflower, Yellow *(Mimulus brevipes)*	March-May
Morning Glory *(Calystegia macrostegia)*	Feb.-June
Mountain Dandelion *(Agoseris grandiflora)*	May-June
Mustard, Common *(Brassica campestris)* *	All year
Mustard, Black *(Brassica nigra)* *	March-July
Mustard, Tansy *(Descurainia pinnata)*	March-June
Mustard, Tower *(Arabis glabra)*	March-July
Onion, Wild *(Allium spp. [2])*	March-May
Owl's Clover *(Orthocarpus purpurascens)*	March-May
Pansy [Johnny-Jump-up] *(Viola pedunculata)*	April-May
Pea, Wild Sweet *(Lathyrus laetiflorus)*	Feb.-June
Pennyroyal *(Monardella hypoleuca)*	June-July
Penstemon, Climbing *(Keckiella cordifolia)*	May-July
Penstemon, Foothill *(Penstemon heterophyllus)*	April-June
Penstemon, Showy *(Penstemon spectabilis)*	April-May
Peony *(Paeonia californica)*	Jan.-March
Perezia *(Perezia microcephala)*	June-July
Phacelia, Branching *(Phacelia ramosissima)*	May-July
Phacelia, Caterpillar *(Phacelia cicutaria)*	March-June
Phacelia, Fern-leaf *(Phacelia distans)*	March-June
Phacelia, Large-flowered *(Phacelia grandiflora)*	April-June
Phacelia, Mountain *(Phacelia imbricata)*	April-June
Phacelia, Parry's *(Phacelia parryi)*	March-May
Phacelia, Sticky *(Phacelia viscida)*	April-June
Phacelia, Yellow-throated *(Phacelia brachyloba)*	May-June
Pimpernel *(Anagallis arvensis)* *	March-June
Pincushion, Pink *Chaenactis artemisiaefolia*	May-June
Pincushion, Golden *(Chaenactis glabriuscula)*	March-April
Pineapple Weed *(Matricaria matricarioides)*	Feb.-May
Popcorn Flower *(Cryptantha spp. [4])*	March-May
Popcorn Flower *(Plagiobothrys spp. [3])*	March-May
Radish, Wild *(Raphanus sativus)* *	All Year

Rattleweed or Locoweed *(Astragalus spp [4])*
Redmaids *(Calandrinia spp [2])* — Feb.-May
Rock-rose *(Helianthemum scoparium)* — Feb.-May
Sanicle *(Sanicula spp. [4])* — March-May
Saxifrage, Calif. *(Saxifraga californica)* — March-May
Scarlet Bugler *(Penstemon centranthifolius)* — April-May
Shooting Stars *(Dodecatheon clevelandii)* — Jan.-March
Skullcap *(Scutellaria tuberosa)* — March-April
Snapdragon, Rose *(Antirrhinum multiflorum)* — May-June
Snapdragon, Twining *(Antirrhinum kelloggii)* — March-April
Snapdragon, Violet *(Antirrhinum nuttallianum)* — April-May
Snapdragon, White *(Antirrhinum coulterianum)* — April-May
Soap Plant *(Chlorogalum pomeridianum)* — May-June
Sow Thistle *(Sonchus spp.)* * — All year
Stream Orchid *(Epipactis gigantea)* — May-June
Sunflower, Canyon *(Venegasia carpesioides)* — March-May
Sunflower, Bush [Shrub] *(Encelia californica)* — March-June
Sunflower, Prairie *(Helianthus annuus)* * — April-Sept.
Sunflower, Slender *(Helianthus gracilentus)* — April-Sept.
Sweet Clover *(Melilotus spp. [2])* — March-June
Tarweed *(Hemizonia spp. [2])* — April-June
Tarweed *(Madia spp. [3])* — April-June
Tauschia *(Tauschia spp [2])* — Feb.-June
Telegraph Weed *(Heterotheca grandiflora)* — June-Aug.
Thistle, Calif. *(Cirsium californicum)* — April-June
Thistle, Bull *(Cirsium vulgare)* * — June-Oct.
Thistle, Milk *(Silybum marianum)* * — May-July
Thistle, Star *(Centaurea melitensis)* * — May-July
Thistle, Western *(Cirsium coulteri)* — March-June
Thistle, Yellow Star *(Centaurea spp [2])* *
Tidy Tips *(Layia platyglossa)* — March-May
Turkish Rugging*(Chorizanthe staticoides)* — April-June
Verbena *(Verbena lasiostachys)* — April-Sept.
Verbena, Beach *(Abronia spp. [2])* — April-June
Vetch *(Vicia spp. [3])* — March-May
Vinegar Weed *(Trichostema lanceolatum)* — May-June
Wallflower *(Erysimum spp. [2])* — March-May
Whispering Bells *(Emmenanthe penduliflora)* — March-May
Windmill Pink *(Silene gallica)** — Feb.-June
Woodland Star *(Lithophragma affine)* — April-May
Woolly Aster *(Corethrogyne filaginifolia)* — June-Sept.
Yarrow [White] *(Achillea borealis)* — May-June
Zygadene [Star Lily] *(Zygadenus fremontii)* — March-April

* alien (non-native) plants

This list of annuals and perennial flowering plants is not meant to be complete. Their abundance or rarity each year is related not only to habitat and seasonal weather variations, but also to the periodic occurrence of fire. Almost all of the listed plants produce an abundance of bloom the first season after fire that is way beyond the normal; some of them only bloom after a fire.

Trees

Alder, White *(Alnus rhombifolia)*
Ash *(Fraxinus spp [2])*
Cottonwood *(Populus spp [2])*
Laurel [Bay] *(Umbellularia californica)*
Maple, Bigleaf *(Acer macrophylla)*
Oak, Coast Live *(Quercus agrifolia)*
Oak, Valley *(Quercus lobata)*
Sycamore *(Platanus racemosa)*
Walnut, Calif. *(Juglans californica)*

Shrubs
RIDGES AND HIGHER SLOPES

Bricklebush *(Brickellia spp.[2])*	Sept.-Nov.
Buckwheat, Calif. *(Eriogonum fasciculatum)*	April-July
Buckwheat, Ashyleaf *(Eriogonum cinereum)*	June-Sept.
Buckwheat, Conejo *(Eriogonum crocatum)*	May-June
Buckwheat, Longstem *(Eriogonum elongatum)*	Aug.-Oct.
Bush Sunflower *(Encelia californica)*	March-June
Chaparral Pea *(Pickeringia montana)*	April-May
Ceanothus, Bigpod *(Ceanothus megacarpus)*	Feb.-April
Ceanothus, Buckbrush *(Ceanothus cuneatus)*	Feb.-April
Ceanothus, Greenbark *(Ceanothus spinosus)*	March-May
Ceanothus, Hairyleaf *(Ceanothus oliganthus)*	March-April
Ceanothus, Hoaryleaf *(Ceanothus crassifolius)*	March-April
Ceanothus, Whitethorn *(Ceanothus leucodermis)*	April-June
Chamise *(Adenostoma fasciculatum)*	May-June
Cherry, Hollyleaf *(Prunus ilicifolia)*	April-May
Coyote Brush *(Baccharis pilularia)*	Aug.-Nov.
Deerweed *(Lotus scoparius)*	March-June
Goldenbush *(Haplopappus spp. [4])*	Sept.-Oct.

Laurel Sumac *(Rhus Laurina)* May-June
Mallow, Bush *(Malacothamnus fasciculatus)* May-Oct.
Manzanita, Bigberry *(Arctostaphylos glauca)* Jan.-March
Manzanita, Eastwood *(Arctostaphylos glandulosa)* Jan.-March
Mountain Mahogany *(Cercocarpus betuloides)* March-May
Poppy, Bush or Tree *(Dendromecon rigida)* Feb.-May
Prickly Phlox *(Leptodactylon californicum)* Jan.-April
Rattleweed [Locoweed] *(Astragalus spp. [5])* March-June
Redberry *(Rhamnus crocea)* January-April
Redberry, Hollyleaf *(Rhamnus ilicifolia)* Feb.-April
Redshanks *(Adenostoma sparsifolium)* August
Sage, Black *(Salvia mellifera)* April-June
Sage, Purple *(Salvia leucophylla)* May-July
Sage, White *(Salvia apiana)* April-June
Sagebrush, Coastal *(Artemesia californica)* Aug.-Oct.
Scrub Oak *(Quercus dumosa)* March-April
Silk Tassel *(Garrya veatchii)* Jan.-March
Squaw Bush *(Rhus trilobata)* March-April
Sugar Bush *(Rhus ovata)* March-May
Toyon *(Heteromeles arbutifolia)* May-June
Woolly Blue-curls *(Trichostema lanatum)* April-June
Yerba Santa *(Eriodictyon crassifolium)* April-May
Yucca *(Yucca whipplei)* May-June

Shrubs

STREAMSIDE

Blackberry *(Rubus ursinus)* March-April
Cat-tail *(Typha latifolia)* Aug.-Oct.
Mugwort *(Artemesia douglasiana)* July-Nov.
Mulefat *(Baccharis viminea)* Jan.-May
Nettle, Dwarf *(Urtica urens)* Jan.-April
Willow *(Salix spp. [3])* Jan.-March

OCEAN FACING

Coreopsis*(Coreopsis gigantea)* March-May
Lemonadeberry *(Rhus integrifolia)* Feb.-April
Prickly Pear *(Opuntia littoralis)* May-June
Saltbush *(Atriplex lentiformis)* July-Oct.

CANYONS AND LOWER SLOPES

Castor-bean *(Ricinus communis)* *	All year
Cinquefoil *(Potentilla glandulosa)*	April-June
Coffeeberry, Calif. *(Rhamnus californica)*	May-June
Currant, Chaparral *(Ribes malvaceum)*	Dec.-Feb.
Currant, Golden *(Ribes aureum)*	March-April
Elderberry *(Sambucus mexicana)*	April-Aug.
Gooseberry, Fuchsia-flowered *(Ribes speciosum)*	Jan.-March
Honeysuckle *(Lonicera subspicata)*	May-July
Lupine, Pauma *(Lupinus longiflorus)*	April-June
Nightshade, Black *(Solanum douglasii)*	All year
Nightshade, Purple *(Solanum xantii)*	Jan.-Aug.
Ocean Spray [Creambush]*(Holodiscus discolor)*	April-May
Poison Oak (Toxicodendron diversilobum)	Feb.-March
(old name: *Rhus diversiloba)*	
Rose, Calif. Wild *(Rosa californica)*	April-May
Snowberry *(Symphoricarpos mollis)*	April-May
Spanish Broom *(Spartium junceum)* *	April-June
Tobacco, Tree or Bush *(Nicotiana glauca)* *	All year

          * Denotes alien (non-native) plant

NON-FLOWERING PLANTS AND GRASSES
Birdsfoot Fern *(Pellaea mucronata)*
Bracken Fern, Western *(Pteridium aquilinum)*
Chain Fern, Giant *(Woodwardia fimbriata)*
Coffee Fern *(Pellaea andromedifolia)*
Giant Rye *(Elymus spp.)*
Goldback Fern *(Pityrogramma triangularis)*
Horsetail *(Equisetum spp.)*
Maidenhair Fern *(Adiantum spp.)*
Woodfern, Coastal *(Dryopteris arguta)*

The list of shrubs and trees for the Santa Monica Mountains is not complete. There are some rarely found plants that are not included because of space limitations. The division of shrubs according to habitat is not meant to be taken literally; there is much overlapping of species in the areas listed. Blooming months are also meant only as a guideline; there can be variations related to both the particular year's weather and the individual habitat.

The information in this index has been compiled by James P. Kenney.

GLOSSARY OF TERMS

alluvium	unconsolidated gravel, sand, and fine rock debris deposited principally by running water.
anticline	a fold of stratified rock, convex upward.
arroyo	stream
barranca	a vertical walled gully cut by an intermittent stream
basalt	a fine grained rock
boca	entrance
brea	tar
breccia	a rock containing abundant angular fragments. They can be sedimentary, volcanic, tectonic, landslide or other
bushwhack	travel through dense vegetation, usually chaparral
caballero	a Spanish gentleman (horseman)
cajon	box
cienega	swamp
conejo	rabbit
conglomerate	a sedimentary rock consisting of larger rounded rock imbedded in a finer, usually sandy matrix, and all cemented together
diatomite	a sedimentary rock consisting of the silaceous skeletons of single celled algae
encinal	grove of live oak

erosion	removal of rock material by any natural process
fault	a fracture in the earth's crust
formation	a rock unit of distinctive characteristics which formed over a limited span of time and under some uniformity of conditions
granite	a coarse-grained intrusive rock rich in silica, potassium, sodium
habra	dale
igneous rock	a class of rocks formed by the crystallization of a molten state
intrusive rock	rock that has injected into other rock, usually in a molten state
loma	top of a hill
milling stone	a shallow stone which was used by the Indians for grinding seeds
mortar	a deep bowled grinding stone used for acorns
muller	a flat sandstone used by the Indians for grinding small hard seeds
mya	one million years ago..
nogales	walnut trees
pestle	a slender pounding stone used for acorn grinding
pismo	tar
playa	beach
potrero	pasture for horses
puente	bridge

ridge	long narrow crest of a mountain
roble	deciduous oak
saddle	a low place on a ridge
sandstone	a sedimentary rock formed by cementation of sand
savannah	a grassland containing scattered trees
seco	dry, barren
sedimentary rock	a class of rocks of secondary origin made up of transported and deposited rock and mineral particles
serrano	mountaineer, highlander
shale	a sedimentary rock made of very fine particles
siltstone	a sedimentary rock made of silt — finer than sand, coarser than clay
slate	weakly metamorphosed shale
strata	sheetlike masses of sedimentary rock of one kind, usually in layers between beds of other kinds
syncline	a downfold in layered rocks
temescal	sweat house
trancas	a barrier
vallecitos	small valley
yucaipa	wet marshy land

HIKING TRAILS OF THE SANTA MONICA MOUNTAINS by Milt McAuley, is a complete guide to finding the known and not so well-known places in this mountain recreational area. This book is destined to be the main reference for the casual as well as the serious hiker. The easy to read descriptions and the clear maps will take you from the beginning to the end of each hike in complete confidence.